ACCESS to MEDIA

A GUIDE TO INTEGRATING AND COMPUTERIZING CATALOGS

SHEILA S. INTNER

Neal-Schuman Publishers, Inc.
New York   London

Published by Neal-Schuman Publishers, Inc.
23 Cornelia Street
New York, NY 10014

Library of Congress Cataloging in Publication Data

Intner, Sheila S.
  Access to media.

  Bibliography: p.
  Includes index.
  1. Information storage and retrieval systems—
Audio-visual materials.   2. Cataloging of non-book
materials—Data processing.   3. Libraries—Special
collections—Non-book materials.   4. Audio-visual
library service.   5. Machine-readable bibliographic
data. I. Title.
Z699.5.A9I58 1984   025.04   84-1035
ISBN 0-918212-88-X

Dedication

I dedicate this book to my husband, Mathew, whose belief in my ability to write it was largely responsible for its completion. His contributions went far beyond good natured endurance of sketchy meals and late nights at the typewriter or word processor, though these were among them. He also provided the environment for what proved to be more than a year's work, as well as reading parts of the manuscript and offering plenty of objective and constructive criticism. Everything had to pass his "Can I understand this even if I'm not a librarian?" test.

I dedicate it, too, to Jane Hannigan, whose interest in the project was a mighty encouragement and whose advice always proved right on the mark, from the time it began as a doctoral dissertation until it went to press as a full-fledged book. Everything had to pass her "So what?" test.

Finally, I dedicate it to all the computer systems I have every known, because each of them taught me something new and useful every time I logged on.

Contents

Preface

*A*CCESS *to Media* is intended to be used as a handbook for change from manual, nonintegrated bibliographic systems to integrated and automated systems as an ultimate goal. Reading this book should provide an overview of the current state-of-the-art as well as the components necessary for changing a library's procedures and implementing more valuable ones capable of giving better service. The book is divided into two parts: Part One is an exposition of the context of media access and its problems, how they developed, and what current practices and attitudes seem to be; Part Two outlines a plan for action designed to improve access to all media through automated, integrated bibliographic systems.

Part One, especially Chapter 3 and Chapter 5, is based on my 1981 national survey of public librarians' attitudes towards access to nonprint materials. The survey questionnaire (reproduced in Appendix C) was sent to the catalog librarians of almost a thousand public libraries in all fifty states. More than 450 replied, also from all fifty states, representing libraries of all sizes in all types of communities.

Chapter 1 provides an overview of media collections in libraries. Chapter 2 gives an historical review of the growth of media collections in libraries and methods of controlling them. Chapter 4 looks at recent research into bibliographic practices in the academic library community as well as in the lower schools to complement my findings of the public library sector.

In Part Two, I examine future possibilities, beginning with a description of automated bibliographic systems in current use in Chapter 6; projections of the skills that need to be developed by members of the library staff in order to use computer systems in Chapter 7; and scenarios for implementing integrated, online bibliographic systems in Chapter 8. There is also a section in Chapter 8 that discusses the integration process in a manual mode. Finally, Chapter 9 describes the advantages of integrated systems for clients of the libraries and the positive results they should enjoy when new systems are implemented.

Each chapter is followed by a list of selected readings that augment and explain in greater detail the material covered in the chapter. Other appendixes include a list of acronyms and a glossary of terms that may be unfamiliar to students of library and information science or to practitioners who are newcomers to computer or media jargon. The glossary is not meant to be exhaustive for either the media or computer fields.

Access to Media was written for the professionals who want to provide better access to their media materials, especially those librarians who participated in my survey and described their own practices as nonintegrated but believed that integrated access provides the best service to clients. Those librarians who are interested in automating part or all of their bibliographic services will find information in the text useful to their purposes. Students of library and information science can use this book as an introduction to important aspects of media librarianship, aspects which have broader applicability to managing collections of any sort of materials for public use. *Access to Media* is intended to sensitize all who read it to the variety of options for managing media services—including books and other printed materials as media.

I like to believe the greatest value of this book lies in the practicality of its approach, style, and judgment as well as in its recommendations for action. I have tried to provide a guide for planning a step-by-step change in bibliographic practices while offering suggestions and cautions along the way. I have also tried to keep the human factor uppermost in mind. Insofar as people have to implement all projects and processes, the reactions and interactions on the part of library staff are addressed. Furthermore, the people who receive the services—the library's public—also interact with all library systems and must be considered part of the process.

This book is dedicated to the hundreds of librarians who have successfully integrated their bibliographic services. The many thousands of people they serve more effectively can attest to the value of having access to all materials in one place. Their example should serve to motivate us all to do a better job of managing media services. EXCELSIOR!

Sheila S. Intner

Part One

History of Media Collections

Chapter 1

An Overview

THE first task of anyone writing about media is to define exactly what is being discussed. What is media? Or perhaps it is more accurate to say, what are media? There is, in fact, no one "media" but rather a multiplicity of physical forms, including books, pamphlets, printed sheets, manuscripts, cartographics, music, sound recordings, motion pictures, videorecordings, graphics, objects, computer-readable materials, micrographics, and serials. A precise definition for the word media is hard to pin down, though writers and researchers have tried to do so for decades.

Media expert Deirdre Boyle, in an article on the subject entitled, "In the Beginning Was the Word ... Libraries and Media," points out that "The 'word' is a medium," and that "when media as a concept is limited to audiovisual aids or nonprint, when media mean filmstrips, transparencies, and simulation games, few are likely to deem such codes equal partners of the powerful and sophisticated language of words. But, when media are viewed as those sources of information which dominate us, print, television, film, radio, telephone, among others, a total concept of a new information environment ... becomes apparent."[1] Boyle echoes the analysis of Marshall McLuhan, who led a revolution in thought about communication in the 1960s, and who demonstrated that the consequences of newer media, i.e., electronic media, were the result of a different scale imposed on our lives by their introduction. McLuhan's slogan, "the medium is the message,"[2] implies, however, that the physical form of an idea's expression makes a difference in how it is interpreted.

Librarians are likely to agree with McLuhan about the importance of the medium in which an idea is manifested. One expert was quoted as saying media are "...the librarian's Excedrin headache,"[3] and this feeling may well hold true regardless of the "message" or content of the materials. Both McLuhan and Boyle

consider books and other printed materials as part of their definitions of media, as, indeed, they are in the strictest sense of the word
—i.e., as physical representations of ideas. Many information professionals, however, distinguish between books and printed
periodicals, pamphlets, etc. Some are even narrower in their meaning, referring to books and other media, excluding even printed
periodicals and similar materials. For such people, though the intellectual message may be the same (e.g., when a play appears in
book form as well as in a film, videotape, or sound recording), the
medium determines its place in the array of information forms commonly collected by libraries.

Why should definitions of media exclude printed materials? In
Dewey's and Cutter's time, library materials were primarily books.
These library leaders of the nineteenth and early twentieth centuries helped to formally define the rules and structures of our profession and its service patterns, and these traditions have not
changed rapidly. As late as 1953, Seymour Lubetzky wrote, "The
prevailing type of material which is found in a library and is recorded in the catalog is the book...."[4] Books formed the bulk of
virtually all library collections during the early decades of the
library profession. The distinction made between books and other
codes of communication, as McLuhan called them, very likely grew
out of this strong early tradition of libraries as storehouses of books
and the perception of books as the norm of their resources.

The notion that library collections could include things other than
books was not new in the 1940s and 1950s. Maps have been part of
the earliest collections at the Library of Congress, and sound recordings go back to the early years of the century, but it was not until
after World War II that these other forms began to assume the functions previously fulfilled by books and, to a lesser extent, by
periodicals. Libraries were presumed to contain books, and the practice of collecting information in other forms required the use of
another term.

The wealth of intellectual and artistic effort constituting
humanity's accumulation of knowledge varies in form as much as in
content. Furthermore, both the forms and the content change in
response to the changing interests, techniques, and environments of
people and their cultures. This constant change may be part of the
reason that a general term like media assumes different meanings
in the library context. It also has a variety of meanings in the world
at large. When nonlibrarians refer to "the media," they usually
mean the mass media, particularly television, radio, and

newspapers. Even librarians use the term this way. Geoffrey What-more explains, "I should apologise for the use of the term [media], which I personally dislike, and so do most journalists and broad-casters, but we have failed to invent a better collective noun."[5] Mass media are well described by Whatmore:

> In a sense, all of the media, radio, TV and newspapers, are in effect in-formation processing factories. They take in raw material—the output of governments and most of the organisations and individuals that make up the social infrastructure bearing on our lives—process it, make it reada-ble, interesting, add background, check the facts—and distribute it to millions of people each day and each hour.[6]

To many professional librarians, the mass media are not the meat of their world. Although newspapers are usually found in libraries, current radio and television broadcasts are rarely part of their offer-ings. Mass media are sometimes viewed as a destructive force con-tinually enlarging the gap between people and books, which are seen as the true focus of human culture and, therefore, library interests.

Three distinct characteristics may be used to describe the various mass media mentioned so far: physical medium, communication mode, and marketing strategy. A fourth, publication pattern, is also a factor in the case of newspapers and magazines designed for mass consumption, though periodical publication also is applicable to scholarly journals and serials which are far from "mass" media. There is not one single thread that could be extracted to help define the "media" half of mass media. It is easy enough to see the "mass" half refers to the numbers of people reached, but the "media" half in-cludes all sorts of things, much as Boyle and McLuhan have defined it.

If mass media are a group of information forms aimed at the millions of people who make up modern mass markets, then are library media, by analogy, the information forms that make up library collections? Yes and no. Yes, in the Boyle-McLuhan sense, but no, in the sense that few librarians mean everything, especially books and periodicals, when they talk about media. A definition of media that explains its usage in the library context needs to be found. Several adjectives used by library writers to modify "media" help explain it further. One of these is "nonbook," another is "non-print," and a third is "audiovisual."

Nonbook media, as mentioned before, should cover the whole ar-ray of materials in library holdings which are not books. However, nonbook media would include a variety of printed media such as printed periodicals and serials, pamphlets and broadsides, music, and maps, as well as manuscripts, all of which, with the possible exception of maps, are excluded from most manuals dealing with nonbook media.[7]

The second alternative, "nonprint," would exclude, in addition to books, all of the print forms that slip through into the array of forms qualifying as nonbook. Nonprint, while less inclusive than nonbook, still includes manuscripts and other handwritten materials such as maps and music, or individual sheets of writing which are not, strictly speaking, manuscripts. There are those who might quibble over considering maps and musical notation as nonprint since, though printed, they are not primarily textual. Related cartographics in three dimensions, i.e., globes and relief models, and related musical works consisting of recorded performances rather than symbols on paper, are clearly both nonbook and nonprint. Why is it so difficult to classify their counterparts recorded on paper?

The third adjective, "audiovisual," is often thought of as the most restrictive in meaning. Audiovisual refers to media that are either visual or auditory in nature, or both. That would cover all the things usually considered nonbook and nonprint—pictures, films, filmstrips, slides, sound and videorecordings, microforms, and so forth—but what about McLuhan's notion that books are visual media, i.e., extensions of the human eye?[8] And what about books of illustrative material? These are still considered books, even though the text may be minimal or even absent altogether.

Looking at the various structures for International Standard Bibliographic Description (ISBD) created by groups within the International Federation of Library Associations and Organizations (IFLA), it is interesting to note their separation of printed music, ISBD(PM), from recorded music, which is subsumed under nonbook materials, ISBD(NBM), as well as that of maps and globes, ISBD(CM), from both of these. Even more curious than this is the explicit exclusion of original paintings and other unique art works, which are assuredly not books, printed music, cartographics, or anything else covered by other ISBDs, because they are not primarily intended by their creators as informational media.[9] This odd distinction could certainly be applied to a great many other works, including some which occur in print-on-paper or manuscript forms.

Media means something different to everyone. The lack of precision to be gained from adding the various adjectives typically used by librarians to modify media—nonbook, nonprint, or audiovisual—

should be obvious. Years ago, Lester Asheim, in his Introduction to an issue of *Library Quarterly* entitled "Differentiating the Media: A Focus on Library Selection and Use of Communication Content," analyzed the notable lack of a suitable definition.

> Our major difficulty lies in the term "media," which carries a variety of connotations depending upon the special outlook or practice of the group perceiving the term ... There were those whose interest in "media" focuses strictly on *non*book devices, ignoring completely our warning that the book is one of the media to which we would pay particular attention, stressing by our very attention to all the media that which is unique and indispensable in each of them, the book included ... Suffice it to say here simply that the librarians' book orientation has led us to see all other media as supplementary or subordinate to the book, as our own standard terminology so clearly reveals. "Nonbook," "nonprint," "audiovisual *aids*," we say condescendingly, leaving no question as to which format we place at the heart of the learning process or the aesthetic experience. With that kind of bias, often unrecognized in ourselves, we tend to expect of the other media that which we like best about the book...."[10]

All of these definitions, whether broad or narrow, are acceptable and applicable, although the materials usually called nonbook/ nonprint/audiovisual are the primary focus of this book. Still, it would serve little purpose to exclude books from discussions about managing bibliographic information and providing bibliographic services to the public. This book proceeds from the assumption that the more advanced and innovative bibliographic techniques are being applied first to books and printed materials before they are extended to other media. It follows that, although books are part of the larger system, it is the other media that need our attention.

Another word with a variety of confusing definitions is "access." Access means availability, and the availability of information is the business of librarianship. In the broadest sense, access to information means making available whatever might be needed from the entire body of recorded knowledge no matter when, where, or how it originated and is stored. This ideal vision of access is not expected to be realized, but it is a goal toward which information professionals strive. It is the essence of the profession, within the limits imposed upon it by the realities of environment.

More and more, unlimited access to information is something consumers desire and expect to be satisfied by their libraries. At the 1979 White House Conference on Libraries and Information Services, delegates (both lay and professional) passed resolutions establishing people's right of access to knowledge—all needed knowledge—in appropriate formats and at the time needed.[11] The library's goal is to maximize access, whether it is physical access to documents themselves or intellectual access to information about knowledge.

Librarians use many complex tools in order to make information available to their clients. Tools that help to provide physical access to library materials include the classifications by which they are arranged on the shelves as well as shelflists (catalogs arranged in classification or shelf order) and indexes to the classification scheme. Tools that help to provide intellectual access are, primarily, an institution's catalog, limited to its own collections, and bibliographies, indexes, guides to the literature of disciplines, catalogs of other institutions, union lists, and other similar aids containing references to information from the world at large outside the individual institution. These may be historical, current, or both; they may cover a single subject or language or many. Each tool has strengths and weaknesses. Most are continually being revised, updated, or otherwise improved. One might question the point of having tools that contain references to information not immediately available in a client's home library. The answer is complex, but it is based in part on the idea that the materials may be obtained for use by the library and its client from other sources. This is one of the notions underlying a national network scheme, that anyone, anywhere, would have access to information about all materials in all collections in the nation. Whether or not having virtually unlimited intellectual or bibliographic access would actually result in accompanying physical access is another issue to be resolved.

Problems of access are not unique to our time. Some of the great early library leaders were associated with tools designed to resolve access problems. Charles C. Jewett dreamed of a streamlined, inexpensive, and higher quality centralized cataloging system that would provide libraries all over the country with cataloging information. Melvil Dewey devised his decimal classification system to facilitate the collocation of related materials. It was Charles A. Cutter who formulated the purposes of a library catalog to show the holdings of the library and collocate materials by an author, editions of a title, and on a subject.[12] William F. Poole began the index bearing his name, the prototype of modern subject indexes to periodical literature, to provide access to the contents of journals which were otherwise inaccessible to the clients of his library.[13] All of these were improvements which furnished better access or a new kind of access.

This book is concerned with the contents of a library's main public catalog, the tool that is supposed to be the key to an institution's own collections, and its clients' first-line source of bibliographic access to materials that are immediately available. What distinguishes a library's catalog from bibliographies, indexes, and other lists of bibliographic entries is the fact that it includes only materials owned by the institution. The purposes of the catalog, codified by Cutter in 1876 and further refined by Seymour Lubetzky in the 1950s and adopted by the International Conference on Cataloging Principles in 1961, are twofold: to enable the user to locate a specific item in the library's collection for which the author, title, or subject is known; and to display for the user the works of an author, editions of a work, or works on a subject owned by the library.[14] Lubetzky's emphasis on collocating *works*, including all the translations, editions, and versions in which a work could be found, is easily extended to accommodate the various media in which a work might appear. Lubetzky later acknowledged the implications for cataloging of a work's medium.[15]

It was also Cutter's idea that a library catalog should be a single alphabet in which authors, titles, and subjects were interfiled as access points. Bibliographic access is a fundamental service of the library to furnish in a form that any person, scholar or novice, educated or not, could use. No other access tool is as prominently located for the public as the public catalog. The establishment of the dictionary arrangement instead of the classified arrangement of entries, more popular in Europe, has been attributed to the democratic nature of the alphabet. Presumably, anyone who can read can use the catalog and have access to the library's collections.

The need for a catalog is obvious. Even relatively small library collections are too large for most people to keep in their heads, and it is easiest to have a surrogate or set of surrogates for each item in a catalog of manageable size. If an item appears in surrogate in the catalog, it can be expected to be found on the shelves as long as no one else is using it—and one would not have to traipse all over the stacks to see the holdings in a particular area even if the various works were not all shelved in the same locations.

Most libraries have more than one catalog—"official" catalogs are so-called because they are available only to staff and contain the official records of identification and inventory; shelflists, sometimes made available to the public and sometimes restricted to staff use only, are arranged in shelf order rather than alphabetic order; and specialized finding lists on specific subjects also exist. In addition, records are kept of materials on order or received, but not yet available to the public for use. Most librarians realize that the main public catalog is not the only access tool one must search in order to know whether or not something is part of the library's collection. At least, they realize it when they think about it, or when they are aware of the possibility that a client is looking for a special kind of material, a newly-published item, or something which cannot be located through the catalog such as a single poem, song, or short story. The development of libraries from small collections of relatively uniform materials to complex and greatly enlarged conglomerations of books, periodicals, films, recordings, microforms, etc., was paralleled by the development of larger and increasingly complex access tools. Nevertheless, most library catalogs contain records only for their institutions' book stock rather than for all of their holdings.

Since Cutter, great debates have raged over the most effective catalog forms. Should there be book catalogs or card catalogs? This question may now be updated: should there be offline or online catalogs? When the catalog grows large, should it be divided? If so, then how? Each institution has had to address its own problems, answering these and other questions about the effectiveness of its catalog and the methods by which it furnishes access to materials, in individual ways.

At the turn of the century, the Library of Congress' decision to sell its catalog cards to the library community was the turning point in the evolution of catalog formats from books to cards. It had already become evident that book catalogs were costly to produce and perpetually out of date. Supplements forced people to do multiple lookups, and often items were overlooked because people did not take the time to search in all the volumes. The change to card format eliminated many of the problems of book catalogs. Card catalogs were infinitely hospitable to new entries and, thus, no one had to wait for new editions or supplements to be printed to have access to the newest acquisitions. All the entries could be maintained in one file, not divided into a series of updates plus a central file/book. It was less costly to interfile new cards than to produce new cumulations of the book catalog. There were other attributes of book catalogs that card files could not match, however. Book catalogs could be produced in multiple copies easily and cheaply once the initial typesetting was done, while reproducing a card catalog required an equal cost in housing and maintenance even though the cards themselves cost only pennies to reproduce. Local libraries, even large ones, couldn't very well sell copies of their card catalogs to defray the cost of production and maintenance. Nevertheless, once the Library of Congress made its cards available, the card format took hold, and since the early 1900s it has been the most familiar kind of bibliographic display in all types of libraries.

For some time the drawbacks of card catalogs have become increasingly obvious, and librarians have cast about for a better vehicle for the ever-increasing stores of information their card files contain. For one thing, cards are perishable. Another problem is the size of the catalog. Some very large libraries have to devote huge amounts of floor space to their card catalogs. Filing has become an endless task requiring an army of filers and revisers. As acquisitions grow, backlogs build, some in large research institutions containing records for more than a year's acquisitions. The flexibility of the card format to accept new entries proved neither limitless nor a guarantee of an up-to-the-minute catalog. Some institutions divide up the main file, either to create smaller files for easier maintenance and searching, or on principle—that subjects should be kept separate from authors and titles, or that children's materials should be separated from adult materials, or any one of several other principles. In this way, the catalog as a unitary structure was replaced by a decentralized series of catalogs which, together, performed that function.

What normally remained in the main catalog? The materials that formed the nucleus of library collections—adult books. In public libraries, children's collections, media collections, and reference collections often had their own catalogs. In branch libraries, there frequently were no union catalogs of the holdings of the main unit and/ or the other branches. In academic libraries, departmental collections, media collections, and other specialized collections remained separate from the main catalog listings. School libraries followed similar practices, though few individual agencies in schools were so large as to have problems because of their size alone.

A catalog format that could resolve the problems of size and the speed and cost of updating for large numbers of entries was a high priority item for many leading institutions at mid-century. By the end of the next decade, it became an acute problem, but during this period, a solution began to loom on the horizon: computerized storage and manipulation of the data. A few pioneers began to design automated bibliographic systems in the 1960s, and notable among these was the Library of Congress. The solutions to design problems were related first to the primary records in their main catalog, i.e., those for books. The result was the MARC (machine-readable cataloging) format for books. The MARC format is a convention for entering bibliographic information about books into a computer, identifying the elements of the records, their order, and, in some cases, the range of values which could be assigned to them. For example, it was designed with a place for the familiar LC card number, and in the special area designated for that data (a field, in computer jargon), digits can be entered only in the form "nn-n...," where "n" is a number from zero to nine—the only style in which LC card numbers are created. This format, which was later adopted as a standard by the American National Standards Institute (ANSI),[16] giving it more of a quasi-official status, did not accommodate other forms of informational materials. It had to be altered and expanded to be applied to serials and a broad range of other physical media.

Throughout the 1970s, the MARC formats gained acceptance throughout the profession, primarily because agencies whose bibliographic systems were designed to accept MARC-formatted records could purchase them from LC and automatically enter (or "dump") them into their database. Libraries or library organizations were already sensitized to the advantages of using LC products. Their quality was a national standard of excellence; their authoritative reference work on names and other access points was unmatched in detail except for a mere handful of institutions; their scope and coverage of books was broad; and their costs were relatively low. Here was a ready-made database for a fraction of what it would cost to create one from scratch by any other agency or organization. The idea of continuing to share in the enormously valuable efforts of LC would have been foolish to ignore, and few, if any, major shapers of automated bibliographic access systems have ignored it. Rather, all the major forces in the U.S. library community have adapted their systems to the MARC standard.

By itself, this initial conversion from card to electronic format and from print-on-paper to images on a cathode-ray tube (CRT) terminal would not seem terribly different from the change from books to cards must have been at the turn of the century. One critical difference, however, lay in the fact that libraries were no longer uniform collections of books but multimedia amalgams, and the time-lag in the creation of MARC formats for media other than books has exacerbated the problem of access to these materials.

Access to media information and managing the processes whereby it is produced and supplied to library clients is the focus of this book. The objectives to be served include the following:

- Appreciation of the origins of the problems of access to media

- Evaluation of solutions previously applied

- Examination of current bibliographic practices in the nation's public libraries as well as other parts of the library community

- Investigation of librarians' attitudes toward media and access

- Projection of future directions for provision of integrated access to all library materials

- Formulation of a blueprint for action which can be adapted for use by libraries.

It may seem peculiar to be concerned with the public service aspects of what has traditionally been perceived as a behind-the-scenes operation. It has always been true that the catalog is a connection between the public (the outsiders) and the staff (the insiders) of any library, as well as between the public services staff (in this case, the outsiders) and the technical services staff (the insiders) within the agency. Often, it has proved to be a bone of contention between these groups, with the public resenting the typical advice of public services staff to "... go look in the catalog"; public services staff resenting what seemed to them an inordinate amount of the library's budget going to technical services staff; and technical services staff resenting what appeared to be unfair criticism of their consumption of resources and the value of their work. For the reference librarian—the public services staff member—the catalog is only one tool with which they do their work. The public, often ignorant of the conventions of bibliographic entries, subject headings, and filing practices, find the catalog an inscrutable maze. The catalogers have one eye on the intellectual standards that govern what they may do and the other eye on the financial restrictions limiting the time and effort that can be devoted to the task. Without blaming or excusing any of these attitudes on the part of the three groups of people who interact with the catalog, it is important to realize that, while far from ideal, the catalog performs crucial functions for each group. Without an appreciation of the various different demands made on it, it is difficult to fulfill many of them successfully.

At the 1983 Midwinter Conference of the American Library Association (ALA), during a meeting of the committee charged with responsibility for descriptive cataloging rules, CC:DA,[17] a discussion arose over a proposal by the Library of Congress to use the place of publication rather than the name of the issuing organization (corporate body) to distinguish between two serials with identical main entry titles. In the ensuing discussion, it quickly became clear that reference/public service librarians preferred having the corporate body precede or substitute for the place of publication, while the catalogers/technical service librarians wanted the reverse, supporting LC's initial position. The discussion resulted in a call for re-evaluation of the proposal and delay in making a decision until more people could be consulted. This exemplifies the conflicts that arise over and over in the construction of catalog entries and displays. That the LC representative agreeably withdrew the proposal dramatizes the willingness of the nation's leading catalogers to assign importance to the needs of librarians other than themselves, something LC has been accused of ignoring on more than one occasion.

Technical services operations do not exist in a vacuum, though in large libraries with relatively isolated catalog departments they may seem to. In small libraries, the public and technical service librarians may be one person, to whom it should be obvious that cataloging decisions have consequences for public services as well as for the cataloger. Large or small, libraries and information centers need to come to grips with the objectives which they want the catalog to serve and the realities of how the job can be done within whatever limits the environment, staff, budget, etc., impose on their institution. That is why this book is concerned with exploring access provided to clients by the catalog (or catalogs) of a library and making suggestions about how to enhance its "access potential" in general by unifying separated cataloging operations and by automating the system.

It is assumed here that effective management of any collection of information can be measured in terms of resulting public service, not only in terms of operational efficiency, though efficiency is clearly an important objective—too important to be sacrificed to serve other goals exclusively. Nevertheless, public service considerations cannot be set aside to serve the demands of efficiency alone. A balance between what is an ideal result and what is a realistic possibility has to be struck. For example, simplifying the cataloging for each item may make it more efficient in the sense that the cost per entry may fall or the production per hour may rise, or both; but the result may not contain enough information to serve the needs of the users of the information. It may be efficient in terms of costs and production, but it is not effective management of whatever resources are invested since the services produced do not satisfy the needs of their users. Both cost-conscious administrative and service-oriented bibliographic goals have to be considered.

This book attempts to point out both kinds of concerns in order to enable the reader to make comparisons between alternatives which will assist them in decision-making. Managing media means making decisions about media from the first one—to collect a particular kind of material—to the implementation of the most ambitious program based on its use. Implicit in this is accountability for the consequences of the decisions made, both good and bad, and being able to defend those decisions on the basis of the objectives they were meant to serve. While the primary emphasis of the book is on bibliographic access methods, their consequences are far-reaching for use of the materials, which reflects this author's belief that the purpose of access is the eventual use of collections. The traditional task of accumulating materials to preserve them intact, and not for public use, is not at issue here. Preservation is a valid objective of archives and, in many other information agencies, some collections are subject to similar treatment, e.g., local history materials may be entrusted to local public libraries or historical society libraries in order to maintain them for posterity. In such cases, use by the agency's public is not the purpose of such bibliographic access systems as are provided for the materials. Rather they are methods for providing ongoing inventory and organization for its own sake, though clients may also occasionally be permitted to use the materials for special purposes and thus, benefit from them. In fact, successfully managing media collections requires that the purpose of the collection and its end uses be clearly identified; and also that one of the most important benefits of enhanced access, if implemented, be in keeping with those purposes. If, for example, the purpose of a collection of films is to enable the institution to show them at its own educational programs and nothing more, one would certainly purchase different titles, process them differently, and design access to them differently than if the purpose of the collection were personal recreational use in-house or at home by a diverse group of clients. In the first instance, it is arguable whether surrogates for the films in the form of bibliographic entries need to be made at all, or if they are, whether it makes sense to file them in the public catalog. The films are not intended for use by the public at all, and, while they are part of its holdings, they are more in the category of internal support materials. In the second instance, however, of films intended to circulate to individual members of the public, lack of inclusion in the public catalog would hardly seem justified.

The arguments to enter holdings into a public catalog even though physical access is restricted seems more defensible than *not* to enter holdings to which the public has direct physical access. The logic involved is that the catalog is a record of the library's holdings, not necessarily only those holdings to which physical access is encouraged; but omission of records from the catalog effectively removes materials from the list of holdings in addition to making discovery by author, title, or subject in the usual way impossible.

The original purposes of early catalogs were not necessarily to assist users in finding materials, but to inventory holdings.[27] The modern library rarely relies on its public catalog as the definitive inventory. Inventories, which include prices paid for items and list the individual copies of a title, are usually arranged in the same order as the materials are physically located on the shelves—the shelflist. These have only one entry per call number/shelf location, and each corresponds in almost all cases to one particular title, though sometimes the same title is housed in several locations and will have an equal number of corresponding shelflist entries. Shelflist inventories are most often available only to staff members for work-related consultation; however, some libraries allow their shelflists to be used by the general public for their own searching. In contrast to the shelflist, a public catalog has more than one entry per title. It will have at least two, one for the title and one for the subject or author, and it is likely to have three or more. It will not have, as a rule, information about individual copies owned by the library. Shelflists and public catalogs serve, essentially, two different purposes and their designs reflect this, even though there is some overlap of the functions and uses of both. A quick examination of catalogs and shelflists reveals the following:

1. In order to find a work on the shelflist, one must know its shelf location, based in most libraries on its subject. Knowing its author and title will not be of any use without first placing the work in its correct position by call number. A public catalog is designed to offer access by several means, namely, by author, title, and subject. The public catalog furnishes a different kind of subject access from the shelflist, since the catalog can give a work covering two subjects a separate heading for each, while the shelflist only reflects the single class number assigned to it.

2. Shelflists give information about specific physical items—copies—of a title. Catalogs give information about titles. This may seem to be a small difference, but it assumes that catalog users are not interested in copy-specific information such as the date an item was acquired, the source of acquisition, price paid, etc. It is assumed that catalog users are interested in the title and that any copy of it is equally satisfying to the client. Only certain copies of the title may be of use to the staff member, however.

3. The shelflist requires knowledge of a specialized code representing subject information, the classification scheme, Cuttering, and any other devices used in a particular agency to identify shelf locations. The catalog requires, in theory, at least, knowledge of only the alphabet. The implication is that catalogs are easy to use, while shelflists are complex and arcane. In actuality, catalogs are complex and arcane, too, but not because of their alphabetic arrangement. Because of the complications we information professionals introduce into the simple alphabetic sequence, catalogs are rendered less straightforward and more confusing.

The purpose of the catalog, as opposed to the shelflist, is to afford ordinary people easy access by multiple access points to the titles in the collections. The purpose of the shelflist, on the other hand, is to provide a record of item-specific information which can be accessed by its location within the collection by trained staff. The call number is, in many libraries, a unique identification mark and thereby an efficient access point as well. The shelflist is intended for specific uses, the catalog for general use.

The catalog is often not a unitary object. For example, in the central unit of the small public library system where I was employed, the catalog was made up of at least five displays. Though there were some overlaps in the holdings listed in each of four smaller catalogs and the main public catalog, none of the five catalogs was a complete record of all the library's holdings, and the main display had full information only for adult books and bound serials. In addition, books held by branch libraries but not by the central unit were not listed at all in any of these catalogs, but were filed only in their respective branch library catalogs. Even the shelflist in the main library, the official inventory for the whole system, was missing records of any kind for sound recordings, either adult or children's, serials, or microforms. No single display contained entries for all holdings, either in shelf order or alphabetic order. This situation is probably duplicated at least in part in libraries of all kinds. In addition, of course, there are holdings for which no bibliographic or inventory records are made.

Try to see this multiplicity of files from the ordinary client's point of view. Isn't the bibliographic control and access likely to appear confusing, complicated, and arcane? It does not have to be. The strategies for managing media in this book are intended to draw the disparate files into one catalog, disparate procedures into one process, and encourage information to be accessed according to the needs and desires of the consumer, rather than the convenience of any of the staff groups within the organization.

For those who are accustomed to dealing with many different files and are paid to do so, the fragmentation of cataloging into several displays is a minor annoyance and raises no insurmountable barriers. Clients of the library, however, may not be familiar with the series of files providing access. The objective of integrating separate catalogs into one display for the public—to which separate lists of the holdings of a departmental unit, subject area, medium, or material type can be *added*—is assumed to be both desirable and feasible.

The possibility of integrating large, separate bibliographic systems for media depends on using computer technology to make the unified file easy to search quickly, since the larger a manual file becomes, the more difficult it is to search. The flexibility and hospitality of computerized catalogs are certainly greater than manual systems, and, it is assumed, are sufficient to accommodate the total holdings of most libraries.

This is not to say there are no limits to what can be stored in a computer, however. Capacity in every computer system is limited, but the factors that determine maximum effective storage can be addressed more easily than those affecting card or book catalogs. One example of this is the public floor space a card catalog occupies. This is one of the factors limiting the size of a card file, but it does not apply to a computer catalog, since terminals occupy more or less the same amount of space whether the catalog contains ten thousand entries or, like OCLC, ten million entries. The behind-the-scenes space required for actual data storage and processing equipment of larger computer systems still needs to be accounted for, but that seems to be shrinking at a rapid rate and does not even have to be located in the library building.

There are also many libraries whose catalogs are so small and whose needs are still so well satisfied by their manual files that they do not intend to employ automation at all. These institutions may wish to integrate all bibliographic data into one card or book catalog. This kind of implementation is also discussed. It is the author's intention, nevertheless, to encourage the use of a standard bibliographic record in all catalogs, since future needs will very likely be met by joining forces with other libraries in networks or other cooperative ventures—all of which depend on exchangeable bibliographic information. For this reason, it does not make sense to make changes in current systems without including whatever steps are necessary to produce standard entries for all materials. Libraries that receive cataloging from regional or commercial sources may be indirect beneficiaries of networks. They may not need to change the level or quality of their data, but only to file it differently, as well as to monitor the quality of their original cataloging.

The size of a library file is not the only factor governing the choice of manual or automated display, though it is probably a major factor. Other reasons librarians consider automating files that have not yet grown into problems of crisis proportions are the costs of alternatives, needs of their clienteles, and future plans for their library. The cost of automating small catalogs is spread over far fewer entries than large ones, but it might be considered worthwhile because there would be no larger conversion effort to be made in the future or because of the added services the computer would provide, so long as the initial investment in equipment, etc., were possible. Often, it is the administrator's familiarity with the capabilities of computer systems which motivates initiation of the project. Once it is decided that a computer is important, the necessary resources can be mustered by a creative and determined library director. Outside funding, cooperative funding, or other methods may generate enough money for the capital expenditures. Some institutions may wish to convert bibliographic data into machine-readable form as part of their preparation for computer systems to be purchased several years down the road.

In general, however, it is the larger libraries with the worst problems which have turned to automation as a solution. These libraries are also most likely to have larger media collections with separate catalogs for them. They will also have the highest costs, overall, though not necessarily per unit in the system, whether measured by individual item or by individual branch or department. For large libraries to enlarge their main public catalogs, they will probably need to consider automation as a necessary part of the project. It should be obvious that no one system or procedure can be applied uniformly to all types and sizes of libraries. Still, most of them are adaptable to a fairly broad cross-section of institutions if they are viewed without rigidity and more as guidelines than as prescriptions.

It is hoped that no one will try to apply the principles of media access outlined in this book without a carefully prepared and documented evaluation of that individual's own library—its clients' needs, staff members' expertise, and current systems. Plans must be tailored to individual budgets and timetables, which will necessarily be unique. While we all try to emulate our colleagues' successes and avoid their mistakes, each situation has unique factors that can affect outcomes unexpectedly. These caveats are not intended to equivocate about the value of the principles of integrated access, but rather to ensure that they are applied with due caution and respect for the effects of change in any system.

NOTES

1. Deirdre Boyle, "In the Beginning Was the Word ... Libraries and Media." *Library Journal*, 101 (January 1, 1976), p. 126.

2. Marshall McLuhan, *Understanding Media, the Extensions of Man* (New York: McGraw-Hill, 1964), pp. vii, 7-21.

3. Unattributed quotation from Ronald Hagler, "Nonbook Materials: Chapters 7 through 11," in *The Making of a Code: The Issues Underlying AACR2*, ed. Doris Hargrett Clack (Chicago: American Library Association (ALA), 1980), p. 72.

4. Seymour Lubetzky, "Design for a Code," in *Reader in Classification and Descriptive Cataloging*, ed. Ann F. Painter (Washington: NCR:/ Microcard Editions, 1972), p. 209.

5. Geoffrey Whatmore, "Current Affairs Information for the Media," *ASLIB Proceedings*, 33 (November-December, 1981), p. 455.

6. *Ibid.*

7. See, for example, the various editions of Jean Weihs' *Nonbook Materials: The Organization of Integrated Collections* (Canadian Library Association, 1970, 1973, and 1979) or either edition of the (British) Library Association's *Non-Book Materials Cataloguing Rules* (1973 and 1974).

8. McLuhan, p. 172.

9. International Federation of Library Associations and Institutions. *ISBD (NBM): International Standard Bibliographic Description for Non-Book Materials* (London: IFLA International Office for UBC, 1977), p. 1.

10. Lester Asheim, "Introduction," *Library Quarterly*, 45 (January, 1975), p. 2.

11. *The White House Conference on Library and Information Services 1979; Resolutions* (Washington: The Conference, 1979), p. 8.

12. Charles A. Cutter, *Rules for a Dictionary Catalogue*, 2nd edition with corrections and additions (Washington: Government Printing Office, 1889), p. 8.

13. In the Preface to his 1853 *Index to Periodical Literature*, Poole says, "Some five years since, while connected with the library of the "Society of Brothers in Unity" in Yale College, I attempted to execute a plan by which the contents of the periodicals could be made accessible to the students of that institution, in the preparation of their written exercises, and the discussions of their literary societies . . . I arranged, under topics which were supposed to be of interest to that community, references to the periodicals in which they were treated."

14. See articles by Charles A. Cutter, Seymour Lubetzky and the preliminary report of the International Conference on Cataloging Principles held in Paris in 1961 in the *Reader in Classification and Descriptive Cataloging*, 184, pp. 208-210 and 211-212.

15. Seymour Lubetzky, *Principles of Cataloging, Final Report, Phase 1: Descriptive Cataloging* (Los Angeles: Institute of Library Research, 1969), p. 13.

16. American National Standards Institute, Inc. *American National Standard Format for Bibliographic Information Interchange on Magnetic Tape.* (New York: ANSI), 1971.

17. Formally identified as the Committee on Cataloging: Description and Access of the Cataloging and Classification Section of the Resources and Technical Services Division of the American Library Association, this committee is charged with responsibility for continually assessing the state of the art of descriptive cataloging and recommending changes and solutions to problems.

RECOMMENDED READING

Avram, Henriette D. *MARC: Its History and Implications.* Washington: Library of Congress, 1975.

Boyle, Deirdre, ed. *Expanding Media.* Phoenix: Oryx Press, 1977.

Dunkin, Paul. *Cataloging U.S.A.* Chicago: American Library Association, 1969.

Freedman, Maurice J., and S. Michael Malinconico, eds. *The Nature and Future of the Catalog: Proceedings of the ALA's Information Science and Automation Division's 1975 and 1977 Institutes on the Catalog.* Phoenix: Oryx Press, 1979.

Henderson, James W., and Joseph A. Rosenthal. *Library Catalogs: Their Preservation and Maintenance.* Cambridge, Mass.: Published for the New York Public Library by M.I.T. Press, 1968.

Malinconico, S. Michael, and Paul J. Fasana. *The Future of the Catalog: The Library's Choices.* White Plains, N.Y.: Knowledge Industry Publications, 1979.

A Nationwide Network: Development, Governance, Support. Washington: Library of Congress, 1981.

The White House Conference on Library and Information Services: Summary. Washington: The Conference, 1980.

Chapter 2

Components of Media Librarianship

THE concept of media librarianship is relatively new, evolving as a distinct pattern of skills with particular kinds of collections and materials only since about 1950. It is not that libraries had no media collections before then, but rather that these were not thought of as requiring knowledge or procedures different from books and serials. Growth of media collections and development of objectives and services based upon them did not begin to assume significant proportions until after World War II, years which were witness to the rise of other new ideas about information materials and services as well.

At first, media collections were few and small. Media were less important as communication modes than as evidence of innovation in materials and services. Special libraries more frequently had sizable collections of certain nonprint media than general libraries, e.g., music librarians were familiar with handling scores and recordings, and art librarians had experience with collections of visual representations of works of art. General public and academic libraries were slow to collect a variety of media until the 1960s and even later, in the 1970s, in contrast to school libraries which quickly converted to the use and collection of "audiovisual aids."

The first part of this chapter provides an overview of the establishment and growth of media collections in libraries, particularly public libraries. Once media collections developed beyond the point where they could be put in a drawer, a box or two, or on a rack without any kind of formal organization, librarians began seeking methods of administering them. Thus, the second part of the chapter is devoted to an examination of the ways in which this was done—the first exploratory manuals, the rise of media cataloging rules, and other standards affecting the way these materials have traditionally been organized in libraries. Experts' arguments over philosophy and treatment of nonbook media, and the eventual compromises contained in the second edition of *AACR2* is a background against which current practices may be understood.

Influence of computer technology on current practices of bibliographic access and control for media is a third element explored in this chapter. A brief examination of automation activities involving nonprint media shows that some projects have served to isolate nonprint media further from books and other printed materials, while in others just the opposite has occurred, at least for some kinds of materials. No examination of current bibliographic practices would be complete without recognition of the prominent role played by computers.

These three components of media librarianship—the development of collections, evolution of organizational rules and administrative practices, and automation—constitute a context in which current practices can be understood and evaluated.

DEVELOPMENT OF MEDIA COLLECTIONS

Libraries have a long history of collecting nonprint materials. Melvil Dewey acknowledged the value of such materials in satisfying users' information needs as early as the first decade of the century.[1] One hundred years earlier, Benjamin Franklin combined collecting scientific apparatus with reading materials in his subscription library in Philadelphia, established in 1731.[2] But Franklin's nonprint materials, like those in the British Museum, while intended for the general edification of library patrons, were more in the nature of museum displays than the informational, recreational, or inspirational materials in printed form with which they shared the space. Indeed, even today it is not uncommon for libraries to devote some of their floor space to displays of various kinds consisting of artifacts from their own collections as well as from outside sources. Two examples of modern day institutions which include such exhibits as an important part of their services to the public are the Morgan Library and the Library and Museum of the Performing Arts at Lincoln Center, both in New York City.

The Library of Congress has been a leader in collecting nonbook media materials, as might be expected, with a map collection going back to 1800,[3] and receipt of photographic prints of motion pictures —the only way early films could be registered for copyright—beginning in 1894.[4] The films themselves were accepted after the 1912 amendment to the Copyright Act, but fire hazards associated with

storage of nitrate film made it impossible for LC to retain them for
their collections after the copyright inspection. Not until 1942 did
revival of interest in collecting films and development of safer
acetate film technology coincide to support efforts to begin developing historical film collections. These collections are now among the
nation's best.[5]

Many city libraries experimented before 1950 with film collections and services. These included libraries in Beaumont, Texas;
Charlotte, North Carolina; Cleveland, Ohio; Dallas, Texas;
Edgewater, New Jersey; Gary, Indiana; Kalamazoo, Michigan;
Madison and Milwaukee, Wisconsin; and Seattle, Washington; as
well as the state library of California.[6] Carnegie grants were made
to public libraries for developing film activities as early as 1941 and
continued until about 1954. During the period between 1947 and
1951, the bulk of the grants designated for collection and service de-
velopment were made. In these years, the libraries of Akron,
Baltimore, Boston, Canton, Cincinnati, Dearborn, Detroit,
Evanston, Knoxville, Louisville, Middletown, Nashville, New
Rochelle, Peoria, Portland, Racine, Rochester, San Antonio, Santa
Monica, Sheboygan, Stamford, and Toledo began to provide film
services to the residents of those cities. Regional groups were organized as well in Ohio, Missouri, Tennessee, Michigan, New York,
Washington, and California to serve smaller library agencies. Some
of these Carnegie funds were allocated to the American Library Association to establish a film office and staff to assist librarians in
these endeavors. Other funds were invested in the development of
the prototype film circuits, whereby village, town, and smaller city
libraries could share the cost of these new materials with larger
jurisdictions, and cooperate in the distribution of all of them by
rotating them among themselves.

In 1950, Robert Leigh reported that fewer than 100 public
libraries in the country were involved in film activities. He declared
with great optimism, however, "It might well be that within a decade practically all public libraries in cities over 75,000 or 100,000
will circulate information films. Extension of film service through
public libraries to smaller communities, however, requires novel cooperative arrangements. . . ."[7] His optimism was probably due to the
promotion of film activity by ALA and the Carnegie grants. The use
of informational films by the military during the Second World War
and the inauguration of public library film programs to support the
war effort were among the moving forces behind the increase of interest in the medium and the participation of the Carnegie Corpora-

tion, at least at the outset of their program.[8]

·Professional activities in the decade before 1950 included the founding of the ALA Audiovisual Committee in 1940 and its incorporation with the Visual Methods Committee, established earlier, in 1934. Also in 1940, ALA was a participant in the Joint Committee on Educational Films and Libraries with the American Film Center, Association of School Film Librarians, and Motion Picture Project of the American Council on Education.[9] Most importantly, in 1947, ALA used the funding of the Carnegie Corporation, about $27,000, to expand film services to smaller communities by organizing the film circuits and hiring a professional adviser for films. Work was begun on a manual to be used by public libraries, too, as part of the project.

The 1940s and 1950s saw expanded film activities in many areas. The Library of Congress was prompted to publish its catalog of films for copyright,[10] as well as its film cataloging rules,[11] and in 1951 it began selling its printed cards for films as it had done half a century earlier for books. ALA's *Booklist* also started to list films and filmstrips at this time. The Resources and Technical Services Division's Audiovisual Committee (RTSD/AV) conducted a survey of audiovisual cataloging practices in 1956 covering films, filmstrips, and sound recordings, based on the belief that films were among the more popular nonprint media collected in libraries, despite their cost.[12] (It should be noted, however, that the institutions surveyed were selected *because* they were listed in a film reference work or directory of film librarians, not at random from the universe of libraries.)[13]

In the sixties, library film activities were enlarged greatly with Library Service and Construction Act funds, including a large project in New York State and the establishment of the National Audiovisual Center in Washington, D.C., whose responsibilities included the distribution of government agency-produced AV products as well as information about them. The Educational Resources Information Center (ERIC) Media Center was also starting to branch out into micrographic format in this period and later computerized. Activities of the National Information Center for Education Media (NICEM), which originated in 1950 as an information, storage, and distribution center for films created by students of the University of Southern California's Cinema Division, began to affect a larger and rapidly growing circle of libraries interested in exerting control over an explosion of media titles. NICEM, whose leadership recognized that Cinema Division products were a valuable resource for the entire educational community, pioneered in applying computer technology to the control and indexing of its resources. In 1967, McGraw-Hill began to publish these indexes, produced from the growing databases for a variety of nonprint media. Today, NICEM's coverage of many media forms and the range of tools it can produce and services it can offer are among the most comprehensive and diverse in the nation. In 1968, the Los Angeles Public Library published its first computerized film catalog, based on NICEM's work.

Other film activities during this period included the founding of film-related publications including *Film Library Quarterly* and the first *Film Evaluation Guide*, participation in groups such as the Educational Film Library Association (EFLA) and the Film Library Information Council (FLIC), as well as the inauguration of film festivals. Much of the work described here was directed toward the lower schools. Even smaller city school districts were enthusiastically collecting educational films and using them in classrooms and auditoriums on a regular basis. These were short documentaries on a great range of topics designed to coordinate with popular curricula. Public libraries were also participating, to a lesser extent, in this fever of collecting activity; while academic institutions, excluded from receiving federal funds for such materials for much longer than their public and school library counterparts, were the least interested in building film collections. The cost of feature length films made them difficult to collect in large numbers, even for larger institutions like the regional film groups, and some, of course, were not even available for sale. For these reasons, film collection building was uneven and, outside of educational films intended for lower schools, did not include a great deal of overlap from one collection to another. Also, it should be remembered that many of the libraries that purchased films did so to use them for programming purposes, not for circulation by individuals outside the library buildings. Though the Fitchburg, Massachusetts, Public Library began circulating films in 1947, this was not a universally provided service, even in 1970.

Introduction of films into college and university libraries may have proceeded more slowly, but was certainly not absent altogether. Interest in contemporary history, popular culture, film as art, and communication studies depended heavily on film and later video resources. Considered nonscholarly by some, they became accepted on campuses across the country, bringing with them a need to collect, control, and organize for use their sources—films and tapes. At the same time, the technique of visual reproduction on film or tape for other, more traditional disciplines, especially science and medicine, was being exploited by more and more institutions, so these collections began to grow, too. Participation in organizations such as the Consortium of University Film Centers (CUFC) and collection of film and video resources by universities was marked in the seventies.

Film is only one kind of nonbook format, however. Edna Hanna claims the first collection of phonograph records in an American library was established in 1914 at the St. Paul, Minnesota, Public Library.[14] Musical recordings became popular in public libraries more rapidly than films. Reporting on the public library inquiry in 1950, Robert Leigh states that the study revealed 73% of the large libraries sampled had sound recordings among their holdings.[15] This is the same study that reported film collections in a hundred city libraries. The contrast speaks for itself.

According to Leigh, the lack of "adequate" music divisions (those) containing scores and sound recordings as well as books about music) in communities under 100,000 was due to their relatively high cost compared to books; thus, smaller libraries with limited budgets could not afford them. Only 11% of the smaller libraries in the inquiry sample had holdings of sound recordings and 9% of the county libraries did. Leigh concludes, "... in terms of numbers of libraries only about one in twenty-five public libraries, at most, has gone in for nonbook music materials."[16] Still, it was a much higher number than had gone in for motion pictures.

Cooper reports on the rapid expansion of collections of sound recordings in public libraries between 1939 and 1968:

> In 1939 there were twenty-five public collections, and by 1940 ... some fifty public libraries had collections of varying types ... The Second World War, like the First, inhibited progress for all American libraries, but in 1945 the number of libraries offering phonorecord lending services to the public or collections of recorded material for use on library premises began to increase in number at a tremendous speed. Microgroove recordings arrived in 1948, and an examination of the *American Library Directory* would have revealed that over 40 percent of general public libraries listed have phonorecords available either for loan or for listening to on library equipment.[17]

During the 1950s the Library of Congress, in cooperation with the Music Library Association (MLA) and the ALA, devised cataloging rules for sound materials and published them[18] as well as a catalog of additions to their collections[19] and began selling printed cards. In

1958, ALA published cataloging rules for recordings prepared jointly with MLA.[20]

While Leigh saw music collections, like film collections, as developing primarily in larger communities, the advent of cheaper and more durable long-playing records revolutionized the industry. Recordings not only of music but also of spoken words—plays, poetry, stories, and lectures on all subjects—were widely available. It did not take an enormous investment to begin a collection, and the recreational and educational value of records was praised in the library and education literatures. Thus, sound materials rapidly became familiar library resources in the quarter-century beginning in 1950.

The development of the excellent Rodgers and Hammerstein Archive of Recorded Sound held by the Music Division of New York Public Library at Lincoln Center—part of the reference collections of the Research Libraries, not the circulating collections open to the public—illustrates quite well this pattern of collection building.[21] No one paid too much attention to the sound materials acquired in fits and starts under the leadership of far sighted Carleton Sprague Smith until the end of the 1930s. During that time, Smith and his assistant, Philip Miller, started using them to provide Sunday afternoon concerts free to the public. Eventually, the collection was expanded, organized, and indexed, and a closed-stacked remote dissemination system was devised so recordings could be used by scholars without unsupervised handling. This occurred in the 1960s after the Music Division moved into new quarters in Lincoln Center.

Once again, the university library community was considerably slower in accumulating collections than public and/or school libraries. Boss[22] reported in 1972 that a survey of sound materials in a sample of 68 academic research libraries revealed only 25% of the collections were worthy of follow-up interviews to determine their details. Fully 25% had no audiovisual collections at all and, presumably, the rest of them had some materials but were deemed inadequate by Boss.

Collection building in other nonprint media such as graphic materials (photographs, drawings, filmstrips, posters, etc.), cartographic materials (maps, globes, etc.), microforms, video, artefacts, and other three-dimensional materials, etc., have proceeded along similar lines in general libraries in many instances. They also have followed other patterns. For example, most general libraries always had some cartographic holdings, usually maps and atlases, although globes may have been provided for reference, too. These were often maintained as reference materials outside the main holdings of that department, often uncataloged and sometimes even without indexing except in the most rudimentary fashion, and were not part of a consciously developed group of materials. Atlases were often cataloged and shelved as books, unless they were oversized. In some institutions, map collections were heavily used, as well as atlases, charts, globes, and models. In such libraries, accumulation of map and cartographic collections did not follow the pattern of sound recordings and films but were developed in sophisticated ways well before mid-century. Access was provided by specialized indexing methods, developed by professional geographers. These collections were usually associated with departments of geography or other research-oriented institutions.

Videorecordings provide a different example. These materials only became generally available in recent years, when more attention has been paid to nonprint issues. Still, Genova reported in his examination of video in libraries that collections were frequently small and uncontrolled.[23] These small collections of newer formats are developing much more quickly and in an atmosphere quite different from that which prevailed in the 1940s and 1950s, when libraries had little experience with media other than books and there were few tools on which they could rely for advice and information.

Perhaps one of the biggest problems with the rapid growth of media collections since 1950 is that librarians have not changed as quickly in their perceptions of media as a single kind of material significant primarily in its differentiation from printed materials. Some years ago, an audiovisual department in a general public or academic library might have been expected to include motion pictures and other filmed materials such as photographs, slides, filmstrips, sound recordings in disc and, possibly, reel-to-reel tape formats, and one or more of a variety of instructional items sometimes collected by non-school libraries, such as flash cards, posters, wall charts, transparencies, and so forth. Maps were usually administered in separate, departmental libraries, as were musical scores, manuscripts, and microforms. In fact, graphic materials related to art programs and musical materials were also frequently administered separately, by art or music librarians who had no idea how to deal with the rest of the nonprint/nonbook/audiovisual formats and who were satisfied with unique arrangements they devised to manage those nonbook items in their charge.

By 1970, there were more than six different and not interchangeable sound recording formats being collected—tapes in reel-to-reel, cassette, and cartridge, and discs in 33⅓, 45, and 78 rpm—and other less common formats, including sound pages, 16 rpm discs, and more. Sound recordings in even more exotic formats existed in historical collections. Thus, sound recordings could hardly be called a medium. Similarly, photographic slides were not one medium; videorecordings could be quite different depending on who manufactured them, and even photographs were not all alike, although they did not require different kinds of equipment to be viewed.

The problem caused by media being lumped together into one entity (libraries had book stock, periodical subscriptions, and nonprint media) is that it rapidly became evident that no single set of policies, procedures, or rules could be created to cover them all; no dealer, producer, or agent could be expected to supply them all; no tool, index, or review journal listed them all; and no environment was likely to be equally hospitable to them all at once. Because a librarian was conversant with current films did not imply he or she was familiar with video, or sound materials, or the latest in filmstrips being issued by the most popular producers. In spite of all this, it was not unusual for libraries to have an audiovisual or media librarian, as if all of these diverse formats were one.

Schools and colleges (as well as public libraries and universities) that created media centers were really creating environments with the flexibility to house these various materials, with a special emphasis on providing electricity for equipment, a number of different kinds of storage areas, and viewing and/or listening areas. Media librarians had to be extremely versatile individuals, able to cope well with many sets of problems. It was not unusual for those libraries without specially designated media professionals to assign responsibility for media to a children's librarian, or circulation librarian, or someone else with other, more basic duties. A survey of Connecticut's public libraries revealed that children's librarians were most often responsible for the library's nonprint media, followed by administrators, designated film staff, reference librarians or subject specialists, circulation librarians, and catalogers, in descending order of frequency.[24] Of the 118 participants in this survey, most had phonograph records, but only eighty-two had some film activity, fifty-three had picture files, thirty-five collected realia, twenty-five had art prints, fourteen had posters, and video activities were reported by only six libraries.

Despite the progress indicated by the events listed in Appendix A, in an introduction to a *Library Trends* issue devoted to nonprint materials and services published in 1967, Stone wrote, "While the case is not made in so many words, a strong negative impression might be gained from reading at one sitting the eleven articles which comprise this issue of *Library Trends*. This impression would be that librarianship has completely missed the boat in developing newer media services; that necessary professional recruitment and training, both pre-service and in-service, are almost totally lacking; and that public library progress in the field is still 'little by little and bit by bit.' "[25]

As one might expect, growth of collections was linked to several factors, not the least of which was the cost and life expectancy of media items as well as the sophistication of the public in their use. Public libraries needed to be convinced that people would use media materials if they were made available; academic libraries, geared to curriculum support and research activities of their faculties and students, needed to be reminded by these users, particularly faculty, that they were necessary and proper as part of scholarly collections. As has already been said, school libraries were the most enthusiastic collectors of media as well as the first to begin using and developing them. Nevertheless, not even the school library sector was successful in meeting standards for holdings set by national professional organizations, according to a study performed for the National Commission on Libraries and Information Science (NCLIS) by Ladd in 1975.[26] The extensively documented report was published two years later and revealed that no segment of the library community had met the standards. Although the total number of audiovisual titles owned in the public library sector exceeded the total needs identified, the only sector in which this occurred, the distribution of resources was so unbalanced that Ladd declared, "... because many libraries fell far short of their indicated needs the aggregate shortage is 56% of the indicated needs."[27] Despite aggregate holdings of a hundred million items, school libraries were shown to have the largest unmet audiovisual resource needs—an indicated need of one billion items.[28] Interestingly enough, in this NCLIS study, academic library needs were measured in volumes for both books and audiovisuals, though exactly how this was done was not clear. In any case, academic library needs—both print and nonprint—totalled 158 million volumes, a far lower number of volumes than the audiovisual needs alone in school libraries.[29] Clearly, Ladd demonstrated dramatically the urgent need for additional resources in libraries when existing holdings were measured against professionally determined standards. This was, however, only part of the disturbing findings of his work. Even more distressing was the contrast between resource-rich areas and resource-poor areas in the country. Once again, this imbalance was found for both printed and audiovisual materials. A statewide survey of audiovisual resources conducted at about the same time in California—a state that was in the forefront of development of film service—in which holdings and services were measured against existing standards for libraries, found the same situation. Bogan reported: "... among the California public libraries and library systems surveyed there were extensive inconsistencies in the range and character of audiovisual services, in the variety and quantity of audiovisual materials provided, in staffing, financing, and in the space provided for audiovisual services."[30]

The unpleasant truth contained in these reports and others like them has not been refuted since they were published. It seems to be a function of library service that, since standards for nonprint materials were established by various interested organizations, they have not been met, despite the astonishing growth of media collections all across the country. It is not that the standards have been set too high, either. Critics of most library standards have agreed that, if anything, they have been set too low, establishing only minimum levels of collections and services, rather than ideals toward which even the best libraries can strive. This sobering picture of media development should be kept in mind as methods for administering and organizing nonbook collections are investigated.

ADMINISTRATION AND ORGANIZATION OF MEDIA IN LIBRARIES

Unlike books, which were collected gradually for hundreds of years in libraries in manageable numbers while organizational strategies were perfected, media collections mushroomed in only about forty years or less. Palmer describes early attempts at defining the role films could play in public libraries:

In December 1940, Alice I. Bryan of Columbia University's School of Library Service submitted a proposal to several national organizations outlining a plan for a "concerted attempt to strengthen civilian morale." She suggested that a series of weekly programs be presented in public libraries consisting of moving pictures followed by a "discussion period under the guidance of trained adult education leaders in the community." ... The American Library Association undertook leadership of the project, in January, 1941, forming a Committee on Film Forums ... it was decided to seek funds—not from the government but from the Carnegie Corporation. A grant was forthcoming in March 1941; demonstrations were undertaken in various public libraries and at the 1941 ALA Conference.

The film forum movement flourished during the next few years. It gained impetus from our entry into World War II and represented the first large-scale use of films in public libraries. By showing that libraries could be used to reach the people with information films, the movement led to public libraries becoming a locus for government deposit of civilian information films during World War II. This in turn led to the development of the first public library film collections of consequence.[31]

The basic thrust of film collections was in support of large audience programming, rather than satisfying individuals' information needs. This has continued through the establishment of film circuits and other film booking systems whereby participating libraries can reserve and use a film for their own programs from a centrally administered store of titles held by a state library, regional or local film group or consortium.

All of this activity had to be based on development of suitable descriptions of the films both for inventory purposes and for use as selection aids for the libraries using them in programming. Carnegie funded a union catalog project for films in Louisiana which resulted in publication in 1952 of a catalog of 855 titles owned by libraries in that state.[32] There was, however, no intention to incorporate these new materials into existing collections or access systems and no such idea arose for years.

Library of Congress cards for films, filmstrips, scores, and sound recordings were available and could be used for creating catalogs, too; however, the match between LC cataloging and the kind of access being furnished in local libraries was not ideal. LC did not catalog everything being produced and purchased; it was slow in its production of cards and cataloging copy; its cataloging was not appropriate for non-research libraries in style, content, and arrangement of information. Many libraries made up their own cataloging styles, entry formats, and organizational procedures. Others turned to commercial services. In assessing the effects on cataloging of commercial services, Hines points out: "Not only have commercial firms made a *de facto* contribution toward providing a standard practice where present rules leave options open, they have been forced into other areas—the cataloging of nonprint materials and the classification of phonorecords and tapes, for example—where conflicting rules existed or no suitable rules were available."[33]

When exercise of control over media became a pressing problem, many manuals, codes, and systems sprang up, some with the authority of national or regional organizations, and others produced by individual libraries for others in need of guidance. In a period of about thirty years, three major national organizations published different multimedia codes in more than one edition; LC's nonprint cataloging publications appeared in later editions; numerous regional or individually-sponsored works for many media and even more manuals covering only a single medium appeared. By the 1970s, when collections were already expanding in size and number, the library literature was filled with articles urging standards be set for nonprint cataloging, and uniformity became a high priority.[34] Since 1967, publication year of *AACR1*, all the major nationally-sponsored multimedia codes were themselves published and revised,[35] achieving a high degree of uniformity after 1978, publication year of *AACR2*. In spite of this rapid transition from many approaches to a smaller scope of differences, the problem of recataloging collections to conform with the changes is enormous and expensive.

The literature relating to media access in the late 1960s and early 1970s reveals two divergent schools of thought. The more vocal group advocated treating nonprint materials exactly like books and serials, using cataloging rules that conformed as much as possible to those for books. Indeed, one complaint voiced by catalogers about *AACR1* was that the entries that resulted were not consistent, and therefore not integrable. Code revision resulting in the second edition (1978) had as one of its objectives to rectify this situation. In the forefront of this group was Jean Riddle Weihs who, with two collaborators, prepared the Canadian Library Association-sponsored media cataloging code titled *Nonbook Materials: The Organization of Integrated Collections*. The authors stated, "... [we] advocate the integration of collections, both in the catalog and on the shelves, because [we] believe that this results in the best public service."[36] After a preliminary edition in 1970 tested the waters, both numbered editions of this code were designed to be used in conjunction with editions of *AACR*, and to produce integrable, consistent entries. Doak went even further than Weihs, insisting that separate audiovisual departments and positions be abolished in favor of decentralizing media responsibilities and materials to wherever they might naturally be expected to be found according to their content, and having all staff members equally adept at their handling and use.[37]

The second school of thought held that each medium's unique characteristics required bibliographic treatment different from books, and frequently, from other nonprint formats as well. Jay E. Daily, an eloquent proponent of this view, wrote in his widely used book, *Organizing Nonprint Materials*, "Preparing [bibliographic] records of nonprint materials represents a special problem.... The rules that pertain to books are frequently not at all appropriate for nonprint materials because the nonprint materials do not lend themselves necessarily to the support of theories of description.[38] Echoing this viewpoint were the first three editions of *Standards for Cataloging Nonprint Materials*, the multimedia cataloging code of the Association for Educational Communications and Technology (AECT) and its predecessor, the Department of Audio-Visual Instruction of the National Education Association. These codes mandated title main entry for all nonprint media and were thus irreconcilable with *AACR* cataloging for books.[39]

Arguments between the two schools of thought centered on several issues:

- Applicability of principles of book cataloging to other kinds of materials

- Proper administation of nonprint media

- Ability of current (at that time) access systems to accommodate nonprint media.

The fundamental issue appeared to be which of conflicting objectives in administering nonprint collections was more important to satisfy: to capitalize on the unique qualities of each medium which differentiate it from all others; or to emphasize the similarities of all media (including books) as library materials in order to integrate them with one another.

As the 1970s passed, national and international professional leaders appeared to endorse the latter view, persuading their peers that bibliographical integration was both possible and desirable. In addition to Weihs and Doak, Ronald Hagler, Suzanne Massonneau, Sanford Berman, Antony Croghan, Janet Andrew, and Christopher Ravilious are some of the experts on both sides of the Atlantic to champion the integrationist viewpoint.

A look at events leading up to the publication of the first omnimedia cataloging code, *AACR2*, illustrates the development of a commitment to bibliographic integration on the part of professional leaders in the U.S. and abroad.

In the chronology in Appendix A, the pioneering efforts of the Library of Congress in the 1950s to formulate and publish rules for the cataloging of nonprint materials it collected (motion pictures, filmstrips, sound recordings, and graphics) are recorded. These publications, together with similar prototypes from such specialized groups as the Music Library Association, were the only codifications of nonprint cataloging rules until 1967, when they were updated and included as Part III of *AACR1*.[40] In the late 1960s and early 1970s, four major professional organizations concerned with access to nonprint materials sponsored the publication of multimedia cataloging codes, though excluding coverage of books and certain other formats. The Canadian code has already been mentioned, as well as the AECT's *Standards*. The Library Association and National Council for Educational Technology, on the opposite side of the Atlantic, published *Non-book Materials Cataloguing Rules...*, designed to coordinate with the British text of *AACR* in much the same way as the Canadian rules did with the North American text. This British code was called the LANCET rules, from the initials of its sponsoring bodies, and it offered different solutions to problems, varying drastically on choice of terminology prescribed for naming the media. This difference still persists, with *AACR2* including two lists of terms for designating media, one for the British and one for North Americans.[41] Appendix B furnishes the full titles and publication dates for all of these multimedia codes.

AACR1's nonprint media rules were not well accepted in the United States. First, they were written to fulfill the needs of research libraries, not the larger library community, as clearly stated in the first page of the text. School librarians, the biggest purchasers of new media products, were not necessarily trained in cataloging and many could not fathom *AACR1*. They had neither the professional commitment to the code nor the pressure of scholarly users to motivate them to conform. What they wanted were simpler rules and helpful illustrations, neither of which characterized *AACR1*. Other criticisms were that only a small number of media were covered; no standard terminology was provided; there were inconsistencies in the rules; the common problem of multiple titles for media was not addressed; medium was not clearly or consistently indicated; application of author-title principles to media was confusing; and, finally, the entries were not integrable with each other and with those for books.

Some of the problems were addressed by the other codes. They all covered more media, though not the same ones. Many more instructional materials were included, such as kits, dioramas, charts, flash cards, and models. The CLA and AECT rules were simplified and many illustrations and sample entries were provided. Only the LANCET rules were more abstruse and less exampled than *AACR1*. All had lists of terms to be used in naming the media and directions on how to apply them. Many were quite different for the same medium, e.g., sound recordings were called *audiorecording* by Weihs and the AECT, *phonorecord* by *AACR1* and LC, and *sound disc* by the LANCET rules. The alternative codes disagreed on where the medium designator should be put in the entry, with some codes opting to put it after the title and others putting it only in the collation or physical description area (*AACR2*'s Area 5). The alternative codes were internally consistent, however, while *AACR1* put the medium designator after the title for films and sound recordings, but not for graphics, where it appeared only in the collation.[42]

The codes varied on their approaches to author-title cataloging, with *Standards* mandating title main entry for all materials until its fourth edition, published in 1976. Even then, the language of the rule implied strict limitations on the number of cases to which personal, or even corporate, authorship could apply. The LANCET rules defined authorship so as to make it difficult, but not impossible, to apply and though the Canadian rules were less strict in their definition, sample entries were divided approximately 41 percent author main entry and 59 percent title main entry. The language and styles of the AECT and Canadian codes were simpler, easier to understand and less theoretical than *AACR1*. The LANCET rules were just the opposite, however, although their method of organization—a chapter of general rules followed by three chapters of rules applicable to each of three broad categories of media, graphics and three-dimensional materials, motion pictures, and sound recordings—made them easier to follow. The entries produced using any one of the alternative codes were integrable with one another; and the British and Canadian codes also coordinated with book entries produced using the appropriate version of *AACR1*.

While the alternative codes did not successfully address all problems, they resolved some of those considered most pressing by the constituencies of the organizations that sponsored them. In the brief period from 1967 to 1973, librarians went from having only LC's guidelines or rules of specialized groups for individual media to having at least four multimedia codes with the weight of various authorities behind them. Clearly, this was a confusing and chaotic situation for general libraries. Nevertheless, there were rules to be followed if an institution chose to do so; and if not, they could use them as guidelines and adapt them for individual use. Manuals of cataloging procedures used in individual libraries or by local groups began to appear, some based on the published codes and others deliberately different. Simplifications of codes and illustrations for using them became popular in this growing body of literature.

By 1975, when it seemed clear that a new code would soon appear, battle lines were drawn over certain issues: (1) terminology; (2) designator placement; (3) author vs. title main entry; (4) integrability of entries; (5) elimination of inconsistencies. Some of these problems were resolved by *AACR2*. Its orientation toward establishing a basic structure applicable to all media, treating all media then being collected, and addressing the concerns of all general libraries, not only research libraries, helped to solve problems of usage, inconsistency, and placement of bibliographic elements. To some degree, the issue of main entry was alleviated by separating creation of the description from selection of headings or access points by which they are filed as part of the basic structure of the work, though this has been criticized by some cataloging theorists.[43] The Canadian and U.S. groups were able to agree on a list of twenty-four terms, but the British found them too specific and held out for a separate one containing only twelve.

On the whole, with some notable exceptions such as newer forms of computer and video materials, *AACR2* seems to have answered most of the problems of its predecessor and represents a large measure of agreement derived from the earlier codes and their sponsors. The British have not brought out any more versions of the LANCET rules, content to use *AACR2*; the Canadians published a second edition of *Nonbook Materials* with appropriate changes to coordinate with *AACR2*; and as of this writing, AECT are supposedly doing the same, with a fifth edition of *Standards* in progress.

Subject headings and classifications are another issue. There has been no effort matching that of developing a multimedia cataloging code to develop a multimedia subject list or classification. On the other hand, any general subject list or classification of all knowledge should be as applicable to nonprint media as it is to books. Thus, perhaps the question is not why has no such effort been made, but rather why should it be made at all? Problems of subject analysis and classification appear to arise with extremely large and/or highly specialized collections in a particular discipline or interdisciplinary group in which nonprint materials may be a significant part of the holdings. In such cases, general subject lists and classifications do not have the degree of specificity necessary to satisfy users of such materials. This is equally true of book collections of like size and speciality. Indeed, all the same criticisms made of the *Library of Congress Subject Headings* (LCSH) or *Sears List of Subject Headings*, or of the Library of Congress or Dewey decimal classifications, are valid whether they are applied to book or non-book collections as well as to combinations of both. Among these criticisms are that they are too slow to change, reflecting new disciplines and terminology, that they are linear and do not adequately reflect the multidimensionality of ideas and their relationships, that they are inconsistent, incomplete, and overly complex.[44]

The more difficult task, perhaps, is demonstrating that the use of an accession number classification or the lack of subject analysis does a disservice to public or college library users who are accustomed to using both subject headings and shelf arrangements to help them find information in books; therefore, they can reasonably expect the same help with all informational materials, regardless of medium. In 1972, the Chair of the Committee on Audiovisual Media in Libraries of the Cataloging and Classification Section of RTSD, reported endorsement by the Committee of the use of standard subject heading lists and classification systems for all media, although it stopped short of recommending that libraries intershelve the materials. A library could do that if it wished, provided all materials were classified according to the same scheme.[45] An observer to a discussion of a specialized slide classification asked, "As a user, I will come to a place of information, wanting a book, a slide, a film, a filmstrip, a tape, a recording. Are you going to send me to ten different systems in ten different ways?"[46] One cannot help asking whether it is more advantageous to the user to emphasize the dissimilarities among media and design subject lists and classifications for them individually, or to concentrate on applying a single, all-purpose system to all materials in the library, while working to improve that system simultaneously?

To sum up, the years between the two editions of the *Anglo-American Cataloguing Rules* saw the development of three nationally sponsored media codes which dealt with some of the inadequacies of the research library, book-oriented code. These became the basis for the second edition, which achieved compromise on many of the thorniest issues and set the stage for uniform treatment of bibliographic description and related access points.

No comparable attention was directed to subject headings and classification schemes by national professional groups. Many schemes for arranging media on library shelves sprang up, developed by local or subject-interest groups or individual libraries. These had important impact on the accessibility of media materials. A review of shelving problems follows:

1. *Nonbrowsable shelf arrangements.* In an article decrying the chaos in classification of sound recordings, Stevenson reported that 38% of the schemes in use in 392 libraries he surveyed were based on accession numbers; and, if arrangements based on manufacturers' numbers was added to these, the figure rose to 43%.[47] The result of using such schemes for arranging these or other nonprint materials on open shelves, or going further and denying physical access to nonprint shelves altogether, is that the client's only approach to nonbook materials is through the catalog.

2. *Closed stacks.* Many reasons have been offered for denying clients open access to nonprint shelves. They include the fact that audiovisual materials usually require the use of playback or projection equipment. Materials that cannot be sampled on the spot as books can do not offer much satisfaction to browsers. Some libraries are well equipped with playback and projection hardware, but even these are not always set up close enough to the storage areas to allow users to sample materials freely. Few libraries have enough viewing or listening stations to satisfy the demand. Patrons are not equally knowledgeable about all kinds of equipment, so in addition to providing the hardware, expert assistance in using it is often required. Another reason given for closing stacks is to avoid theft and vandalism. Sound cassettes, slides, film spools, videorecordings, diskettes, and more media, are all small enough to fit into a pocket or handbag. To keep materials on open shelves, administrators must operate on assumptions of honesty, good intentions, and respect for property. Some are simply unwilling to do so, pointing to mistreatment of other facilities by the public. Even when no damage is intended, carelessness or ignorance can do harm. Slides, films, and photographs are easily smudged with fingerprints; tapes can be stretched, erased, re-recorded, or demagnetized; disks can be scratched or ruined by careless handling or a bad stylus and warped by heat or poor shelving. Heat, light, and humidity cause damage to nonprint formats just as they do to books, and so do many other environmental pollutants. A third reason is economy—closed stacks eliminate higher replacement costs and are efficient to maintain.

3. *Packaging.* Some nonprint items, e.g., many films, are stored in

nearly blank cans that offer little information to the casual browser as to their contents. Repackaging items such as this to provide enough information to the browser adds considerably to th , cost of the materials. One of the problems of lumping the diverse f·r·ns which constitute media into one category is that it misleadingly implies uniformity. A single medium such as videorecordings really contains many video formats, few of which are either physically identical or interchangeable. There are single slides, multislide carousels, five-inch 45 rpm sound disks, ten-inch and twelve-inch 33⅓ rpm sound disks, sound cassettes, videocassettes or videodisks, and computer-readable materials on cassettes, multiplatter disk packs or 5¼-inch floppy diskettes. These are only a few examples of the seemingly endless variety of dissimilar shapes and sizes of nonprint media. Each is packaged differently by different producers and would be most easily and efficiently stored in a different environment.

4. *Lack of foresight.* Accession numbers and other "idiot" numbers are attractive to use as the initial ordering system for a new and very small collection of materials. They do not require any intellectual effort to assign and they are unique identifiers. Manufacturers' numbers are used by discographies and catalogs of sound recordings, making them somewhat official and more meaningful than accession numbers. To ordinary library users, their meaning may well be lost. In any case, unbrowsable systems like these force the patron to do two look-ups for any one item, one in an index or catalog and another on the shelf. By the time such a collection has outgrown the advantages of class numbers unrelated to content and the library would like to have built-in browsability, reclassifying has become a costly burden.

The ultimate result of using nonbrowsable classification schemes for nonprint materials is a barrier to their use, especially for clients accustomed to having intellectual access to books directly from their shelf arrangement. However imperfect the retrieval capabilities of general classifications currently in use, they are better than nothing. The price paid for using meaningless location symbols is the added effort to obtain a specific item, or a type of item. This is, however, not the only access problem where saving intellectual effort at the outset creates much more work for the user. A still more serious barrier to use is raised by the treatment of sets.

In 1974, Freudenthal commented that librarians have ignored the problem of intellectual access to slides.[48] Slides and other graphic and micrographic materials are often parts of large sets. If they are cataloged, they are usually treated as a unit. They might relate to a single subject or have some other intellectual commonality or they may not. Their relation could be that they belonged to the same collector or collection or were the output of the same studio or laboratory or artist. Large sets pose economic problems for libraries, since careful and accurate cataloging of each component could add up to a great deal of money. Cataloging the unit, however, shifts the burden of unravelling the content of individual components to the user. Scholars in pursuit of research evidence they suspect is contained in a set might track down individual slides or frames or photographs they need, aided by their experience in doing such research. But what of the non-scholar? The public library user rarely has the motivation, knowledge, or persistence to pursue that kind of search to a successful conclusion.

Efforts to create analytics, or otherwise identify components of sets, have been confined for the most part to the research library community. The problem for micrographics has been documented by Simonton,[49] Thompson, [50] and Myrick.[51] Recently the Association of Research Libraries inaugurated a project to provide access to individual works in micrographic sets.[52] This is one of the most promising efforts to date, but whether it will have any benefits for college, public, or lower school libraries is doubtful. The greatest benefit would be to provide a model for imitation in other areas where this problem exists.

Liebman reported a computer-based index to previously inaccessible elements of sound recordings in the California State University (Los Angeles) collections.[53] The elements made accessible by the new system were additional subject headings and data about individual selections on a single recording. This additional information is assigned as needed up to a maximum for any single recording of 384 characters of text. In this way, individual bands of a disk or tape may be described instead of only the larger unit which is standard practice in our cataloging rules.

Bibliographic access to a collection as a unit when it is composed of many individual works is not really giving users enough information to find what they want easily unless each component is identified. In general, there are economic factors that make libraries reluctant to do more. The California experiment may prove to be a viable method of creating analytics inexpensively, especially for libraries that already have access to an automated system. The question of policies concerning analytics may well require a new examination in light of the fact that newer media, e.g., videodisks, are being created especially to store large amounts of data of various kinds—text, sound, and visual—in a very small amount of space such as a few bands on a disk. If libraries continue to catalog such items as a unit, they will lose access to the works on them and destroy much of the effectiveness of the medium. Yet the videodisk and microform both represent methods of dealing with physical space and storage problems faced by libraries today. Clearly, a new view of collections, sets, and other multiwork units needs to be found.

The foregoing discussion describes developments in bibliographic objectives and services in libraries over time, including the growth of media collections, lack of uniform rules for their organization at first, development of media cataloging rules, problems of classification and shelving, and access to works in collections or sets. These peculiarities of media organization have not promoted access, but tended, instead, to inhibit it, raising especially formidable barriers to casual or unsophisticated clients. To complete this review of media administration and organization, a look at other tools which helped establish a measure of bibliographic (or, better yet, mediagraphic) control follows.

No description of tools for mediagraphic control can proceed without mention of the early efforts of the Library of Congress in this area. LC published its catalogs for sound and motion materials, as well as music, maps, and manuscripts. Just as bibliographies of books provide needed information for technical processing as well as acquisitions, bibliographies of media or mediagraphies are important for the control of nonprint materials and LC's were among the first and most inclusive media listings. They did not provide multimedia coverage, however, i.e., of the entire gamut of physical forms. Since the media "industry" is really a great many different industries and has not enjoyed the benefits of mutual associations and relationships as did the book publishing industry, it is no wonder that comprehensive cross-media tools were lacking for some time.

Another mediagraphy which now has cross-media coverage are the NICEM indexes, which began with film information in the 1950s and expanded to more media gradually. Today there are eight sections, for films, filmstrips, transparencies, 8mm motion cartridges, videotapes, audiotapes, disks, and slides. All the indexes except films began publication since 1967.

Two periodical guides to commercial sound recording resources began publishing in the late 1940s, *Phonolog* and the *Schwann*

Record and Tape Guide. They offer the most complete "in print" listings with *Phonolog* emphasizing popular music, though it has sections for spoken, classical, and specialty recordings, while *Schwann* emphasizes classical music though it has sections for other types of materials. *Phonolog* also provides analytics for popular recordings as well as access by performer for both popular and classical music. More recently, in the 1970s, *Phonolog*'s publisher began to list sound tapes in a parallel publication called *List-o-Tapes*, including similar broad coverage, analytics, and access by performer as well as title.

Even earlier than the 1940s, H.W. Wilson pioneered in publication of single-medium listings, introducing its *Educational Film Guide*, a quarterly periodical, in 1936, with the title *Educational Film Catalog*. In March 1948, filmstrips were added to the *Guide* and a separate *Filmstrip Guide* was begun in September of that year.

Coverage of other kinds of educational materials in a mediagraphy lagged, with individual producers and distributors making their own efforts to reach the school and library markets for some of the media and occasional book selection periodicals also including some of these materials. An example was ALA's review guide *Booklist*, which began including filmstrips and filmloops in 1969 and added more media later. Interested organizations such as AECT, EFLA, MLA, and others also made efforts to keep their membership informed of new materials being produced in increasing numbers and formats through reviews and mediagraphies in their own periodical publications. Audiovisual bibliographies produced for educators, such as the *Educators Guides*, which offered listings of free nonprint materials, the *Learning Directory*, and *AV Index*, filled the gaps, although they never reached the comprehensive coverage of their print counterparts. Other important cross-mediagraphies included *Media Review Digest, International Index to Multi-Media Information*, and *Index to Instructional Media Catalogs*. The catalog of the National Audiovisual Center, mentioned earlier, titled *A Catalog of United States Government Produced Audiovisual Materials*, an irregularly updated listing, as well as LC's nonprint catalogs, contributed to the advancement of mediagraphic control.

Guides to the literature, pioneered by Rufsvold and Guss in 1961, sponsored by ALA and now in its fourth edition, have been appearing for educational media of all kinds. Some recent ones include, in addition to Rufsvold and Guss' *Guides to Educational Media* (1977), Sive's *Educators' Selection Guide to Media Lists* (1978), and Mirwis'

Guides to Educational Media Software (1977).

Complaints about mediagraphies tend to focus on inaccuracies in the entries resulting from using producers' data sheets or other surrogates instead of the items themselves in preparing the entries. Solutions to this problem are not readily apparent. Furthermore, comprehensive coverage is often lacking. A number of current sources for media information were reviewed by Doughty, who posed the possibility of more of what she called "integrative bibliography" in the future, especially in the automated environment likely to prevail. She recommended Neal-Schuman's *Alternatives in Print*; *Information America: A Guide to Print and Nonprint Materials Available from Organizations, Industry, Government Agencies and Specialized Publishers*; and *Children's Media Market Place* as furnishing multimedia coverage of nontraditional topics and/or less familiar producers.[54]

The library profession has been accustomed to a unified front on the part of book publishers. Many of these also produce educational media. Yet it remains to be seen whether the elements of the media industries, educational and information communities will pull together and form a new omnimedia coalition for the distribution of information about new materials. The future may well be shaped by the development of automated systems in place of the labor intensive preparation of bibliographies, indexes, and catalogs.

INFLUENCE OF NEW TECHNOLOGY

It has been forecast that computers will make as far-reaching an impact on information service as the printing press did in an earlier age. The computer, which began to be applied to library problems in the 1960s, has already become the basic tool for more complex systems in technical services, reference services, and administrative planning. Branscomb identifies the computer-accessed videodisk as a more viable format for information storage and retrieval than the book, citing as advantages the ability to store the equivalent of 1,600 books on one side of a plastic disk the size of an ordinary phonograph record, to use a computer to access small portions of information from anywhere on the disk, and the small cost to duplicate information in this format and to transmit it for low cost over telephone and television screens instantaneously over long distances.[55] He declared that the computer is the key element in the management of our information-rich society and in overcoming the existence of information-poor individuals in an age of plenty. Echoing McLuhan's message that books are not efficient as either a storage or a communication medium compared to electronic media, he speculated on the impact on libraries of the computer and electronic media revolution. The computer is at once versatile, efficient, and cost-effective in storing, managing, and producing information products of great diversity once initial implementation of the systems are completed. The greatest expense of computer technology is in this first stage.[56]

Branscomb is not alone in wondering about the changes to libraries brought about by the conversion to a "paperless society." Roberts predicts far-reaching changes in response to what he deems "...this shift from materials orientation toward communications orientation...,"[57] including different building designs with emphasis on the flexible modular constructions and wiring adequate for the electronic load. He sees information systems becoming like "giant nervous systems," with the warning that, "If [libraries] are not integrated into these 'nervous systems' [they] will be excluded from them."[58] Lancaster has proposed several viable electronic models as alternatives to the old bibliocentric model.[59] The question of these experts is, in view of the money necessary for the initial establishment and ongoing expenses of their operation, how may libraries become part of the new systems and also, how may they use the computer to serve their clients? While some libraries may be able to justify charging fees for information services to their public, others believe this is antithetical to their mission. Without supporting either side in the "fee or free" debate, and recognizing that all services cost more than any fee that might be charged for them, one type of service that has been outside the debate should be examined, namely, computerized cataloging.

The bibliographic utilities demonstrated on a large scale that the costs of automation could be borne by sharing them among a network of institutions, all of which contribute to its operation and to the database it builds, achieving savings and service through their mutual inputs. On a smaller scale, groups of libraries have banded together to finance and implement automation projects of various kinds as well as to use the computer systems to facilitate and expand previously established interlibrary loan (ILL) systems. Through cooperation, the twin problems of development and implementation costs have been overcome and services maintained or extended. The key to success for these projects is agreement on sharing information central to the systems and a uniform design for its exchange. This requirement of much more rigid standards for entering data into the large computer system so that anyone can retrieve it has led to greater emphasis on the rules themselves, their design, and their interpretation.

The revisers of *AACR1* were aware of the need to create a code that could be applied in an automated context and did several things to facilitate this. First, they decided to use a single overall structure for the cataloging of all print and nonprint media. Second, they removed the selection of access points from the creation of a bibliographic description for an item, believing that in the automated environment there was less importance attached to main as opposed to added entries since all would be indexed and were, therefore, equally accessible. Third, they conformed to the International Standard Bibliographic Description (ISBD) format and punctuation—an effort on the part of the International Federation of Library Associations and Institutions (IFLA) to establish a grand design of Universal Bibliographic Control, dependent on the automated exchange of bibliographic data among nations.[60] The idea was to provide a uniform structure for preparation of national bibliographies by each country of its national output of information which could then be combined into a worldwide bibliography of publications. Even before an international database was created, ISBD could aid catalogers by standardizing the elements, their order and punctuation, permitting recognition of author, title, etc., regardless of language or even the script of a language. This has practical value in acquisitions work as well as for a variety of tasks involving bibliographic data.

Another standard affecting the bibliographic record is the Machine-Readable Cataloging (MARC) format developed by LC for the encoding of data.[61] Originally designed for printed monographic books and then serials, MARC formats have been devised for films, maps, and music (including sound recordings), but LC has made it clear it does not have the resources or the desire to expand into other media. The MARC standard is being adapted and used by the bibliographic utilities to provide cataloging information to thousands of libraries in the U.S. and abroad. The databases being built now include all kinds of nonprint materials, not only those for which LC designed MARC formats. Beyond the MARC standard set by LC, the machine readable formats are being controlled by the managers and users of the networks who, in turn, seek to codify their protocols through such committees as ALA's interdivisional Committee on

Representation in Machine-Readable Form of Bibliographic Information (MARBI). MARBI's objectives include:

> To encourage the creation of needed standards for the representation in machine-readable form of bibliographic information; to review and evaluate proposed standards; to recommend approval of standards in conformity with ALA policy ... to maintain liaison with concerned units within ALA and relevant outside agencies.[62]

The American National Standards Institute (ANSI) published the MARC format as a standard in 1971, lending more formal authority to what is certainly the *de facto* standard anyway.[63] In addition, it has an omnimedia standard for bibliographic references, published in 1979.[64] While citation practice does not affect library catalogs, the interrelation between cataloging and bibliography, at least from the users' point of view, bears examination. Both library staff members and clients alternate between searching in reference tools and library catalogs. One item cited in various forms in different publications or databases may go unrecognized in the library catalog or in two different indexes or bibliographies. It would seem logical that greater uniformity in both areas of information retrieval could not help improving access for library users.

Catalogers and other staff members who use the bibliographic networks have also formed organizations to focus their efforts, get their problems addressed, exchange information with others, and generally lobby for useful action with their utilities. Not only are there representatives from the general libraries within each network, but also specialized groups such as the Music OCLC Users Group (MOUG) and the On Line Audiovisual Catalogers (OLAC) who are primarily concerned with items cataloged by the Audiovisual Media Format, as well as discipline-specific rather than format-specific interest groups such as the law catalogers, medical catalogers, etc. Regional networks, e.g., SOLINET, the Southeastern Library Network, ILLINET, the Illinois Library Network, AMIGOS, the southwestern network, and others, also work to obtain new services and more advantageous operations. User groups will be an important factor in shaping future directions of network services, and they fulfill an especially useful function in large organizations such as OCLC, which tend to have many layers separating the management of the organization from its end users. The user group provides a forum for voicing common concerns as well as interacting more directly with managerial staff. In smaller networks, where individual institutions are more immediately involved in the management of the organization, there may not be as pressing a need to formalize the process and create structured groups for this purpose.

The standards described so far are an interlocking set of requirements for creation and transmission of bibliographic data among growing portions of the library community. The codes used for description and access—MARC formats, ISBDs, and citation standards—all affect what information is presented to bibliographic searchers and in what form it appears. The automation of library catalogs is forcing libraries to use sophisticated computer hardware—video display terminals with a variety of capabilities— instead of cards and drawers. An ALA committee devoted to monitoring such activity is the Library and Information Technology Association's Technical Standards for Library Automation Committee (TESLA), charged with responsibility for encouraging development of automation standards and acting as a clearinghouse for information on them as well as interfacing with ANSI and other standards-making bodies.[65] Many computer keyboards are unable to reproduce all the symbols needed for languages other than English. These are problems that require hardware and software development—solutions that demand a costly investment on the part of manufacturers.

In sum, complex access systems are governed by a variety of standards affecting all aspects of the preparation, communication, and display of bibliographic information. Many of these were created in response to new technologies, while others have been adapted to account for their translation into computer systems. Although recently developed catalog codes and computer conventions have been extended to accommodate nonprint media, coverage is neither comprehensive for all media nor for treatment of works within a medium. In 1967, NCLIS and AECT jointly established Project Media Base, an effort to develop guidelines for a national computer database of entries for nonprint materials.[66] The aim of the project, like that of other cooperative ventures involving books, was to provide the user with as large a pool of entries as possible from which desired items could be selected. After several years' investigation of the problems of mediacentric (i.e., nonbibliocentric) materials, the Task Advisory Committee of the joint project concluded in their 1979 report, "The non-audiovisual, or library, community and the audiovisual community are different in a number of important ways...," among which were that the library community was more successful in establishing bibliographic control over printed materials than the audiovisual community had over nonprint.[67] In addition, they concluded that attempts to unify efforts and standards for nonprint materials were not productive, and disparity among database structures was a major barrier to development of a national audiovisual network. It remains to be seen whether the inclusion of nonprint entries in the databases of the bibliographic utilities will permit a national network to emerge. It appears that such links between databases are under development as well as links of a different kind between types of libraries and information providers in the public and private sectors. These networks or series of large and small networks made possible by computers may have the greatest impact of all on access systems. To date, agreement on entry uniformity and standardized structures for bibliographic exchange is the most dramatic effect. The future may see still greater changes as the channels for producing and communicating information continue to reflect advances in technological capabilities.

SUMMARY

The components of media librarianship, historical development of collections, development of bibliographic objectives and services, availability of access tools, establishment of standards, and other impacts of new technologies have all contributed to the current situation. The points which bear special emphasis are the short time in which libraries have had sizable holdings in nonprint formats, the chaotic period between 1967 and 1978 (or, *AACR1* and *AACR2*) when different nonprint cataloging codes emerged and experts fought over treating media uniquely or together with print materials; the lack of comprehensive cross-media tools; and the rapidly developing changes in all access systems resulting from application of computer technology and cooperative ventures based on automation.

The relatively brief time during which libraries have dealt with nonprint materials greatly telescoped the natural evolution of bibliographic access systems which took hundreds of years to develop for books. Experience with books was both helpful and harmful in the search for optimum media access. It was helpful in providing a model for media organizers to follow but harmful because media could not be made to follow that model exactly. Nevertheless, in 1978, publication of *AACR2* furnished catalogers with a unified bibliographic code for all library materials, representing the success of a vocal group of professional leaders who believed that integrating access for all media resulted in better public service.

Another factor that contributed to the lack of availability of media information was the absence of a media-in-print tool providing comprehensive coverage. Media librarians must still maintain extensive files of producers' catalogs, advertisements, reviews, etc., in order to assemble authoritative data for acquiring and organizing media materials. This also discouraged practitioners from mainstreaming nonprint materials and viewing them as equivalent to better-controlled print forms.

Development of standards for creation and exchange of bibliographic information and their relation to new kinds of recording and communication modes has already had an important influence on attitudes toward access as well as its practice. The computer has become the key component in access networks. Cooperative ventures to share the cost of automating or increase the extent of an institution's resources have given rise to networks, which require a high degree of uniformity from all participants. The inclusion of nonprint data in the files of national bibliographic utilities is adding new options for the future.

Understanding the status quo and the predispositions of professionals clearly has value in planning for the future. The traditional role of the library as a bibliocentric institution may wither away and it is not certain what its new role may be. Survival may be related to dramatic changes in the library's ability to exert control over the new media of information and communication and furnish new products and services to clients who perceive information as central to success in their endeavors.

NOTES

1. Melvil Dewey, "Libraries in the Twentieth Century: A Symposium," *Library Journal*, 26 (March 1901), p. 122.

2. See Franklin's *Autobiography* for details.

3. Charles A. Goodrum, *The Library of Congress* (New York: Praeger, 1974), p. 11.

4. Katharine Clugston, "The Library of Congress and Nonprint Media," in *Bibliographic Control of Nonprint Media*, ed. Pearce S. Grove and Evelyn G. Clement (Chicago: ALA, 1972), p. 155.

5. *Ibid.*, p. 157. Clugston reported that the Library of Congress had printed catalog cards for 72,000 motion pictures and filmstrips of which 3,600 were theatrical films cataloged before 1958. Since that time, the Library has added thousands more titles, making their collection a unique resource in that medium.

6. Much of the information in this section is based on the following articles: Ronald F. Sigler, "A Rationale for the Film as a Public Library Resource and Service," *Library Trends*, 27 (Summer 1978), pp. 9-26; and Joseph W. Palmer, "Contributions of the Carnegie Corporation to the Development of Public Library Film Service," *Journal of Library History, Philosophy & Comparative Librarianship*, 12 (Fall 1977), pp. 325-41.

7. Robert D. Leigh, *The Public Library in the United States: The General Report of the Public Library Inquiry* (New York: Columbia University Press, 1950), pp. 86-89.

8. Details of this development may be found in Palmer's article.

9. Evelyn G. Clement, "Previous Nonprint-Media Activity in the American Library Association," in *Bibliographic Control of Nonprint Media*, ed. Pearce S. Grove and Evelyn G. Clement (Chicago: ALA, 1972), p. 276.

10. Library of Congress, *Library of Congress Catalog—Motion Pictures and Filmstrips* (Washington: Library of Congress, 1953-). Entries for some films cataloged between 1950 and 1953 appeared in issues of the *Library of Congress Author Catalog* and *Library of Congress Subject Catalog* during that period. At the time of this writing, the film catalog title is *Films and Other Materials for Projection*, a change dating from 1973.

11. Library of Congress, Descriptive Cataloging Division, *Rules for Descriptive Cataloging in the Library of Congress: Motion Pictures and Filmstrips*, preliminary ed. (Washington: Library of Congress, 1952), p. 12.

12. The report of the survey, prepared by Frances Hamman, was published in the Fall 1957 issue of *Library Resources and Technical Services.* Its findings are discussed in detail in Chapter 4.

13. Frances Hamman, "Bibliographic Control of Audio-Visual Materials: Report of a Special Committee," *Library Resources and Technical Services*, 1 (Fall 1957), pp. 181-82. The existence of more than 2,000 16mm film collections at the time of the survey is certainly an indication of the popularity of film.

14. Edna Frances Hanna, "First Steps Toward a Record Collection," in *Readings in Nonbook Librarianship*, ed. Jean Spealman Kujoth (Metuchen, N.J.: Scarecrow Press, 1968), p. 45.

15. Robert D. Leigh, p. 87.

16. *Ibid.*

17. Eric Cooper, "Gramophone Record Libraries in the United States of America," in *Phonograph Record Libraries, Their Organization and Practice,* 2nd ed. (Hamden, Conn.: Archon Books, 1970), pp. 248-49.

18. Library of Congress, Descriptive Cataloging Division, *Rules for Descriptive Cataloging in the Library of Congress: Phonorecords,* preliminary ed. (Washington: Library of Congress, 1952), p. 10.

19. Library of Congress, *Library of Congress Catalogs—Music and Phonorecords* (Washington: Library of Congress, 1953-). Like the catalog records for films, some sound recording entries cataloged before 1953 appeared in the *Library of Congress Author Catalog* and *Library of Congress Subject Catalog.* The title of this separate work was changed in 1973 to *Music, Books on Music and Sound Recordings* to reflect its expanded coverage.

20. Music Library Association, *Code for Cataloging Music and Phonorecords* (Chicago: ALA, 1958), p. 89.

21. An excellent and detailed history of the NYPL collections is contained in volume 36 (1979) of the Music Library Association's publication *Notes,* by Philip C. Miller and Frank C. Campbell.

22. Richard Boss, "Audio Materials in Academic Research Libraries," *College and Research Libraries,* 33 (November 1972), pp. 463-66.

23. B.K.L. Genova, "Video and Cable: Emerging Forms of Library Service," *Library Trends,* 28 (Fall 1979), pp. 297-309. See especially the discussion on page 300.

24. Joanna Foster Dougherty, "Media in Connecticut's Public Libraries," *Connecticut Libraries,* 18 (Spring 1976), p. 31.

25. C. Walter Stone, "Introduction," *Library Trends,* 16 (October 1967), p. 179.

26. Boyd Ladd, *National Inventory of Library Needs, 1975; Resources Needed for Public and Academic Libraries and Public School Library/ Media Centers* (Washington: NCLIS, 1977), p. 277.

27. *Ibid.,* p. 49.

28. *Ibid.,* p. 111.

39. *Ibid.,* p. 157.

30. Mary E. Bogan, "A Survey of Audiovisual Resources in Selected California Libraries and Library Systems," *California Librarian,* 37 (October 1976), p. 53.

31. Joseph W. Palmer, pp. 327-28.

32. *Ibid.*, pp. 336-37.

33. Theodore C. Hines, "Commercial Cataloging Services," *Library Trends*, 24 (April 1976), p. 781.

34. See, for example, C. Walter Stone, "AV Task Force Survey Report," *American Libraries*, 1 (January 1970), p. 42, as well as writings throughout the 1970s by such expert observers as Suzanne Massonneau, Wesley Doak, Jean Weihs, and others.

35. These include four editions of *Standards for Cataloging Nonprint Materials* sponsored by the Association for Educational Communications and Technology, two editions of the Canadian Library Association's *Nonbook Materials: The Organization of Integrated Collections*, and the (British) Library Association's *Non-Book Materials, Cataloguing Rules*.

36. Jean Riddle Weihs et al., *Nonbook Materials: The Organization of Integrated Collections*, 2nd ed. (Ottawa: Canadian Library Association, 1979), p. 1. The same sentiment was expressed in the authors' Introduction to the first edition, p. vii.

37. Wesley A. Doak, "Administrative Problems and Their Solutions," *Library Quarterly*, 45 (January 1975), p. 60.

38. Jay E. Daily, *Organizing Nonprint Materials* (New York: Marcel Dekker, 1972), p. 5.

39. *Standards for Cataloging Nonprint Materials*, 3rd ed. (Washington: AECT, 1972), p. 1 states: "The entry for all audiovisual materials will be by title. According to widely accepted cataloging principles, printed materials are generally entered under author or, lacking a specific author, under title. The extent and nature of the collaborative authorship of most audiovisual materials, however, makes author entry inappropriate. Entry under title is therefore recommended for all audiovisual materials." This was changed in the fourth edition to: "Main entry may be made under title, series title, or creator." (1976, p. 6.) Note that creator main entry is still not preferred.

40. *Anglo-American Cataloging Rules, North American Text* (Chicago: ALA, 1967), p. vii.

41. *Anglo-American Cataloguing Rules*, 2nd ed. (Chicago: ALA, 1978), p. 20.

42. *Anglo-American Cataloging Rules, North American Text*, pp. 282, 322, 333-37.

43. Seymour Lubetzky, "The Fundamentals of Bibliographic Cataloging

and AACR2" in *The Making of a Code: The Issues Underlying AACR2*, ed. Doris Hargrett Clack (Chicago: ALA, 1980), pp. 16-25.

44. See Jesse Shera, "Classification: Current Functions and Applications to the Subject Analysis of Materials," in *Reader in Classification and Descriptive Cataloging*, ed. Ann F. Painter (Washington: NCR-/Microcard Editions, 1972), pp. 69-70.

45. Richard L. Darling, "Nonprint-Media Organization in the American Library Association," in *Bibliographic Control of Nonprint Media*, ed. Pearce S. Grove and Evelyn G. Clement (Chicago: ALA, 1972), pp. 330-31.

46. Quoted in Wendell Simons, "Development of a Universal Classification System for 2-by-2-inch Slide Collections," in *Bibliographic Control of Nonprint Media*, ed. Pearce S. Grove and Evelyn G. Clement (Chicago: ALA, 1972), p. 372.

47. Gordon Stevenson, "Classification Chaos," *Library Journal*, 88 (October 15, 1963), p. 3790.

48. Juan Freudenthal, "The Slide As a Communication Tool," *School Media Quarterly*, 2 (Winter 1974), p. 112.

49. Wesley Simonton, "The Bibliographical Control of Microforms," *Library Resources & Technical Services*, 6 (Winter 1962), p. 29-40.

50. June Thompson, "Cataloguing of Large Works on Microforms in Canadian University Libraries," *Canadian Library Journal*, 16 (November 1969), pp. 446-52.

51. William J. Myrick, "Access to Microforms: A Survey of Failed Efforts," *Library Journal*, 103 (November 15, 1978), pp. 2302-304.

52. Reported along with an interesting list of suggstions for immediate remedies by Scott Stebelman, "Bibliographic Control of Microforms: Suggestions for Improved Local Access," *Microform Review*, 10 (Summer 1981), pp. 162-65.

53. Roy Liebman, "The Media Index: Computer-Based Access to Nonprint Materials," *RQ*, 21 (Spring 1981), pp. 291-99. Projects of this kind are proliferating, some based on OCLC or other networks, such as the OMRAC (OCLC Musical Recordings Analytics Consortium) project of the MLA and Music OCLC Users Group, and Rutgers University's Institute of Jazz Studies project, under the direction of Marie Griffin.

54. Esther C.D. Doughty, "Bibliographic Control of AV Materials: Current Signs of the Integrative Approach to Access (A Very Condensed Overview)," *Collection Building*, 3 (1981), pp. 3-12.

55. Lewis M. Branscomb, "Library Implications of Information Technology," in *An Information Agenda for the 1980s*, ed. Carlton C. Rochell (Chicago: ALA, 1981), p. 44-45.

56. Lewis M. Branscomb, "Information: The Ultimate Frontier," in *An Information Agenda*, pp. 29-31.

57. Don Roberts, "IFLA and Audiovisual Materials, From a Media Specialist," *IFLA Journal*, 7 (1981), p. 337.

58. *Ibid.*

59. F.W. Lancaster, *Toward Paperless Information Systems* (New York: Academic Press, 1978), p. 179.

60. Eva Verona, "A Decade of I.F.L.A.'s Work on Standardization of Bibliographic Description," *IFLA Journal*, 6 (1980), pp. 216-33. An excellent article giving the background and history of these activities.

61. Historic background material on the MARC system may be found in the Library of Congress' publication *Information on the MARC System*, 2nd ed. (Washington: Library of Congress, 1972), p. 34.

62. American Library Association, *ALA Handbook of Organization* (Chicago: ALA, 1981), p. 115.

63. American National Standards Institute, Inc., *American National Standard Format for Bibliographic Information Interchange on Magnetic Tape* (New York: ANSI, 1971).

64. American National Standards Institute, Inc., *American National Standard for Bibliographic References* (New York: ANSI, 1979).

65. *ALA Handbook*, p. 91.

66. Results of this project were documented in its final report, *Problems in Bibliographic Access to Non-Print Materials: Project Media Base, Final Report* (Washington: NCLIS, 1979), p. 86.

67. *Ibid.*, p. 43.

RECOMMENDED READING

Excellent chronologies of the development of nonbook media activities are found in the following works:

Olson, Nancy B. *Cataloging Nonbook Materials: A Manual Based on AACR2*. Mankato, Minn.: Minnesota Scholarly Press, 1981, 143-153. (Appendix C)

Problems in Bibliographic Access to Non-Print Materials; Project Media Base: Final Report. Washington: National Commission on Libraries and Information Science, 1979, 52-64.

Additional readings on history and background of nonbook media collection development may also be found in the following works:

Brown, Karline. "What Libraries Are Doing in the Audio-Visual Field." *Library Journal,* 72 (January 1, 1947), pp. 39-44.

Goldstein, Harold. "A/V: Has It Any Future in Libraries?" *Wilson Library Bulletin,* 36 (April 1962), pp. 670-73 +.

Grove, Pearce S., and Evelyn G. Clement, eds. *Bibliographic Control of Nonprint Media.* Chicago: American Library Association, 1972.

Stone, C. Walter. "Audiovisual Materials and Services," *Encyclopedia of Library and Information Science,* ed. Allen Kent and Harold Lancour. Vol. 2. New York: Marcel Dekker, 1969.

Development of nonbook media cataloging rules are found in the following works:

Frost, Carolyn O. "Chapter 1: The Development of Bibliographic Standards for Nonbook Materials: A Historical Survey," *Cataloging Nonbook Materials: Problems in Theory and Practice.* Littleton, Colo.: Libraries Unlimited, 1983.

Hensel, Evelyn. "Treatment of Nonbook Materials," *Library Trends,* 2 (October 1953), 191-96.

Chapter 3

Current Bibliographic Practice in U.S. Public Libraries

T HIS chapter examines the ways in which public libraries in this country provide bibliographic access to nonprint materials in their collections. The access system is made up of several parts, including methods for identifying individual items, selecting filing points from the identification, displaying this information, and providing subject access through application of subject headings and classifications. Decisions must be made in each of these areas, e.g., the rules to be followed in making bibliographic descriptions, the subject list to be followed, and so on, which together form a kind of policy concerning the services being produced. This kind of policy formulation may be explicit and prescriptive, or it may merely result, after the fact, from the combination of individual decisions made by different staff members without clearly defined objectives.

The organization of the chapter will follow the process itself, asking and answering a series of questions:

- Is there a written bibliographic policy?

- How are bibliographic data obtained?

- What rules are used to create entries?

- What subject headings and classifications are applied to provide subject access?

- How is the information presented to library users?

- How does this system for nonprint materials relate to bibliographic information for books and other printed materials?

BIBLIOGRAPHIC POLICIES

Since Cutter formulated his objects of the catalog in 1876, these have been the ultimate bibliographic objectives of all libraries in the country. In recent years, however, the idea of policy formulation has received attention, possibly carried over from the world of business and industry, in which measurable objectives are defined in more specific terms. Once these specific objectives are written, procedures can be devised to reach them, or, at least, they can be evaluated in terms of how well they are doing the job. This evaluative function of a bibliographic policy is relatively new for libraries, but has been growing in acceptance in general, particularly in other functional areas of library work, e.g., selection and collection development. It has received special emphasis when automated systems are involved in the execution of a service area. Application of a well-defined and coherent policy to cataloging and classification tasks and procedures is far less typical, with Cutter's objects still providing the main goals for the entire bibliographic system.

A growing number of institutions have adopted written policies for their bibliographic services. In the group of libraries queried by the author, 12 percent said they did no cataloging at all for their nonprint materials; 23 percent said they had a written policy statement that covered all their materials and 5 percent more were in the process of preparing one; and the rest, about 60 percent, replied they had no written policy but did furnish cataloging for their nonprint materials. The size of the library alone was not the deciding factor, since some very small libraries do not maintain catalogs even for their books, while others with equally small collections have several. In one small town in the author's recent experience where there was no catalog, all the books were shelved in alphabetical order by author's last name. The person in charge said there were few complaints about the lack of a catalog, but clients did not like having fiction and nonfiction intershelved. Such a lack of bibliographic or inventory control is acceptable in a very small minority of information agencies, largely because it prevents adequate evaluation of collections and services required for reports to their funding authorities.

The fact that almost one quarter of the libraries surveyed already have written policies for their bibliographic services and more are in the process of writing one came as something of a surprise. An investigation of the contents of these policy statements—whether they are defined in measurable terms or merely new wordings for the more abstract and theoretical concepts of a catalog embodied in Cutter's objects—would reveal whether they are likely to be used to upgrade substandard products and services, maintain a desired level of services, and provide a means for evaluating current levels of service.

One public library system with a well-defined bibliographic policy is the Hennepin County (Minnesota) Library.[1] In this system, adequate bibliographic access is achieved by enriching standard products obtained through a national network with more access points and nonstandard access points devised by its own staff members. In addition to covering these aspects of service, Hennepin's policy covers classification, shelving, and other factors in the display of the data. This commitment to bibliographic services for the library's public is not typical, but it might serve as a model for what can be done when cataloging and classification are seen as critical components in clients' actual physical access to library materials.

OBTAINING BIBLIOGRAPHIC DATA

In the not-too-distant past, most libraries prepared the majority of their own catalog entries, ordering cards from the Library of Congress when they were available, but essentially relying on their own catalogers for the information that went into their catalogs. Alternatives to original cataloging or LC cards were to purchase catalog cards from commercial sources—either the wholesalers who supplied the materials themselves, or another service—or to become part of a centralized cataloging service in one's own region. These are still the operative methods for obtaining bibliographic data. What seems to have changed is their relative importance. The rise of national nonprofit cataloging networks based on computer databases, the bibliographic utilities, has changed earlier reliance on commercial suppliers of cataloging and on the Library of Congress. Now, even cataloging done within a library's walls may be part of a national network even though the individual library considers it in-house work. Bibliographic utilities were employed by 40 percent of the libraries surveyed. Cataloging for printed materials was obtained outside the library by 30 percent of the libraries, with almost one quarter of these using nonprofit central services and a little over half of them using commercial services. In contrast, only 10 percent said they obtained nonprint cataloging from outside, with a little over one quarter of these using nonprofit central services and approximately one third more of them using commercial services. Though the local libraries would not have been expected to relay this information, it is likely that either or both of these outside sources for bibliographic information are also using bibliographic utilities. Considering the predominance of academic libraries in the membership of bibliographic utilities, this large proportion of public libraries using them represents an important segment of recipients of database services.

What is interesting to note is the much smaller proportion of libraries obtaining their nonprint cataloging outside the library. Even among those libraries which used bibliographic databases for in-house cataloging, more than one third did not catalog any of their nonprint materials with it, preferring to catalog them separately.

The survey indicates that public libraries still rely primarily on their own catalogers, though many of them are doing their work on network terminals rather than beginning from title pages (or equivalents in nonbook materials) and using only their own original efforts to provide entries. Nonprint materials are frequently accorded treatment different from books. For example, less than half of the libraries using bibliographic databases for cataloging books also claimed to use them for their nonprint cataloging. These statistics indicate that original cataloging may still be much more important for nonprint materials than for books and other printed items.

RULES FOR DESCRIPTION AND ACCESS

Nationally endorsed cataloging rules have evolved over the years, with major codes being published in 1908, 1949, 1967, and, most recently, in 1978. While LC rules have not always been identical with these four codes, they have matched closely enough to be compatible in most respects, eliciting vociferous complaints when discrepancies caused problems for catalogers in the community at large. The most recent code caused much sound and fury upon its publication, especially in research libraries, because the changes it required were sufficiently far-reaching to necessitate a great deal of repair work on existing entries. This kind of work, when done in ordinary, people-operated card catalogs, is very costly to do. In a move that terrified many catalogers, LC announced its intention to close its card catalog, containing millions of cards representing the output and collections of decades, and begin a new one to which the new rules would apply. The library press abounded with articles debating this technique as well as others available to catalogers, i.e., to upgrade all of their existing entries or to leave the old entries alone and create new files under the new rules with cross references to relate them. Some libraries threatened to shun the new rules altogether and continue using the 1967 code despite the many complaints about its inconsistencies and omissions. In spite of this outcry, most catalogers expected to use the new rules at least for their books, since there was no question that LC and the bibliographic utilities—major sources of cataloging information—were going to do so. How soon they would begin to implement the new code, what method they would use to integrate new and old style entries, and whether or not they would use the new rules on other materials remained to be seen. Regarding the other materials, including nonprint, the 1978 cataloging rules were the first to integrate all media into one structure and produce entries that could be interfiled into one catalog. Thus, application of the new code to all of a library's materials might well have more than just the usual result, but might also encourage libraries to incorporate all of their cataloging into one display.

The author's survey of public libraries found that the new code was followed in more than half of them and was the most popular code in use. This was not an anticipated result since implementation by LC had been delayed for one year beyond its original deadline, to January 1, 1981, and the survey was conducted only a few months after the new deadline during April and May of 1981. Most experts believed that small and medium-sized public libraries, and even many of the larger ones, would wait to see how the major research and large university libraries fared before making a commitment to the new code themselves. Nevertheless, the local libraries were not waiting for other institutions to lead them and had quietly begun changing over to the new rules. In fact, responses to the survey indicated that only a small percentage of those who intended to use the new code had not already done so. However, only about half as many libraries were using the new rules for their nonprint materials, and far fewer than half of the rest intended to apply them in the future.

Most of the survey participants decided not to close their old catalogs, but to interfile old and new style headings with cross-references to link them. In fact, of those who had not yet implemented *AACR2*, just 2 percent said they were going to close their old catalogs, while 15 percent said they were going to upgrade all cataloging. In contrast, the rest, 83 percent, were going to interfile all cataloging, linking the split files with cross-references. When questions were asked about selected elements from the bibliographic descriptions of print and nonprint materials in order to compare their entry profiles, a number of differences between them emerged. Five elements were compared: (1) title, i.e., the fullness of information included in the title area; (2) general material designation, the users' early warning system of the physical medium of a work; (3) edition; (4) notes, often an important source of information about nonprint items which would be hard to determine from mere perusal of items without playback or projection equipment; and (5) alternate elements unique to particular media, such as directors and casts for films or video, or performers for sound recordings.

Responses indicated that the fullest information was usually provided more often for printed materials than for nonprint—56 percent transcribed complete title information for printed works and 44 percent did so for nonprint—and more than twice as many libraries transcribed only main titles for nonprint as for print. Approximately the same number of institutions, a third of the entire group of participants, did something in between using only the main title and transcribing everything prescribed by *AACR2* for the title area, using their judgment about the amount of additional information beyond the main title to be included in an entry.

Use of the general material designations for all materials was not a popular practice, followed in only 14 percent of the libraries, and for all nonprint materials but not for printed items by only an additional 24 percent. Most libraries either did not use them at all or only used them some of the time. This finding of frequent disuse of general material designations was in sharp contrast to the dramatic debate in the professional literature over the concept of such indicators of the physical medium of a work in the title area instead of the area normally devoted to physical description, as well as over the terminology to be used to name the media. One of the complaints about the 1967 code was that it lacked a list of standard terms for naming the media and the only failure to reach a compromise agreement with the British in the 1978 code was over these terms.[2] It appears that for the libraries in this sample, at least, this battle was much ado about nothing.

Edition statements, much more difficult to ascertain for nonprint materials than for books, were nevertheless given for all materials in the great majority of libraries. Only 7 percent of the participants did not provide edition statements when applicable; however, 22 percent supplied this information only for printed materials. On the other hand, complete notes were not usually supplied for any materials by the majority of those surveyed, although some 20 percent did provide them for all materials cataloged. This might be taken to indicate that notes are considered less important or less valuable to the catalog user than information about the edition of the work.

The use of alternate elements of identification for nonprint media if they were known seemed to be an intermittent practice, with half the libraries using them some of the time, a little more than one quarter never using them, and the rest always using them. While the rules of the current cataloging code do provide for such elements to be included in the entry, more often than not they are expected to be put into the notes, seen to be an element infrequently used in entries.

Selection of main and added entries, those filing points or headings derived from the bibliographic identification of the work, were determined in the same way for print and nonprint materials in almost 86 percent of those responding. Again, the rules of *AACR2* do not distinguish between media in the determination of access points; however, several factors might have led to the expectation of more access points to be provided for nonprint media materials: the frequency with which media items have several "authors"; the occasions when a library might want to have access by performers as well as authors, composers, etc.; and also the frequency with which many individual works appear on what is considered one unit as far as the cataloger is concerned. Thus, the fact that most public libraries do not add extra access points to nonprint media entries to account for these less usual attributes is indicative of simpler treatment than might have been warranted.

SUBJECT ACCESS

Subject access, or access to the intellectual content of materials, is provided by libraries in two ways: first is the verbal subject access furnished in the catalog by means of subject headings arranged in dictionary order; second is the classified physical arrangement of the materials on the shelves according to a classification scheme. Although the indexes to classification schemes might be considered equivalent to subject headings from an organized list or thesaurus of terms, in actuality these two operations are quite disparate in most libraries even when they are performed by the same person. One of the advantages of subject cataloging is that more than one heading can be assigned to a single item in order to describe multisubject contents, while library practice has usually been to assign only one class number to an item no matter how many numbers might actually reflect some portion of its contents. In fact, it has become so difficult to have class numbers accurately reflect the contents of materials that many classifiers simply have given up trying and assign something that will enable items to be placed on the shelves and located through the catalog's subject headings or indexes—the "mark it and park it" philosophy.

In view of the foregoing, it is interesting to compare the results of the survey for subject access. Most of the time, nonprint materials were treated identically with their print counterparts when subject headings and subject heading lists were involved; but when classification was being considered, nonprint materials were perceived as requiring different schemes from those applied to books and other printed materials. *Library of Congress Subject Headings* were used by more than half of the respondents, with all but a few of the rest following *Sears List of Subject Headings.* More than 75 percent of these libraries used the same subject heading list for all materials, confounding those critics who claim that general lists are not suitable for nonprint materials. In contrast to the widespread practice of uniform assignment of subject headings, the assignment of classification numbers in the same way for all materials occurred in fewer than one third of the libraries in the survey. Printed materials were classified according to the Dewey decimal classification in 97 percent of the institutions, but almost 70 percent of them did *not* use it for their nonprint items.

One factor affecting the use of a browsable scheme such as Dewey might be the restriction of nonprint materials to closed stacks. However, when asked about this, most libraries responded that all, or at least some, nonprint collections were shelved on open stacks, with only 10 percent keeping all nonprint materials on closed stacks. Comments on the shelf arrangements indicated that films and video were most often kept on shelves closed to the public, while sound recordings, filmstrips, and other graphics were usually open to the public. Thus, this cannot adequately explain the use of separate schemes for arranging nonprint materials.

Subject access through library catalogs appears to be the same for all media in most of the public libraries surveyed. Shelf access is also usually open, at least in part. But subject access through classification directly to materials on the shelves is usually quite different for nonprint materials than for books and other printed materials, in spite of the generally uniform practice of using the Dewey classification for public library book collections.

INFORMATION DISPLAY

The value of bibliographic information carefully combined into a catalog entry, with headings assigned to reflect both the work and its contents, and then filed with other entries into a catalog, depends on what the user of that information is able to find. Information professionals know what they intend for the client to find and do their best to insure they can succeed in finding it, but various surveys of catalog use seem to indicate that problems exist, nevertheless.[3]

Over half of the libraries participating in the survey did not integrate print and nonprint entries into a single catalog display for their clients. Fifty-five percent said they did not have multimedia or omnimedia catalogs. Of these, most offered alternatives in the form of separate catalogs or finding lists for nonprint materials. In slightly less than half of the libraries with separate media catalogs, the nonprint files were located near the main public catalog. In 51 percent, they were located elsewhere. A few librarians responded they had both a multimedia main catalog and separate media catalogs, bringing the total absolute number of separate files to slightly more than the number with unintegrated files.

Interestingly, if the responses to the question of integrated versus separate catalogs for nonprint materials are broken down by the size of the library (i.e., small libraries serving populations of less than 50,000; medium-sized serving populations of 50,000 to 150,000; and large serving populations over 150,000) it is the small libraries that are more likely to have an integrated public catalog containing entries for all of their holdings, and medium-sized libraries that are the least likely to integrate all cataloging. It is also the small libraries that most frequently locate separate nonprint catalogs together with their main catalog. Large libraries are most likely to keep nonprint catalogs physically separated from the main catalog.

The overwhelming majority of main public catalogs containing entries for books and other printed materials were in card format in the libraries surveyed, over 85 percent. Book catalogs were the least favored catalog format, with only 2 percent having them. Computer output microform (COM) catalogs were in use in 8 percent more.

Card catalog format was the most frequent display medium for separate nonprint catalogs, too, though the proportion, not quite 73 percent, was lower than for main catalogs. Book catalogs were next in frequency for separate catalogs and COM was used least often. Display media other than these—card, book, or COM—were used in 13 percent of the libraries for separate nonprint catalogs, but in only 5 percent for main public catalogs.

Patrons usually encounter main card catalogs containing information about printed materials alone. Card catalogs for nonprint materials are usually available, too, though more often than not in different locations. Each medium may have its own catalog, or they may be combined into one or more different catalogs. Thus, for the person who approaches the catalog with no specific kind of material in mind, nonprint forms may be missed altogether or, in most cases, would require additional searching in separate files.

RELATIONSHIP OF PRINT AND NONPRINT CATALOGING

Results of the survey of nonprint cataloging in public libraries indicate that these materials are still subject to unique or nonstandard practices much more often than are books and other printed materials. One example of this is the fact that, for printed materials, only 15 percent of the libraries used nonstandard cataloging rules for original cataloging, while for nonprint materials, 27 percent were applying rules other than those in the current or previous edition of *AACR*. More libraries responded that they did not intend to use *AACR2* for nonprint materials at some time in the future than for printed materials, which would indicate a lack of desire to bring their nonprint cataloging into greater harmony with standard practice. Classification seemed to be the area of greatest difference in practices between print and nonprint materials, with very few libraries applying the Dewey decimal classification to their nonprint materials, although it was universally popular for arranging book collections.

Continuing in this vein, more nonprint materials were cataloged within the institution than printed materials. In libraries having access to bibliographic utilities for cataloging, fewer than half of them used it for all their cataloging. As for the entries themselves, nonprint materials were more likely to have brief titles or have full title information on fewer occasions, as well as not often having alternate elements relating only to specific nonprint formats added to their entries. Fewer libraries included complete notes for materials than did not, or only did so sporadically. For nonprint materials, the note area contains extremely important information such as casts and credits, summaries, contents, audience level, and so forth; thus, they provide some things that would not be immediately apparent from looking at the materials themselves without projectors, players, or other equipment.

Most libraries did not integrate all their cataloging into one main public catalog for their clients, preferring to keep nonprint catalogs separated from entries for books and other printed materials. Up to the time the survey was done, the card catalog did not seem to be in danger of being displaced from its supremacy over either book or COM catalogs. In the case of printed materials, however, the runner-up was COM format, whereas in the case of nonprint materials, the runner-up was book format.

The area of greatest uniformity in current practice was subject cataloging, with three quarters of the libraries applying the same subject heading list to all their materials. The *Library of Congress Subject Heading* list had a slight edge over its rival, *Sears List of Subject Headings*, in spite of the preponderance of small and medium-sized libraries in the survey. It would seem that, for general public libraries at least, there is no great problem in assigning the subject headings designed for books to nonprint media, contrary to the opinions of some individuals or groups who have spent time designing their own thesauri for certain media.[4]

Readers may well be wondering why this is significant. If most public libraries do provide bibliographic access and similar kinds of catalogs for nonprint, what difference can it possibly make that they are not all in one main catalog or that full title information or notes are not always included on the entries and that materials are arranged differently on the shelves? Investigating the implications of these current practices for the people who use the nation's public libraries may reveal the reasons for concern.

IMPLICATIONS OF CURRENT PRACTICE

At the beginning of this chapter it was speculated that many libraries have an unwritten bibliographic policy about where cataloging and classification information will be obtained, what rules will be applied to the information to create entries and access points, and how the entries will be presented to the public. These decisions are usually governed by a number of factors—a need to save money, increase productivity, and demonstrate greater efficiency in bibliograpic operations. Sometimes, the lack of trained personnel within an institution limits the number of options available to it for either cataloging or classification, with heavy reliance on regional groups or other cooperative programs necessary as an alternative to more costly individualized services. There is also a tendency for libraries to continue to do things in the same way once a pattern or procedure has been established, even though the pattern or procedure no longer satisfies the demands placed upon it. In fact, one of the great problems for all libraries regardless of their budgets, staffing situation, or operational size, is the need to recatalog and reclassify materials already in their holdings when new rules or new class numbers are put forth as part of the ongoing development of bibliographic standards. The same librarians who complain about the slowness with which the rules change may be those who react with surprising anger when they are faced with implementing within their libraries whatever changes do occur. This is not always so—there are many people who welcome the changes and manage to deal with them successfully—but it is true that some people simply ignore change and cope with problems by patching up the older rules, headings, or class numbers, and continuing to widen the gap between their systems and the standards endorsed by the profession at large.

One of the most disturbing findings of the survey is the relative frequency with which nonprint materials are *not* being cataloged according to *AACR2*; indeed, still the majority rule. The main implication of this finding is that ever larger numbers of items being cataloged all over the nation are still outside the bibliographical mainstream. If tradition continues to prevail, it is likely that these items will never enter the mainstream at some future point, since recataloging is an unpopular practice in libraries. Another implication is that nonstandard cataloging for growing nonprint collections will make them less attractive candidates for upgrading to standards the larger they become. This may serve to perpetuate the popularity of separate cataloging for nonprint materials. Unless a policy-maker makes an overt effort to change this situation, it will continue in a vicious circle creating greater inertia as time passes, especially in larger institutions which have more nonprint materials in their holdings. The survey revealed that libraries serving a population of fewer than fifty thousand were the ones most likely to have integrated catalogs for the public. These are also the libraries with the smallest budgets, staffs, and resources. Large and medium-sized libraries were more likely to have separate nonprint catalogs, with less pressure to conform to the same set of rules for cataloging, and more of an investment in the status quo.

If this seems insignificant, consider some of the questions a person uses the catalog to answer, and the different ways in which an integrated and nonintegrated catalog will furnish information for them.

"What have you got by Dylan Thomas?" The main public catalog will list any books by or about the poet and his works. It would not have an entry for sound recordings of Thomas reading his poems unless it were an integrated catalog. If it were, it might also list film, video, or microform versions of his works, filmstrips, and graphic materials such as posters, pictures, photographs, or other materials related to him and his writings.

"Have you got a critical analysis of Beethoven's Fifth Symphony?" A critique in book form devoted to this major musical work would be listed in a nonintegrated catalog. A person could also look up the subject heading, "Symphonies," with or without additional subheadings such as "Addresses, essays, lectures," indicating the book contained critical analysis of symphonic works. Also, the person could look up "Beethoven, Ludwig van. Symphonies," or "Beethoven, Ludwig van. Works," as a subject heading and would find any book covering those topics which might contain the desired material. But a catalog devoted entirely to books and printed materials would not include a score of the work with critical analysis, or a sound recording of it with valuable program notes on its slipcase, or a videorecording of a performance, such as the one by Leonard Bernstein and the Vienna Philharmonic, in which the conductor prefaces the performance with an analysis of the work itself. All of these nonprint works would be entered into an integrated catalog, giving the searcher looking for criticism on Beethoven's Fifth several sources of information alternative to a book on the subject as well as furnishing all entries for all reproductions of the work within the holdings of the library.

"Do you have a copy of *The Knight's Tale* by Geoffrey Chaucer?" This time the catalog would list, if integrated, not only the printed versions of the single part of *The Canterbury Tales*, if they had them, but also the parent work, sound and videorecordings of both, and any other version of this classic. If the catalog were not integrated—more likely, according to the survey—only the books would be listed, and the part might or might not have a separate entry.

From these examples, it is obvious that a good deal of valuable information will not be found with ease. It seems unlikely most people would have gone to a separate nonprint catalog in order to search. It is probably equally unlikely that reference librarians, accustomed as they are to finding books or periodical articles to answer questions, would direct someone to a sound recording jacket as a place to find musical criticism, even though many classical sound recordings do have extensive notes including such analysis. What then is the rationale for failing to include this kind of work in the main public catalog? It is even less understandable why a faithful reproduction of a book of poetry, a play, or a story is not included in the main catalog of the public library unless it is in the form of print-on-paper. Nevertheless, that is the result of excluding nonprint media from the catalog. The most serious implication of maintaining separate nonprint catalogs is the fragmentation of the works in the holdings of the library as well as limiting what people might do with them if they were unified. The fragmentation of works is a purely theoretical problem, but limiting people's options is a practical and real public service problem.

The survey demonstrates that, despite all one reads about innovative electronic display systems, the card catalog has not yet given up its hegemony over the other forms—book, computer assisted COM, or online—of displaying bibliographic information for the public. After all, only thirty-six out of almost 450 institutions were using COM for their main catalog displays, less than 10 percent, and still fewer opted for other than book, COM, and card catalogs. Thus, if all the newest systems were in this category they would make up less than three percent of the whole. In the context of the card catalog, the addition of a great many entries to the system might well create problems for the people who have to maintain them as well as for the ones who have to use them. This is certainly one of the reasons that large and even medium-sized libraries have avoided making their main catalogs larger than they already are by adding traditionally separate catalogs to them.

Studies have shown that the larger a file becomes, the more difficult it is to search in it; and a corollary might be, the longer it takes to file something in it.[5] The very unification of works in different physical formats beneficial for answering clients' questions would create filing and searching problems for both clients and staff, for it might increase the number of cards having the same author and title—just think of what would happen to the Shakespeare file—requiring that these cards be filed according to another, less recognizable, element on the card in order to keep things straight. If general material designations (GMDs) were used on the cards, these would be a convenient sorting element, but if not, then date, or publisher, or some other element would have to be employed to arrange the cards. In any case, whatever secondary or tertiary element was used for the sub-arrangement of these cards, it would certainly be a mystery to the lay people using them and probably to many of the library's staff as well.

Furthermore, the survey showed that, while most of the separate nonprint catalogs were also in card form, the next most popular display medium was book form. This finding is interesting in light of the parallel finding that book catalogs are the least-used method for displaying bibliographic data for printed materials. Presumably it is not their expense that makes them a more viable format for nonprint catalogs—this would certainly make them less appealing. So what other factors could make libraries choose to retain book format for this purpose? One reason for selecting book form for nonprint catalogs might be that the collections are so stable there is little need to make extensive changes to it, or change it very rapidly. Another is that patrons are not expected to consult it as frequently as are the staff, and the presence of supplements or other updates do not bother professionals or escape their notice as much as they would for the public at large.

A third reason might be to make the nonprint book catalog available to persons and places outside of the library building. Certainly, for those nonprint collections that rotate, or circulate to many individual libraries, the book catalog form is a convenient way to supply information about materials to everyone in the cooperative system in the most compact way—more attractive, for instance, than sending around packs of cards or drawers of filed cards. Finally, of course, there is the reason that book catalogs were popular in earlier centuries for book collections—to create beautiful tools for reference and other purposes such as the solicitation of gifts. Somehow, having seen a variety of nonprint book catalogs that are less than beautiful, I doubt sincerely this motivates many libraries who have them. For a collection such as the New York Public Library's circulating films, however, the book catalog is a useful and attractive reference tool and, for all I know, may also be used to obtain additions of gifts for the collection. The option of the book catalog for nonprint might also indicate the limited size of the many nonprint collections they represent. It seems more unhandy to have one or two drawers of cards for a small collection than it would to have a pamphlet, notebook, or other book-style list of entries. The book catalog is acceptable for controlling small numbers of items and this may be another reason for their use in conjunction with nonprint cataloging.

Separate nonprint catalog display, whether it includes all the media or only one medium per catalog, seems to follow no pattern at all according to the survey. If most libraries put all nonprint cataloging into one separate display, uniformity in the records between media could then be assumed. This, of course, is not the case, so no such assumptions can be made. Almost as many libraries combined several media into one catalog, but had other catalogs for other media and/or put some of their media cataloging into the main catalog together with print cataloging. The largest number, unfortunately, had one catalog display per medium, resulting in the greatest possibility for variation in cataloging styles and forms. The proliferation of monomedia catalogs might also indicate the parcelling out of responsibility for each of them to different departments or staff members.

The location of more than half the separate nonprint catalogs in places other than the main public catalog area would seem to imply a likelihood they will be overlooked by the casual catalog user. Even the location of separate nonprint catalogs within the main catalog area does not insure they will be used. It is possible to imagine these as drawers at the end of the main files or a separate set of drawers at one side of the main file, or as a book or books piled on top of the main file, and so on. There is no guarantee that any of these locations are better than others in terms of their visibility to the library's clientele; however, the assumption is that they are more visible when put near the main catalog than in a different area.

To sum up, answers to the questions about the catalogs themselves have some interesting implications, the most obvious and emphatic of which is that public libraries still have card catalogs. When discussing changes in the contents of these catalogs, one of the considerations must be their present format—the limitations and problems of cards for both integrated and separated cataloging—which will have effects on plans for change. Another is the more frequent use of book catalogs for separate nonprint catalogs not in card form, which may indicate collections which are small and slow to change as well as catalogs expected to perform functions other than the control of individual collections in individual libraries. These must also be taken into account when planning for change. The lack of a clear-cut pattern about separate nonprint catalogs, some of which include all media, some only a single medium, and other a combination without including all media, will require different methods for change and these will also depend on the contents and numbers of the various catalogs.

Aside from the catalogs, methods used to obtain and manipulate information for nonprint materials were shown by the survey to be different from these processes for books and other printed materials. The survey found that the presence of an online bibliographic database for cataloging books did not necessarily mean it was used for nonprint, too. One might well want to know why not, since it should be cheaper and faster to use the database for the additional entries at least some of which would be found online and would, therefore, not require original cataloging. Among the possible answers to this question is that the nonprint cataloging is not done by the catalogers who have access to the database, but by some other person in another location without such access. It may be that the kind of cataloging done for nonprint materials is not standard library cataloging, but brief listing or title entry plus summary of contents or some other kind of cataloging too different from the entries found in the bibliographic utility to warrant its use. It could be that the materials are so unusual and are found so rarely in the database that most require original cataloging anyway and then do not also have to be searched, but in such a case, one might argue in favor of doing the original work online anyway. It may also be possible that the terminal for the bibliographic utility is not located in the individual library at all and the decision not to use it for nonprint cataloging has not been made by the local library, but by some other authority altogether. In all of these cases, the implications are that nonprint materials receive nonstandard treatment. This kind of problem feeds upon itself, i.e., not entering nonprint records in a bibliographic database makes it less likely they can be found online, which, in turn, makes the database unattractive as a data source for these items. The impressive statistics for nonprint materials already available in the databases of the utilities belies this reasoning and leads me to believe it is more likely nonprint materials are not cataloged in standard ways when excluded from online cataloging, not that they aren't found often enough to warrant its use.

A surprise revealed by the survey was the very small number of libraries using commercial processing services to obtain their nonprint cataloging. Once a major source of nonprint cataloging, only fourteen libraries claimed to use commercial services. Is the implication that, like Wilson catalog cards for books, commercial cataloging for nonprint material is disappearing? Or should this finding be interpreted to mean it is there but is not being used? The latter interpretation does not seem sensible, since the market for such services should include a proportion of public libraries larger than these replies would indicate in order to be profitable. While the survey sample is not necessarily the same as the entire public library population, in general it should reflect similar findings for print and nonprint materials within the institutions that participated and not too dissimilar findings for the larger public library community. However, while only fourteen of these used commercial processing for nonprint, seventy-five used it for books and print materials. Since even fewer survey participants (twelve) used non-profit central services for cataloging nonprint, one must conclude that most libraries are doing their own original cataloging for these materials, making the rules and standards by which original work is done for nonprint more important than ever before.

More than twice as many libraries surveyed used *AACR2* than *AACR1* for cataloging print materials, and only 15 percent of the total used rules other than *AACR*. though the proportions are about the same for those using the two editions of *AACR* for nonprint, the absolute numbers are smaller. While, for books, ninety-three libraries used the first edition and 216 used the second, for nonprint media, only eighty-one used the first edition and 168 used the second. Also, the number of libraries using variant rules was much larger—almost twice as large. Since so many libraries are doing original cataloging for their nonprint materials, the use of standardized rules for this work would indicate that nonprint catalogs were approximately equal in content to their print counterparts. As the numbers demonstrate, *most* libraries are using either the new standard or the old one—a heartening result at the time of the survey. Nevertheless, almost twice as many were applying other cataloging rules to media as were doing this to books and other print items. Also, survey participants were asked about future plans for implementing *AACR2,* if this had not already been done. Among a total of 179 replying to this question for books, ninety-seven, or more than half, said they had no plans for using the new code. Contrast this with a total of 203 institutions replying to this query about nonprint media, to which 145 (or more than 70 percent) said they would not implement the new code. One might conclude from this that the future will not bring a larger proportion of public libraries into harmony with currently endorsed standards, but a smaller proportion. If these libraries are representative of the public library community at large, it does not appear promising for nonprint media.

With respect to shelf arrangements for nonprint media, there is even less evidence that standards acceptable for general collections of printed materials are being used for media collections. Although replies about permitting clients open access to the materials themselves, as has been the public library tradition for books, are generally in favor of open stacks for media, too, there were many qualifications, with films and videorecordings most frequently being mentioned as exempted from open areas. As for the numbers, while only forty-three institutions had closed stacks for media, 117 more limited physical access to some portion of their media collections. Thus, while 231 libraries kept open stacks, 160 did not. This does not indicate widespread and hearty endorsement of open access for nonprint media. On the other hand, there are also portions of book collections that are put outside the generally accessible areas and are protected from ordinary handling; therefore, it may not be as important to have immediate physical access to all holdings as it is to exercise some cautionary measures against unnecessary or undesirable handling of those items that can be easily damaged and also replaced only with difficulty. Further investigation of the kinds of print and nonprint items kept on closed shelves might reveal whether there are parallels in the decisions made or whether nonprint materials are shielded from public access for less acceptable reasons.

The question of classification of nonprint media is also difficult to analyze. The simple numbers test shows that most of those surveyed use Dewey for books and something else for media. Only 123 libraries use Dewey for their nonprint materials, while 225 do not. Those who used variant schemes were asked to describe them briefly. The comments indicated two things: First, that many libraries used different shelf arrangements for different nonprint media rather than a single scheme for all of them; and second, many of the variant schemes were based on nonbrowsable systems, especially accession numbers. Typical of the descriptions are the following quotes:

"By date of receipt."

"Phonorecords are classed as REC."

"Alphabetical."

"Sequence number ..."

"By medium symbol, then accession number."

"...numbered consecutively, i.e., movies are M1, M2, etc. Cassettes are Cas 1, Cas 2, etc."

"Records—cassettes—film are arranged chronologically..."

The fact that these nonstandard, nonbrowsable schemes are working in the libraries that use them is not in question. If the books in those libraries were suddenly to be found in such arrangements, people would still find what they want through the catalog or through their memories. There are many people, both library users and professional librarians, who believe Dewey and LC classifications do only a spotty job of collocating related works anyway. Adding to this the habit of "marking and parking" materials, the growth of interdisciplinary materials, and massive workloads that have characterized the last two decades of intellectual production, perhaps the nonstandard or nonbrowsable schemes are not much worse than their alternatives.

There are problems, however, with the use of different schemes for print and nonprint materials. In the first place, books are almost always arranged in open stacks by Dewey classification in U.S. public libraries. Nonprint are not. This means that people using the various kinds of materials in the same library have to learn different schemes to find them even though the subjects covered may be the same. It also means that when these people go to another library, while every book will not be assigned the same Dewey number, in general they can transfer what they know about the location of books to the other public libraries and to college, school, and even university libraries that use Dewey too, while they cannot do this for the nonprint media. They may be faced with closed stacks for nonprint materials more frequently, too.

One result of this situation is that nonprint media materials are harder to locate than are books and other printed materials. A person has to do more catalog work to locate them in most places, and cannot use what is learned in one place to make the job easier or faster anywhere else. The second implication is that in many cases people have to rely on the catalog to find desired, known media items. At the same time, the catalog for nonprint media items is likely to be someplace other than near the main catalog so there is a double barrier: the catalogs, which are more important even for known items, are in less prominent places; and the materials are in less familiar locations.

Readers might be led to think nonprint media are in some way essentially or inherently different from books and other print forms so that Dewey is inapplicable to them. Its use by more than one hundred libraries, however, would not be possible if that were truly the case. Also, the fact that the general subject heading list used for books by three hundred libraries is also being successfully applied to nonbook materials indicates no special subject-related problems offered by media.

The two kinds of subject analysis are theoretically related, as already pointed out, and the relationship can be seen most vividly by looking at the indexes of classifications and/or the classed lists in various subject areas or a general list such as the *British National Bibliography*. The fundamental difference between verbal and symbolic subject application is that one can assign more than one verbal subject heading to a single work, while only one symbolic one is generally applied in our libraries. Theoretically, a work could have as many symbolic as verbal subject assignments and copies or dummies could be placed in each of them in order to accurately reflect a multiplicity of subjects in one work.

Why aren't the same rules for classification applied to nonprint materials? Perhaps because when the collections were established, the decision-maker thought the scheme chosen would be adequate considering the small size of the collection, its location on closed stacks, its supervision and classification by noncatalogers, or adoption of a model from another library. Although there has been a number of examinations of the effectiveness of various kinds of organizational schema, none comes to mind that has compared the use of a browsable classification and an accession number scheme. Just think again of the example raised about arranging nonfiction books by their accession number. What might this do to clients' ability to find what they want—especially when they are not sure what they actually want? Is it possible that, if this arrangement were the case for books, one might use this collection only when it was absolutely necessary? I believe the answer is yes.

A frequent complaint about Dewey classification which is also leveled at the LC classification is that they are not specific enough to organize a relatively large collection of such items as musical sound recordings or slides of art works. One example of such a collection is the nearly 20,000 sound recordings owned by the small public library where I worked for several years as music librarian. There were hundreds of titles representing symphonies or symphonic performances. No doubt the Dewey numbers for these works would have been very long or they would not have provided unique shelf locations for the records.

The solution devised by this author's predecessor was to adapt the LC classification's M schedule in order to provide, for symphonic works, several additional numbers to encompass symphonies, concertos, symphonic band music, symphonic suites, etc. For symphonies, however, there was still only one class number. The unique shelf location each one of the many symphonies was to occupy was identified by an elaborate system of Cutter numbers and other shelf marks. There was no reason these same works could not have been assigned an equivalent Dewey number and been Cuttered and otherwise uniquely identified in exactly the same way for shelving. As a matter of fact, the books about symphonies, or symphonic music, or sometimes a critical edition of a symphony in notation form—all of which were shelved with the rest of the Dewey 780s—were treated in exactly this fashion and did not seem to present many problems to clients who browsed the shelves. Very few people, however, ventured alone to the record stacks on the other side of the aisle, without first being pointed in the direction of the work or works they sought. A few caught on to the scheme, and others simply learned which were the shelves where operas or Broadway shows were placed so they could retrieve sound materials unaided. The fact is that the nonstandard scheme worked well.

One reads over and over in analyses of LC classification that it was designed to arrange the works in that great library, so it will not "fit" any other collection in just the same way. All who have had experience using LC with other collections can probably find truth in that statement. When any general classification scheme is used with a collection other than the one for which it was created, the specificity of the scheme often does not match the needs of the collection. What is normally done? Libraries struggle along with the scheme and, if the professionals have activist hearts, devote their professional energies to lobbying for changes in the scheme to suit their collections better.

It is interesting to see how many libraries had no problem with specificity for their nonprint materials in the application of the same subject heading list used for books. In the collection of sound recordings this author supervised there were as many difficulties caused by poorly defined subject headings as there would have been in the use of Dewey classification. Take, for instance, the LC subject heading "Music, Popular (Songs, etc.)." In the 1970s all the folk, pop, soul, blues, rock, country and western, folk-rock, punk, and other kinds of popular vocal records went into this category. (Other more specific headings have since been added to LCSH.) The same was true of a number of other headings, especially the ones naming a form of music in which the library collected heavily, e.g., symphonies, concertos, and operas. Nevertheless, we struggled along with LCSH and added headings of our own when individual files became so large they were no longer useful. There were also places in the subject heading list where the specificity was far too closely delineated to be used for the library's materials, especially in the area of early music where we may have had a total of fifty or sixty recordings. Again, we did the best we could with the list, grumbling about LC's extensive holdings in this area. Since the materials were shelved with a browsable, though nonstandard, classification scheme, clients did not have to rely solely on the catalog if they were interested in a particular genre of music. The lack of specificity in subject headings was somewhat mitigated by the ability to find related forms of music in more or less related groupings near one another on the shelves. Also, people who were not familiar with the shelves felt free to ask for help, and the policy we established was to ask people if they were looking for a particular record *before* they wandered away without success. If we had been using a nonbrowsable arrangement based on accession numbers or the manufacturer's numbers, the value of the catalog for locating materials would have been critical and, in the particular areas mentioned here, it would have failed miserably. By the way, the non-musical sound recordings in the collection being discussed were arranged by the first three digits of the appropriate Dewey number and shelved after all the musical works. There were about two thousand of these, with language, typing and dictation, and literature the largest subject categories. Dewey was quite satisfactory for the arrangement of these works.

The survey showed that despite their intellectual relationships, verbal and symbolic subject cataloging—or subject cataloging and classification—were applied in very different ways to print and non-print collections in public libraries. The problems of broad and close classification are often avoided altogether by the use of numbers that identify but do not organize the materials they represent. The use of the same subject heading lists to assign verbal headings to nonprint materials, however, is both widespread and without insurmountable problems.

Implications of the contents of catalog records for nonprint materials also merit attention. The most important element in a catalog record, after the headings, is the title. Not only is the title the first element of bibliographic description, but it is also the only element which will never be missing in any record, even if it has to be supplied by the cataloger. According to *AACR2*, the title area is made up of several parts: Title proper, defined in the code's glossary as "The chief name of an item . . ."[6] and also called the main title, first title, or principal title; general material designation, an optional addition in this area to tell the entry's reader what kind of physical package the work is contained in; parallel title, or the title proper in another language or script;[7] and, finally, other title information, which consists of all other title information appearing on the chief source of information.[8] The full treatment of the title area would also include a statement of responsibility for the work, provided this information was displayed on the item being cataloged.[9] All of these subelements, with the exception of the optional GMD, were included on catalog entries for print materials in 216 of the libraries surveyed, but for nonprint materials by only 170. Title proper alone, sufficient for what the code calls a first level bibliographic description[10] was used for books and other print items by thirty-one libraries, and for nonprint materials by sixty-four institutions. This clearly points to greater simplification for the nonprint entries. The conclusion that nonprint cataloging is more often at the first level of description is not borne out by the evidence. Statements of responsibility, edition statements, and physical description statements are all supplied for all materials cataloged with greater frequency than full title information. These elements, with the exception of edition statements, are not required for a first level description. Only series information, complete notes, and standard numbers—not currently assigned routinely to all nonprint materials—are provided in entries for all materials cataloged with less frequency than full title information. They are all found at the bottom of the catalog card, and it has been found that fewer people read that far down anyway, making their appearance less crucial than title statements.

Of all the standard elements of a catalog entry prescribed by *AACR2*, the one least likely to be used in its entirety in any kind of cataloging is the note area. Only eighty-nine libraries included complete notes in their cataloging—both print and nonprint—and more than twice as many said complete notes were given only sometimes for some materials.

The two entry elements probably of greatest importance for many nonprint items are their titles and notes which summarize their contents and otherwise furnish information usable when actual perusal of items themselves is difficult or even impossible. Titles of films, for example, are often made up of statements like "Alfred

Hitchcock presents Laurence Olivier in William Shakespeare's Hamlet adapted for the screen by J. Arthur Rank Associates...." The Library of Congress, whose lead has been followed by major cataloging bodies, does not transcribe everything when faced with a title proper such as this, using instead a shorter statement determined by the work, the typography of the statements in the chief source, and the cataloger's good judgment.[11] By the same token, full notes for such a work, whether or not the title proper is shortened, would include the credits, cast, and a summary of the work, among other items of interest about the film. A full entry for such a film, with all its elements intact, at the second level of description, would include every one of the people considered to have made an important contribution to the film as well as any important relationships it might bear to the work on which it was based. It is easy to see how such an entry, in card form, could go on for several cards, and in book form for columns or pages. It is difficult to find the balance between what is practical, in terms of the time it takes to transcribe and produce an entry as well as its cost, and what is most helpful to the people who will use the entry. The survey shows that notes are definitely an area where librarians feel justified in cutting corners, even for their book cataloging. On the other hand, since most books are available for personal perusal, unlike many of the nonprint media, the justification may be valid for them and not for the materials unavailable for review because they require playback or projection equipment or because they are kept on closed stacks.

The other area where librarians seem to be giving less than full information for nonprint than for books and other printed materials is in the title area. For libraries that opt for first level description, only the title proper is required for any materials, and there is no need to include subtitles, etc. Other institutions would do well to examine their practices for nonprint cataloging in this most critical area. Abbreviating title information for nonprint means that users of nonprint entries may have greater difficulty determining whether the item they see in the catalog is the one they really want, but it also implies that this work is substandard. Survey results about the use of the GMD seem to imply a feeble popularity for using this optional element with nonprint materials (eighty-three libraries never used it; sixty-four always used it; more than one hundred used it for nonprint materials). Several possibilities might explain the limited use of GMDs, the most obvious of which is that if nonprint entries are not included in the main public catalog with entries for books, no one needs to be alerted to the fact that they are not looking at a book entry. Libraries having separate catalogs for each different medium also have no need for GMDs. As for the rest, the GMDs' failure to satisfy many catalogers has caused problems with their use. Take, for example, the case of cataloging a photograph. The GMD which would have to be used is "picture," since the others in this category—art original, chart, filmstrip, flash card, slide, technical drawing, and transparency—are even less appropriate than this. If a GMD as specific as "art original" or "flash card" can be accepted terminology, then why not add "photograph" to the list? The same argument could be made for "poster" and many other kinds of physical media. The main difference in the two lists of GMDs in *AACR2* is that the British decided to keep all of their terms extremely general, while the North Americans wanted to have a larger number of more specific terms. Thus, in the example of the photograph or a poster—as well as any of the other terms named above—the British would use the term "graphic" and no other. The British contend that the idea of having a *general* material designation was to keep the entry reader alerted to the fact that the work represented by the entry was one of twelve broad kinds of media families, not to tell them exactly what specific kind of material was involved. The more specific material designation, the British believe, belongs in the area set aside for physical description, the fifth area of description according to the code. On the American side of the Atlantic, however, libraries were already using the more specific terms in their entries since they were prescribed in the nonprint cataloging codes already being used, *Nonbook Materials* and the AECT *Standards*. The debate between the factions raged in the library literature and at professional gatherings. In the end, compromise was reached on eight terms; a ninth term to designate items made up of more than one medium was called "multimedia" by the British and "kit" by the Americans; and the remaining three British terms, "graphic," "cartographic," and "object," were matched by fifteen different terms on the American list. American cataloging leaders have been having doubts over the efficacy of some of the GMDs for nonprint, not only those kinds of items mentioned here, but also whole categories such as "machine-readable data files," which does not represent all kinds of computer-readable materials, and the various terms used for three-dimensional materials which are misleading for some of the things in the category, e.g., toys.

All the problems with GMDs, plus the fact that LC decided to use only eight of them in their own cataloging,[12] partly because they don't catalog materials in the other categories and partly because they chose not to do so in some cases, has caused some uneasiness about their use. Since they are optional anyway, every library may choose to use them or not without departing from strict adherence to standards. The survey certainly reflects less than wholehearted acceptance of GMDs, which might also be viewed as reluctance to use them, even for nonprint media alone.

One of the practices about which survey participants were questioned which has not been described in this chapter is their resource-sharing program—their lending of materials to other institutions for use by the borrowing library's clientele. Most of the respondents said they shared all of their materials with other libraries; and a small minority, 14 percent of the total, said they did not share resources at all. Resource-sharing is based in some part on having adequate bibliographic information about the materials being shared. Many state and regional bodies devote a large part of their energies to compilation of union lists, i.e., catalogs or lists including the holdings of many libraries within their jurisdiction. These union lists become the basis for cooperative programs, including resource-sharing. This widespread participation in resource-sharing would imply use by many libraries of the cataloging and standard cataloging practices would seem to be important for such use. Standardized cataloging promotes efficient retrieval by the group. Furthermore, if a library shared its nonprint resources and had to search several catalogs to fill a series of requests, it would certainly take more time and cost more than if they could all be searched in one catalog. Once cataloging is intended for use beyond the walls of the institution producing it, some attention has to be paid to making it understandable and useful to these "outside" users. Following nationally accepted standards seems to be the most convenient way to do this. Thus, for the more than three hundred libraries surveyed that share some or all of their holdings with other libraries, there should be a selfish interest in producing standard cataloging, at least for the shared materials.

SUMMARY

From examining the bibliographic practices of a good-sized sample of U.S. public libraries, the following profile may be drawn. Most public libraries provide access to all materials in their collections, including nonprint media, but this service is seldom codified into a written cataloging policy. Public card catalogs are most frequently the display vehicle for bibliographic information, and they usually do not contain nonprint entries, although similar nonprint catalogs are available somewhere in the library.

Most materials are cataloged in the library, especially nonprint items. Entries for print and nonprint look very much alike, although more of the nonprint entries are done following locally developed rules, while print materials follow standard rules. *AACR2* is the most popular code for print materials. Adoption of *AACR2* was already complete in most of the institutions intending to implement it, though a minority were still in the planning stages. New and old-style entries are being interfiled with linking references rather than upgrading all old-style cataloging or closing old catalogs. While the majority of nonprint cataloging also follows *AACR2*, there are more variations on it in use.

Bibliographic elements least likely to be included in all entries are GMDs, complete notes, and, to a lesser degree, standard numbers, i.e., ISBNs, sometimes also assigned to nonprint materials as well as to books. Full title information is furnished less often for nonprint entries. Filing points are created in the same way for all entries whether they are subject headings or descriptive headings.

Once patrons obtain bibliographic information for nonprint items, they can retrieve most of the materials from the shelves themselves, unless they seek videotapes or films. The classification scheme for media items is not necessarily the same as for books, but is more often a nonstandard arrangement.

The bibliographic information in libraries is not uniform for all media, but there are several similarities between print and nonprint cataloging. The number of libraries with a uniform approach for all materials is sizable but still a minority of the total in the sample group.

The lack of specific written bibliographic service policies makes it more difficult to decide when the existing level of services is adequate and tends to impede, or at least does not motivate, changes in the process. The number of libraries with written policies is encouraging but does not indicate a trend. The use of *AACR2* for both print and nonprint materials is widespread, but nonstandard rules are still more prevalent for nonprint than for books and other printed materials. The results of a continued gap in standard cataloging for nonprint items may well be to create large collections of materials that will never enter the mainstream of bibliographic control, and also collections that become less and less attractive as candidates for upgrading to standards. Overt efforts on the part of library policymakers will be required to change this situation so that potential benefits to the public can be realized. This is also true for changes from card catalogs to electronic forms, or even to computer-assisted forms such as COM. Though the library literature seems to indicate otherwise, the card catalog is still ubiquitous among the institutions surveyed.

The most serious implication of current practice appears to be the likelihood that clients of public libraries will not have equal access to nonprint materials because of the separation of nonprint catalogs from main public catalogs as well as their physical arrangement according to nonbrowsable classification schemes. Adding to this the frequency with which the nonstandard cataloging accorded some collections acts as a barrier to access, real problems in the field are still present despite some gains.

A comparison of entry profiles for print and nonprint shows that the two elements usually affecting access to nonprint—full title information and complete notes—are less likely to be given for nonprint. Complete notes are infrequently given for any kind of materials, compared to the other areas of bibliographic description. On the positive side, the same subject heading list was used for print and nonprint materials in most places. The idea is that subject cataloging is quite different in practice from classification although they are related intellectually. The use of GMDs appears to be insignificant, implying either rejection of the compromises over terminology or the principle of applying them, or both. For libraries with fully or partially integrated catalogs, GMDs have more validity than for those who separate print and nonprint catalogs. Since these are a minority of the sample, the use of GMDs may reflect this situation.

The conclusion of this discussion is that nonprint cataloging has come a long way in a very short time, considering there were no nonprint cataloging rules at all only thirty-five years ago. Nevertheless, there is no general equality in the total bibliographic treatment afforded nonprint materials. There is, however, a large minority of institutions in which nonprint media have been integrated into the cataloging system and bibliographic service through the public catalog is equal for all of their holdings.

NOTES

1. A brief statement of policy concerning audiovisual materials appeared in the article "Rules for Cataloging Audio-Visual Materials at Hennepin

County Library,'' $T*H*E$ $U*N*A*B*A*S*H*E*D$ $L*I*B*R*A*R*I*A*N$, 7 (Spring 1973), p. 6.

2. *Anglo-American Cataloguing Rules*, 2nd ed. (Chicago: ALA, 1978), p. 20.

3. The results of several such studies are summarized in F.W. Lancaster's *The Measurement and Evaluation of Library Services* (Washington: Information Resources Press, 1977), pp. 69-72. Chapter 2, pp. 19-67 has a detailed exposition of them.

4. For example, the film thesaurus developed by the California Library Association.

5. The summary in Lancaster's *Measurement and Evaluation* includes this point; however, the classic statement on the problem of catalog complexity (which includes unmanageable size) was made by Andrew D. Osborn in "The Crisis in Cataloging," *Library Quarterly*, 11 (October 1941), pp. 393-411.

6. *Anglo-American Cataloguing Rules*, 2nd ed., p. 571.

7. *Ibid.*, p. 568.

8. *Ibid.* For a more detailed explanation, see pp. 22-23.

9. *Ibid.*, pp. 23-26.

10. *Ibid.*, pp. 15.

11. Library of Congress rule interpretations are disseminated through their publication *Cataloging Service Bulletin*. No. 12 (Spring 1981), pp. 3-4, and No. 13 (Summer 1981), p. 15, deal with this issue and its resolution.

12. *Cataloging Service Bulletin* No. 11 (Winter 1981), pp. 6-7.

RECOMMENDED READING

Berman, Sanford. "Cataloging for Public Libraries," *The Nature and Future of the Catalog: Proceedings of the ALA's Information Science and Automation Division's 1975 and 1977 Institutes on the Catalog.* ed. Maurice J. Freedman and S. Michael Malinconico. Phoenix: Oryx Press, 1979.

Grove, Pearce S., and Evelyn G. Clement, eds. *Bibliographic Control of Nonprint Media.* Chicago: American Library Association, 1972.

Clugston, Katherine. "The Cataloging of Audiovisual Media at the Library of Congress," *Reader in Media, Technology and Libraries*, ed. Margaret Chisholm. Englewood, Colo.: Microcard Editions, 1975.

Hagler, Ronald, and Peter Simmons. *The Bibliographic Record and Information Technology.* Chicago: American Library Association, 1982.

Hyman, Richard Joseph. *Shelf Access in Libraries.* Chicago: American Library Association, 1982. (See especially the chapter on public libraries.)

Mendenhall, Kathryn. *Final Report on a Survey of the Cataloging in Publication Program.* Washington: Library of Congress, 1982.

Nesbitt, Susan. "Analysis of Subject Heading Lists Applied to Nonprint Materials." M.L.S. Thesis, University of Minnesota, 1983.

"Rules for Cataloging Audio-Visual Materials at Hennepin County Library," *T*H*E U*N*A*B*A*S*H*E*D L*I*B*R*A*R*I*A*N*, 7 (Spring 1973), pp. 6-9.

Weihs, Jean Riddle. "Problems and Prospects in Nonbook Cataloging," *The Nature and Future of the Catalog: Proceedings of the ALA's Information Science and Automation Division's 1975 and 1977 Institutes on the Catalog.* ed. Maurice J. Freedman and S. Michael Malinconico. Phoenix: Oryx Press, 1979.

Chapter 4

Bibliographic Practices in Other Libraries

PUBLIC libraries represent one very important part of the U.S. library community and a long look has been taken at what a fairly large sample of them do to provide access to their nonprint media materials. In this chapter, a similar look, although, perhaps, in not quite so much detail, is taken at the bibliographic practices of other kinds of libraries, in public schools and in colleges and universities, as they have been reported by other researchers. First the findings of a large national survey conducted by a special committee of ALA's Resources and Technical Services Division in the 1950s are examined. This survey covered all types of libraries and gives an historical perspective in which to place the several studies that follow. Then the findings of several much more recent surveys are compared, each covering a particular sector of the library community—public schools surveyed by JoAnn Rogers, two-year colleges surveyed by Doris Dale, and colleges and universities surveyed by Nancy Olson. All of these studies were performed since 1978. Of course, each of these researchers was interested in different things and asked different kinds of questions. Finally, a look is taken at other evidence including a recent Canadian study by Isabel McLean and some investigations of other factors in media librarianship besides cataloging and classification. Included here are three statewide reports on media services and some reviews of nonprint media resources together with their projections for future developments. These will give readers needed familiarity with the more general issues and problems existing in the field as seen by both practitioners and scholars having different points of view.

THE ALA STUDY

This oldest survey was sponsored by the ALA Resources and Technical Services Division's Audiovisual Committee.[1] It was part of a needs assessment for cataloging rules and manuals of procedure for media which, up to that time, were almost totally absent. In 1955, the Executive Board of the Division established a special committee on the Bibliographic Control of Audio-Visual Materials, charging it with responsibility for surveying needs and practices in the field, and making recommendations for action. The committee was chaired by Eunice Keen, a school specialist who was herself the author of a manual of practice for audiovisual materials first appearing in 1949 and later revised and issued in 1955.[2] Keen's committee administered a brief mimeographed questionnaire mailed to libraries with collections of films, filmstrips, and sound recordings. It asked what cataloging systems were used and why, and requested samples of catalog products and tools.

A broad national sample distributed among public, academic, and school libraries and including one special library concentrated on large, well-established institutions with audiovisual experience as criteria for selection. Both size of collections and length of time they were held were factors in the selection process. Three hundred libraries with sound recording collections and 203 film libraries were sent the questionnaire, developed by members of various interested groups within ALA. Approximately 60 percent responded, divided fairly equally between types of libraries and the kinds of media they held.

The bibliographic profile developed by the committee and queried by the questionnaire covered nine important points:

1. Which library department was responsible for audiovisual cataloging

2. Whether LC printed cards, colored cards, or cards produced by the library were used

3. What cataloging rules were followed

4. Which bibliographic elements were considered essential

5. What classification scheme, if any, was used to arrange materials on the shelves

6. Whether subject headings were used and, if so, what standard list was employed

7. Whether bibliographic records were filed in the public catalog and/or audiovisual catalogs

8. Who had access to the catalog

9. Whether printed audiovisual catalogs were provided for patrons

Two additional questions asked for respondents' opinions about using LC cataloging rules as the basis for standardizing nonprint cataloging and whether there was a need for a published manual of procedure. Finally, comments and suggestions were invited.

The responses suggested that most of the cataloging of nonprint materials was done outside the cataloging department, and most libraries produced their own catalog cards. One third of the film libraries and a little more than one half of the record libraries used LC or LC and MLA cataloging rules or adaptations of them. It was not reported what the others did, but in the absence of published alternatives, one must assume they used locally developed systems. Regarding classification, about half of the film collections and slightly less than half of the record collections were classified, with Dewey decimal classification the most popular scheme used. Most of the libraries applied subject headings, and LCSH were most frequently mentioned. A small minority of cards was filed in public catalogs. A significant proportion had separate audiovisual catalogs in the appropriate department of the library, while school libraries tended to have catalogs in all departments. Most film catalogs were for staff use only, and while a higher percentage of record catalogs was also available to the public, it was still less than half. Printed lists were popular among film libraries, but not record libraries, for consultation by the public.

A clear majority of librarians felt that LC cataloging rules were a valid basis for standardization. The objections raised by those who dissented from this view centered on the time lag in LC's card production, its inflexibility, and, interestingly, either the lack of needed information or overly detailed entries. Two thirds of the respondents wanted a manual of procedure in addition to standardized cataloging rules.

The results of this study presented, for the first time, a profile of institutional practices and procedures. Its findings are a valuable starting point for tracing the development of nonprint bibliographic practice, taking place at a time when collection development was out of its infancy, but a body of literature on organization had not yet materialized. Indeed, this effort was one of several originating primarily within concerned professional organizations occurring more or less simultaneously, which stimulated creation of cataloging codes, bibliographies, indexes, and the entire range of bibliographic tools already commonplace for books. Perhaps the major contrast between the way things were done in the 1950s and what libraries are doing now is less a matter of achieving standards, though assuredly this is a valid point of departure between the findings of this study and those done in the last several years, but the fact that so many of the audiovisual catalogs, such as they were then, were not open to the public for their use in determining what materials held by the library might be of interest or importance to them. The most fascinating replies were those that criticized LC's printed cards for being, at one and the same time, too simple and too complicated. It is a good guess, without scrutinizing each individual reply, that school libraries complained about their complexity while academic/research libraries took exception to the lack of needed data. Today there are few complaints about the complexity of LC cataloging; the problems focus on the complexity of *AACR2* and its application to media as well as the complexity of the media themselves and the way bibliographic information is presented by producers.

Another startling change from the fifties is the widespread classification of nonprint media collections and the much more limited use of Dewey to classify them. Back in the 1950s, many college and university libraries were classified with Dewey, and one wonders whether these were the collections using Dewey for nonprint, too, or if the public libraries in the ALA sample were also using it in greater numbers than they do today. It is reasonable to suspect that academic libraries were more likely to classify nonprint media than public libraries, and also that, once classified by a subject-oriented scheme, they would not revert to accession number schemes—something more likely to be done at the outset of a new collection. Thus, the reported popularity of Dewey for classifying nonprint may possibly have been limited to the academic group within the study.

If the 1955−56 study is taken as a baseline of organizational activities for nonprint media, it shows the general lack of emphasis placed on access services for the public. Many nonprint catalogs were for the use of staff only; many collections were not classified at all; most nonprint cataloging was not part of the rest of the libraries' primary bibliographic services, as conducted by the cataloging department. The importance of standards to the respondents may have meant different things to different librarians, since the only available measure—LC cards for films and records—were considered too much by some and too little by others. What seemed to be desired were standards that worked better than the LC rules. That so many also wanted a manual of procedure for media indicated the need not only for a set of satisfactory rules, but explanations of how to apply them. This echoes much of what is heard today.

CURRENT SURVEYS

In 1977, JoAnn Rogers questioned state coordinators for public schools in the fifty states and the District of Columbia about bibliographic practices for media within their jurisdictions. Her study was reported two years later in *American Libraries*.[3] In 1980, Nancy B. Olson explored the bibliographic practices of almost six hundred U.S. academic libraries and published the results in her nonprint cataloging manual, *Cataloging of Audiovisual Materials*, published later in the year.[4] The most recent study, of a small sample of two-year community colleges, was performed by Doris Cruger Dale and published in 1981 in *College & Research Libraries*.[5] Within four years of the public library study done by this author, all but the special library sector had some report published based upon observation of more than a handful of agencies, of the process of providing bibliographic access to nonprint materials. While there is wide variation among these studies in the numbers of people questioned, the kind of data requested and methods of gathering it, each provides a view of nonprint bibliographic practices for a sector of the larger library community.

Rogers' survey of school media cataloging practice was designed to learn how the hundreds of millions of dollars' worth of materials being purchased each year by school media centers were being made accessible for use. A mailed questionnaire was sent to each state supervisor and the supervisor for the District of Columbia. Five questions asked for the following information:

1. Which of ten cataloging codes listed were used in the state or district?

2. Which other codes or manuals were used?

3. Which code or manual was most frequently used?

4. Which codes or manuals were recommended by the state department?

5. What comments did the respondent have to make about media cataloging?

The list of cataloging codes included the four editions of AECT's *Standards,* the preliminary and first edition of *Nonbook Materials* by Weihs, and *AACR1* plus its three revised chapters on monographs, audiovisual media, and sound recordings.

Forty-five replies were received. The responses revealed a general disinclination to use the codes sponsored by national professional organizations—all those listed—although of all of them the various editions of the AECT *Standards* were the most popular and *AACR1* was the least used. Rogers stated simply, "...school media specialists and state school media supervisors may be unaware of some existing codes and guidelines for descriptive cataloging of nonprint material. Many school media specialists have not responded to the need to adopt codes and procedures sanctioned by national and international professional organizations—codes which are becoming standard in other library settings."[6]

What were these schools using? They were using locally developed rules or one of the following manuals or guides mentioned on the replies: *AV Cataloging and Processing Simplified,*[7] *Developing Multi-Media Libraries,*[8] *Cataloging Manual for Nonbook Materials in Learning Centers and School Libraries,*[9] *Commonsense Cataloging,*[10] and the LC catalogs for films and sound recordings.[11] Rogers' pessimistic conclusions about the adoption of nationally endorsed standards by schools were also cognizant of a paucity of accurate reporting mechanisms on the part of the state officials for their schools as well as a lack of knowledge about local practice at the state level. There seemed to be little motivation for standardizing rules and procedures and a forecast of little likelihood that *AACR2* would be adopted because of its complexity. Rogers believed, upon *AACR2's* publication, that without additional training for school librarians in its use, the code designed to accommodate the wide variety of nonprint forms and the differences in cataloging needs of schools and other smaller, nonresearch institutions would be ignored.

Rogers was primarily interested in descriptive cataloging and did not question what school library supervisors recommended for classification, display of the catalog entries, etc., nor did she inquire about resource-sharing or the compilation of statewide union lists of materials. Of the states named which reported the use of locally developed cataloging rules—Wisconsin, South Dakota, Hawaii, California, and Indiana—several have information- and resource-sharing programs underway. Examination of the rules they recommend would have to be carefully done before rejecting them as non-standard. They may well have adapted nationally accepted rules or merely provided a restatement in simpler terms of the rules from the national publications. Certainly texts such as Piercy's and Hicks and Tillin's recognized and acknowledged the existence of national standards. In fact, Hicks and Tillin were the author-editors of the latest edition of AECT *Standards* (1976) as well as authors of *Developing Multi-Media Libraries*. Rogers' study was conducted prior to the publication of *AACR2*, which engendered a new edition of *Nonbook Materials* to conform to it just as the earlier editions conformed to *AACR1*. Thus, the picture of school library cataloging may not be as devoid of standards as one might believe from Rogers' work.

Olson's 1980 survey of media cataloging practice in academic libraries contained a seven question survey sent to more than fifteen hundred academic audiovisual librarians, of whom 599 replied. In addition to asking for information on the size and composition of their collections, she requested the following information about cataloging:

- What rules were used to catalog

- What classification, if any, was used to arrange the materials

- What subject heading list was used

- What kinds of cataloging, i.e., OCLC, printed cards, or locally-produced cards were used

Almost all of the responses indicated cataloged collections of media (94%), but many did not indicate what rules were used for descriptive cataloging. Of those who did answer (approximately half of the total), *AACR* was the most frequently mentioned cataloging code. A smaller percentage (74%) also classified their collections, with LC and Dewey classifications being used in about equal proportions. All the respondents applied subject headings, and more than three quarters used LCSH. A very small proportion (11%) used *Sears*, and the balance used specialized headings such as the *Medical Subject Headings* of the National Library of Medicine.

Olson presumed catalog cards were the display format, reporting that over half of the respondents relied on OCLC card production with more expecting to do so in the future. A significant proportion used LC printed cards (29%) and other purchased cards were used by a very small group (9%). Self-generated cards were used by very few of Olson's participants. She did not ask whether the cards were filed in the main catalog or in separate media catalogs or both.

Widespread use of the bibliographic network system for cataloging media is undoubtedly an important factor motivating the use of *AACR*. Academic libraries accomplish several positive goals at once by doing this, including lowering the per-unit cost of cataloging for all the materials cataloged online, obtaining the finished cards more quickly than if they had opted for LC cards, doing less original cataloging though how much less is uncertain, and last but not least, obtaining cataloging of relatively high quality which they could, if they wished, integrate with the cards obtained for books.

The most recently reported work, Dale's survey of a sample of two-year, community-based colleges, examined cataloging practices for all materials, both print and nonprint. One hundred colleges were chosen at random from the *Community, Junior, and Technical College Directory* and these received a four-page questionnaire divided into six sections covering the cataloging and classification of printed materials, audiovisual materials, the catalog, shelving of audiovisual materials, computerized cataloging networks, and the cataloging staff. Less than half (48%) of the sample answered, but the replies came from all parts of the country. Focusing on the audiovisual shelving, Dale found the colleges used a wider variety of classifications than for printed materials, with Dewey the most frequently used scheme. More than half of the respondents used shelf arrangements based on accession numbers. In contrast, all but two libraries used the same subject heading list for all materials. As for cataloging, *AACR1* was used to catalog twenty-six print and nineteen nonprint collections, while *AACR2* was used for sixteen print and fourteen nonprint collections. The only other media code named, applied in five institutions, was the 1976 edition of AECT *Standards*. Fully half of the libraries displayed the entries for audiovisual materials together with print entries in integrated catalogs.

After noting that librarians disagreed on the physical arrangement of audiovisual materials and made more exceptions from their print shelving patterns for them, Dale reported that six libraries intershelved audiovisual and printed materials on open stacks and thirty-nine kept their audiovisuals on closed stacks or locked cabinets. Dale summed up methods used for nonprint materials:

> Audiovisual materials are classified and cataloged in a variety of ways; call number designations for these materials are shelved in closed-access areas.... More original cataloging is done for audiovisual materials than for books ... it seems evident that they have not been fully accepted or integrated into the book collections.[12]

These three studies described different approaches to bibliographic access for nonprint materials in the three sectors of the library community they investigated. Olson's findings about academic libraries were virtually the reverse of Rogers' conclusions about school libraries, and Dale's survey demonstrated that two-year colleges are much more like their senior college and university counterparts in that they evidence much greater conformity to national cataloging standards. All of the studies reflected a perceived need for more bibliographic information for nonprint materials to be made available for librarians and media specialists.

THE CANADIAN STUDY

A detailed study of nonprint resources in Ontario, Canada, was made by Isabel McLean in 1974 and published a year later by the Canadian Library Association.[13] McLean examined the size and scope of collections in seventeen formats, describing the ways in which they were stored, organized, and used. She was interested in whether or not they were cataloged and classified, and if the bibliographic information was in the main catalog or in a separate nonprint catalog or catalogs. Forty-six libraries were surveyed. McLean investigated the degree of integration with print materials; the extent of reciprocal borrowing arrangements with other community agencies and interlibrary loan services between libraries; the physical and bibliographical access available for the user; the users' profile—if individuals, schools, or other community groups were using materials—the extent of library-produced materials and means of publicizing them, as well as the actual size of collections and their subject content. Analysis was done by medium and by size of libraries.

After providing much interesting information about the history and traditions of the libraries and the contents and makeup of their collections, McLean concluded that cataloging of nonprint materials was increasing, as were integrated shelving and integrated catalogs. She did not report on the specific cataloging rules followed for description or subject headings, or the classification by which the intershelving was being done. It might be assumed that in 1974, only *AACR* and the Canadian rules which advocated integration in both cataloging and shelving, were candidates for the task. *Nonbook Materials*, by Ontario-based Jean Weihs and her colleagues Janet Macdonald and Shirley Lewis, became popular in Canadian libraries as well as developing a following in the U.S. and earning official endorsement by the Audiovisual Committee of ALA's RTSD. It is reasonable to assume the use of this code may have influenced McLean's positive findings about nonprint cataloging and shelving.

STATEWIDE SURVEYS

Three state surveys, in California in 1974, Connecticut in 1975, and Wisconsin in 1976-77, were designed to identify existing media resources and compare them with then-current standards as well as with an assessment of current and future needs within each state.[14] The Wisconsin State Division of Library Services was interested in expanding on information about the status quo of media in public libraries appearing in annual reports so state plans for future activities could be formulated. In Connecticut, the Media Section of the Connecticut Library Association wanted to identify their potential audience as well as some general information about media resources and services, also in public libraries across that state. The California survey was directly aimed at comparing state public library media resources and the ALA *Guidelines for Audiovisual Materials and Services for Public Libraries* (1970). In many ways, these smaller studies parallel the national survey of needs and resources done by Boyd Ladd for the National Commission on Libraries and Information Science (NCLIS) for the country as a whole in 1975. Ladd's lengthy and detailed report was published in 1977,[15] documenting the gaps in perceived needs among three sectors of the library community—public school, public, and academic libraries—for various materials. Current holdings were evaluated according to the several nationally endorsed standards proposed by various professional groups, including those used by the state of

California a year later. Ladd reported no segment of the library community had successfully met the standards and supported the contention with dramatic statistics. Although the total number of
audiovisual titles owned in the public library sector exceeded the
total needs identified—the only sector in which this happened—the
distribution of these resources was so unbalanced that an aggregate
shortage of more than half the indicated need was assigned for
public libraries as a whole. School libraries were shown to have the
largest unmet audiovisual needs despite aggregate holdings of 100
million items, the largest of any group. However, Ladd compared
these holdings to an indicated need of one billion items. As for
academic libraries, nonprint collections were measured in volume
equivalents and were located primarily in universities, not in two or
four year colleges. Overall collection needs for academic libraries
were reported totalling 158 million volumes, but how much of this
was nonprint was not defined. Nevertheless, even a small percentage would be a great many titles in absolute numbers.

The California study surveyed twenty-one public libraries and
twenty-one public library systems all serving populations of more
than 150,000. Responses were received from fourteen of the libraries
and eleven of the systems. Like the Wisconsin study, the purpose
was to provide information for future planning in the state. The investigators selected twenty-six standards from the ALA *Guidelines*
relevant for both individual libraries and systems and designed a
questionnaire based on them. The standards dealt with budget,
amount and variety of holdings, facilities, staffing, and the range of
services offered. They found that only eight of the standards tested
were being met by even half of the libraries surveyed. One of these
was provision of a separate audiovisual catalog. The findings of the
NCLIS study were echoed here: "... among the California public
libraries and library systems surveyed there were extensive inconsistencies in the range and character of audiovisual services, in
the variety and quantity of audiovisual materials provided, in staffing financing, and in the space provided for audiovisual services."[16]
Despite the shortfall on the majority of standards, most respondents
were positive in their "philosophy" of AV and indicated media
should be equally funded and accessible as printed materials.

In their recommendations, the California investigators noted that
revised standards had been published by ALA since their survey for
the libraries under investigation, i.e., large libraries, and new ones
had been created for small and medium-sized libraries.[17] They suggested comprehensive studies be done using these new standards

and also investigating the financial problems inhibiting growth in some places.

The Connecticut study covering 118 of the state's 153 public libraries was primarily concerned with people—who was the media librarian? It was learned that the children's librarian most often had responsibility for nonprint materials and services, followed, in descending order, by administrators (directors or assistant directors), film librarians, reference librarians or subject specialists, circulation librarians, and catalogers. It was also learned that phonograph records were the medium most frequently collected, often accompanied by a collection of sound tapes. Variation in the size of holdings was considerable for all media. Thirteen libraries had slide collections, twenty-five had art prints, fourteen had posters, fifty-three had picture files varying from one thousand to four million items, thirty-five had realia, and films were either loaned from the State Library, rented, or owned by at least eighty-two institutions. Video activities were reported by only six libraries.

The only other element of Connecticut's media programs surveyed was the ownership and circulation of media hardware. The report indicated clearly that ownership of materials wasn't always accompanied by ownership of related equipment—e.g., 102 libraries had phonograph records, but only seventy-two had phonographs. Hardware circulation was limited to just two of these. Slide projectors were owned by thirty-seven libraries (more than owned slides) and four reported circulating them; 16mm film projectors were loaned by twenty out of seventy-six libraries.

The results of this survey indicated that media were not uniformly distributed in Connecticut's libraries, except for films, often loaned or rented, and sound recordings. Distribution of media resources was not pinpointed, but several libraries were named as having many different kinds of media collections, leading to the assumption they were the state's leaders. The lack of a common pattern within the state for media staffing indicates a good possibility that there are substantial differences in the character and subject matter of the collections. It may also indicate differences in the kind of access furnished, e.g., since most children's materials are afforded simpler treatment, media may be, too.

The Wisconsin study, funded by a Library Services and Construction Act (LSCA) grant, surveyed 364 public libraries in the state. A two-page questionnaire asked about holdings, services, staffing, hardware, philosophy, and funding, as well as the use made of state media services and materials. Nonprint holdings in at least one

medium existed in more than 80 percent of the libraries. Phonograph records were the most popular here, as in Connecticut, and
video was the least. (At this time, video was both expensive and relatively new, explaining, possibly, its rarity in public libraries.)
Libraries belonging to systems had nonprint holdings more often
and in a wider variety of formats than those not part of a system.

Circulating media seemed to be much more frequent than in-
house use of materials, except for video. Attention to hardware was
not usually systematic, but done on an as-needed basis. Nevertheless, few libraries said they lacked someone on the staff with training in operating the equipment, and more than one third claimed all
staff had this expertise.

Although 60 percent of the libraries claimed to look at media in
the same way as books, the report noted many fewer budgeted an-
nually for media services in the same way they did for books and
printed periodicals. Replies to questions about the use of state or
system resources indicated many people were not informed about
the materials and services available to them. Some requested information on free or inexpensive materials. Few believed they could
successfully propose added funding for media to their governing
boards.

All the state surveys noted the uneven distribution of nonprint
media resources among their individual institutions and systems.
All cited the need for more information about media, staff training,
and funding. The California and Wisconsin studies, exploring
philosophy, reported overwhelming expressions of positive attitudes
without key indicators of any transference to concrete implementation in programs or expanded budget allocations.

SURVEYS OF RESOURCES AND SERVICES

In none of the library sectors studied did the resources on hand
compare favorably to the levels of need cited by any of the existing
standards, even though most of these standards were minimum
levels of service, not ideal visions of the best possible service. Ladd
exposed the uneven distribution of all resources including media
collections, also described by the state surveys.

This division of the nation into information haves and have-nots
has been noted often in library literature. It is not a new problem,
and various solutions have been proposed to resolve it over the last
half-century. Nevertheless, media in libraries seem to be like the

weather—everybody complains, but nobody does anything about it. The state survey which specifically asked if librarians thought they could propose added funding to their boards was resoundingly denied. The dismal picture of limited collections, untrained staff, limited access, and inadequate funds, while not universally true, appeared to be more prevalent than glowing descriptions of abundant resources also described in library literature. A look at the successes is in order, too.

James W. Brown's *New Media in Public Libraries*[18] (1976) detailed the activities of the fifty state libraries and District of Columbia as well as 235 more local public libraries nominated by their state librarians as being particularly innovative with newer media. The emphasis of this survey was on special rather than general use of media collections, and its coverage was of selected media formats, including films, filmstrips, video, photographs, kits, and sound recordings. Access services were not separated from those activities dependent upon them, such as reference, circulation, and interloan, but were often described in terms of the totality of services offered. Brown's study identified a large number of public libraries nationwide whose diverse audiovisual services and collections indicated sophisticated means of access. The State Library of Pennsylvania reported funding seventy academic and public library online cataloging projects for audiovisual materials through OCLC, and the Montana State Library provided regularly updated film card catalogs to all public libraries in the state. A striking characteristic of the reports was the large number of cooperative media projects, also requiring mutually available and accessible bibliographic information. In fact, the only projects which did not depend to some degree on the use of bibliographic records were media production and broadcasting, and even these often resulted in archival bibliographic work.

Brown included eighty-six longer case studies in addition to the 286 state and local descriptions. The case studies detailed the most innovative programs and were selected to include a broad range of activities, formats, locations, library types, and community orientations.

After considering the responses to his survey and all the activities they represented, Brown concluded by forecasting five trends he believed would require continued use of new media in libraries despite funding shortages:

1. Increased independent study by adults

2. Increased need to meet clients on their own ground

3. Increased knowledge of the special contributions of various formats

4. Increased recognition that communications and information technology are not being fully exploited

5. Increased acceptance and use of the systematic, behavioral approach to the solution of community information problems.

This cheerful estimate of the future development of media may yet be borne out, though there does not seem to be any indication that it is better now.

Another relatively recent survey, this time of existing machine-based systems of bibliographic information for nonprint media, was sponsored jointly by AECT and NCLIS and published in 1979.[19] Its purpose was to determine whether the foundation for a national network for media was already in place and to define functional specifications for linking existing databases into such a network. Two parts of the study were particularly relevant for this review, an inventory of media databases in the U.S. and Canada describing their entry formats, and a list of functional specifications derived by comparing the results of the inventory with a list of user needs developed as another part of the study.

A questionnaire was developed containing twenty-five questions asking for information on the origins of each database, the number of titles it contained with their inclusive dates, formats and subjects covered, rules used for descriptive and subject cataloging, reasons for deleting items if any, bibliographic elements and their searchability, user profile, kind and level of activity, types of output, provision of documents, charges if any, technical specifications, and the relation of each database to other systems. A final open-ended question invited comments. Two hundred institutions and individuals were queried and resulted in the compilation of statistics on forty-three systems.

Over half of the forty-three systems had five thousand or fewer titles, including those for printed items; only eight systems held more than twenty thousand items overall. All but five of them began in 1970 or later. The kinds of formats held by at least ten or more systems included films, videorecordings, filmstrips, slides, kits, sound recordings, transparencies, prints, games, realia, models, charts, maps, and other two-dimensional graphic forms. Thus, although the databases were generally small, they held a broad range of media formats.

Approximately half the systems used one of two standard cataloging codes, *AACR* or the AECT *Standards*, while the rest used locally developed rules for descriptive cataloging. *AACR* was more frequently named than the AECT rules. Less than half used a standard subject heading list such as LCSH or *Sears*. The data showed adherence to standards increased as the size of the system increased. Of twenty-four bibliographic elements listed, sixteen of them were present in the entries of at least half the systems; however, the only element present in the entries of all the systems was title. Subjects were present in over 90 percent, but authors were included in only two-thirds of the systems and were ranked eleventh in frequency of use. The ten most frequently included elements, in addition to title and subject, were producer, call number, running time, number of physical units, series, summary of contents, sale distributor, and size/format. The least-used element was evaluation, present in only 15 percent of the systems, though that comes as no surprise to anyone familiar with library cataloging. However, media experts had been recommending that evaluative reviews be included in the creation of automated systems for media for some years before this survey and they had hoped to make an impact.

Findings about users were less clearly defined, with many respondents failing to reply fully. Some twenty-five systems were available to in-house users only, while fourteen more served both in-house users and an outside constituency. The range of end users went from zero—for systems used to produce a printed product—to 75,000. Many of the systems were in academic institutions or lower schools, and all but one of the rest were part of government, commercial, or nonprofit agencies. The exception was in a public library. Few provided document delivery services—only sixteen systems. Services were free in seventeen systems, twelve more charged their users varying fees, and the rest did not respond to this question.

The list of functional specifications developed included three provisions for the uniform entry of materials: that the MARC format should be used; that LCSH should be used for subject access; that a standard code for description should be used; but no code was recommended since agreement couldn't be reached on which one to select; however, since the MARC format is loosely based on *AACR*, that might well be the only choice possible. Additional specifications were for modular design, liberalized access, provision of many access points with a list of eighteen recommendations, online database management, accommodation of non-MARC elements, ability to accept a variety of inputs, and to produce a variety of outputs. Finally, some familiar sounding recommendations were made, including encouraging shared cataloging in the audiovisual world, encouraging media producers to furnish accurate and complete bibliographic data on items they produce, and using the item itself, not data sheets or other surrogates, for cataloging. Aspects of national network development were also addressed, among them continuing and expanding the inventory of audiovisual databases, establishing liaison with the international community, and developing a proposal for funding more work toward a national network. Earlier, James W. Brown's report of the Seminar on Nonprint Media Information Networking[20] had concluded that cost effectiveness of automated bibliographic networking for media was attainable only through existing systems established primarily for the cataloging of printed materials. No new work on Project Media Base was funded, but efforts to link the major bibliographic databases, now containing growing numbers of audiovisual titles, have not ceased. The possibility of greater success in the future has by no means ended.

A third survey meriting brief description here is the international study of nonprint cataloging conducted by Christopher Ravilious prior to development of an ISBD for nonprint materials.[21] It covered the practices of national libraries and professional organizations in thirty-four countries around the globe. The survey was done in 1974, originating the year before in a proposal of IFLA's Committee on Cataloguing. National cataloging bodies such as LC were contacted and asked the following questions:

1. Was the body drawing up rules for nonbook materials?

2. If not, would they contact another national body concerned with nonbook materials?

3. If the national bibliography contained nonbook items, would a sample be sent with an explanation of rules used to create the entries?

4. If recently published cataloging rules existed, would a copy be sent, too?

One purpose of the survey was to determine how close to already established ISBD standards for books and serials were the existing cataloging rules for media. Particular attention was paid to problems of terminology and punctuation. An important decision of the

IFLA Working Group's leadership was to exclude realia such as museum specimens and original works of art from the scope of the survey as well as from coverage in the proposed standard. This decision was based on their observation that these materials were not inherently conveyors of information. (Some experts would disagree with this assessment.)

Summaries of the bibliographic activities of twenty-four national bodies, including the national libraries of Australia, Canada, New Zealand, and the U.S. provided a state-of-the-art review of media cataloging and a larger context in which to evaluate U.S. efforts. The U.S. summary indicated a great deal of activity at the national level by several concerned organizations and the employment of several different cataloging codes with others being promulgated below the national level. This fragmentation may be disappearing after several years' experience with *AACR2*, still several years in the future at the time of Ravilious' study.

After a careful analysis of the materials gathered by his survey and comparison with existing ISBD structures, Ravilious' assessment of ISBD-readiness based on adoption of standards at the national level was negative. However, proposals for national standards did exist and led him to conclude they could be the basis for an ISBD(NBM). He wrote,

> There is, it would appear, something in the nature of a groundswell of interest in the projected ISBD(NBM): a movement of thought which noticeably antedates any large-scale traffic of information across national frontiers ... ISBD(NBM) will display a recognizable kinship with other International Standard Bibliographic Descriptions; it may not be too much to say that the appearance of a standard for non-book materials will underline rather than qualify the likenesses between books and non-books.[22]

Thus, the international community was led by a positive recommendation to develop an ISBD for nonprint and nonbook media, excluding nondocumentary materials. That ISBD was not completed in time to be incorporated into the provisions of *AACR2*, and thus the code departs from it to some degree.

These three surveys of resources and services at national and international levels demonstrate the kind of activity being encouraged for media materials in several directions, including incorporation into library programs of media-based services using newer formats, development of automated databases, and development of national and international standards for creation and transmission of bibliographic information. What might the implications be for media cataloging in general?

IMPLICATIONS OF SURVEY FINDINGS

Comparing school and academic libraries with the public library survey described in Chapter 3, as well as the smaller public library surveys summarized in this chapter, reveals differences and similarities between the practices of various groups. If a continuum is imagined as stretching from maximum individuality of practice, i.e., neglect of nationally accepted standards and adoption of unique treatments, to an opposite point representing maximum conformity to standards, the groups can be placed along it. Lower school libraries would fall somewhere toward the maximum individuality end, while large university libraries would be at the other end, and colleges and public libraries would be, in aggregate, somewhere between these extremes. If another continuum is imagined stretching from total integration of print and nonprint cataloging to total separation of the catalogs of different media, lower schools and two-year colleges would fall toward the integration end, while larger public and university libraries would be at the opposite end, and smaller public and senior college libraries would be somewhere between.

The general lack of a single pattern to which most libraries adhere, except regarding classification and physical separation of the media followed by virtually all of them, is somewhat disconcerting. Perhaps the most telling findings were those of Project Media Base which observed the extent to which media databases were at variance with standard library practice. In fact, they termed the libraries "bibliocentric" and clearly intended both the literal and figurative meanings of the word to apply. The shocking fact that only one bibliographic element was universally present in all databases is evidence of their conclusion that the bibliocentric and mediacentric communities might, like East and West, never meet. On the other hand, the great interest on the part of some leaders, e.g., state libraries, NCLIS, and less recently, IFLA, in the degree of uniformity existing in the field demonstrates that change is both possible and increasingly attractive.

One implication of these findings is the need for a deeper commitment to change on the part of many individual libraries. The growth of nonprint media entries in national networks must be considered in light of the fact that most libraries cataloging online with them are academic and/or larger public libraries. This larger number of computerized entries will also provide a viable means to support change through automation. The situation now and for the foreseeable future appears to be unstable insofar as the trend toward uniformity seems to run counter to the actual practices of some leading institutions. Fortunately, this period of instability coincides with a general atmosphere of instability as individual libraries deal with the changing nature of automated systems.

The libraries with online catalogs today are themselves the testing grounds. As new hardware and software are developed, they enlarge the capabilities and capacities of online catalogs-in-progress. Only a few years ago, the number of machine-readable nonprint entries in the primarily book and periodical databases of the bibliographic networks was extremely small, and experts despaired of their successful incorporation. Now the situation is dramatically different, with most types of nonprint media being included in the largest networks, OCLC and UTLAS. The foundation exists for current mainstreaming of media with online cataloging of books and printed periodicals.

Whether or not the systems such as those surveyed by Project Media Base can be linked with the utilities to provide extensive retrospective data is an open question. A great deal more is known about linking systems today than in the 1970s, but all systems may not be made linkable regardless of their characteristics. Naturally, it would be advantageous if such large systems as the NICEM database could simply be dumped automatically into the memory banks of OCLC or other networks; however, it requires enough of an investment in development to make it a questionable use of funds. On the other hand, no one knows what new processes or programs may be devised somewhere soon that could link these disparate conglomerations of machine-readable surrogates for media materials produced since the middle of the century and earlier, and transform them into usable catalog entries for all members of the several systems.

An interesting speculation is the status of school libraries' automation plans, and how current bibliographic practices will be affected by the introduction into schools of computerized bibliographic systems, assuming they will not be radically different from their counterparts in other sectors of the library community. Two factors lead to greater emphasis on conformity to standards in school library cataloging: (1) The addition of schools in larger numbers to the rolls of national networks; and (2) The attention to standards of the large, well-established commercial vendors of bibliographic data, from which many schools receive their cataloging. Lower schools have, since the late 1950s and 1960s, been the largest collectors of media materials and, therefore, have the greatest potential contribution to make to retrospective coverage of nonprint media. The entry of school libraries into national networks can only add to the networks' overall comprehensiveness. The use of MARC-formatted data on the part of the commercial vendors, on the other hand, makes libraries that would never do their own cataloging the recipients of the same kind of information as colleges, universities, or LC itself—provided they use it. If school libraries ask the vendors to transform the data from a standard format to some unique version with which the school has been familiar, they will overlook the twin advantages of saving money and obtaining standard cataloging.

Where schools will eventually fit into state and regional plans for automation may also determine how quickly they move along the continuum toward their public and academic library colleagues. Economic necessity may force state and regional level bodies to cooperate more closely and dissolve the invisible lines between public and school library organizations. Both have much to gain from mutual association.

Plans for automation do not, however, affect patterns of in-house storage and physical arrangement used to house materials. Unlike pressure to employ standard treatments for bibliographic identification, physical organization is not affected by MARC formats or other structures for machine entry. Libraries using standard classifications such as Dewey or LC schemes have always been free to create additional symbols or locational devices unique to their own institutions. Complete call numbers are rarely identical in any two unrelated libraries, though they may be quite similar. In some libraries, materials that circulate elsewhere are considered reference collections; items classed as children's materials are put into adult collections; and titles classified variously as short stories, mysteries, science fiction, or romances are all classed as fiction. Some children's materials are classified according to the difficulty of their texts as well as their subjects, and still others may be classified according to their publication form, physical form, or the fund from which they are purchased. Much of the call number is a symbolic representation not of the content of the item being classified, but of the administrative policies of the institution. Also, there are no national endorsements of a single classification system for all libraries, or even all of one type of library. It is more convenient to follow Dewey or LC than to make up one's own scheme—although some libraries do. In fact, it is when the particular scheme in use fails to meet a need that libraries devise unique classifications. Many libraries employing Dewey or LC for the bulk of their general materials also use different and specialized arrangements for special collections for which the general scheme might not be as effective or useful, e.g., music, medical works, art works, or language materials.

Greater use for nonprint media of classification schemes which vary from standard published schemes seems to be the one characteristic equally applicable to all types of libraries surveyed. It is unlikely that any current trend will contribute measurably to altering this pattern since it is unaffected by either automation or resource-sharing. When titles are shared among several institutions, uniform location tends to be unimportant. Once the item has been classified, it will be available for use to the entire group so long as they are informed of the classification through mutually-accessible cataloging. The person who requests the item as an interloan will probably not use the call number, but rather author and/or title, producer, date, ISBN, etc. When the item arrives, the receiving library will have a separate area for storing interloans. The patron who goes to the owning library to share the resource will have to obtain the call number there, without reference to where the home library would have placed it had they bought it. People using libraries don't seem to demand uniform call numbers everywhere, perhaps because they don't realize it would expedite browsing or perhaps because they don't realize they can make such demands successfully. The symbolism of library classification tends to be a mystery to most clients, just as it often is to the shelvers. A common complaint of shelving supervisors is that their staff don't seem to pay enough attention to more complicated combinations of numbers and characters and they have a hard time understanding the symbolic relationships sufficiently to shelve accurately and quickly. If the shelving staff have these problems, what can be expected from clients? At least clients have the option of asking for help.

One trend likely to continue which would motivate libraries to streamline their shelving policies is the diminution of numbers of staff available to provide assistance for patrons. One of the by-products of automation is supposed to be staff time released from repetitious drudgery to be used in other ways—preferably in direct service to patrons. What actually has happened in places where more staff time is made available by computer systems is not simple and hasn't necessarily resulted in a noticeable increase in direct service to clients. For one thing, libraries sometimes plan to reduce the staff long before more staff time is even available, sometimes to the detriment of the implementation of the computer system. Even when no staff reduction is made before or during implementation of the new system, it may be planned to follow it, or a change in the composition of the staff is planned to maximize the use of non-professionals. This is done partly to realize as much savings in over-all expenditure as possible and partly because library administrators expect the computer to enable fewer and less highly paid staff to handle more work. While this may well be true, time must be spent with the new system before surplus staff time can be applied to other functions. Rarely do libraries plan to use the released time to put more people out on the floor with clients, perhaps because of the crossover in departmental staffing that kind of rearrangement would entail—an increase in reference or readers' advisory services may not be perceived as a benefit of a technical services computer system. More likely, libraries plan to use the increased availability of technical services staff to do other technical services work or eliminate the technical service positions without adding them elsewhere.

If financial hard times continue to put more pressure on library budgets, any process facilitating clients' access to materials would seem to have value. Applying one system to all materials for shelf access would certainly seem easier than having ten different systems for ten different media. In my experience, a nonstandard scheme for media materials requires much more time in helping people to find (on open stacks, with all call numbers visible on the items and in the catalog) the particular titles they want. Had these materials been shelved by Dewey numbers as were the books, there probably would have been some grumbling about long numbers, but people would have been able to get along on their own. There are even advantages for libraries that close their stacks to use only one scheme for all media, namely, that training staff is easier and the same people can work with all media equally well.

The implication of the college and university library studies that classification needn't provide browsability or subject access to media materials, evidenced by the large number of accession number classifications used, needs to be made an explicit policy consideration of the access system as a whole. Perhaps the first decision to be made is whether the policy is intended to encourage or to discourage self-help by clients. Closed stacks and nonbrowsable classifications certainly don't encourage self-help. The decision ought to depend on various questions. Are materials in the collections irreplaceable, expected to last indefinitely, or ordinary trade items to be replaced by newer materials? Will the investment in a browsable, open shelf scheme pay off with greater use in terms of added circulations per item as well as by eliminating the need for staff time for supervision and retrieval? Can the space in the stacks accommodate the materials comfortably in an open shelf arrangement, or is it too limited for open access? Is the clientele accustomed to browsing or do people need to be reoriented to help themselves? How important is circulation to the library? How important is preservation and elimination of unnecessary handling? How likely is it that someone will ask for help and get it? How likely is it they will go away without a desired item rather than ask for help? How easy to use is the catalog? How much information does it provide? Can one tell from any catalog entry whether an item is on a desired subject and at a desired intellectual level? If not, what will substitute for direct access to the material to test its suitability? Many more questions like these need to be answered before determining whether to use a browsable classification or an accession number scheme, or whether to open or close stacks.

If people begin to have remote access to library catalogs, or beyond this to the material themselves, will open stacks be necessary? Perhaps efforts should be focused on other things, e.g., the need for establishing constructive relationships between grassroots school librarians and administrators at higher levels. There seemed to be a closer working relationship between state and local public library personnel, although the lack of knowledge on the part of local librarians about statewide services evident in the Wisconsin study did not support the assumption strongly. However, the ties and channels of communication between individual school librarians and state-level school coordinators seemed even more confused and tenuous.

Another potentially constructive relationship is between different types of libraries with common locations, subject interests, materials, or clients. Again, it is often at the state or regional level that common characteristics are recognized, let alone acted upon; but more and more the profession is witness to the establishment of multitype library networks or other cooperative projects that no one part of the group could have done alone. Not every library views such cooperation or participation positively; not every state, region, or authorizing body does, either. Sometimes big plans come to nothing and a great deal of individual librarians' time seems to be wasted on the planning of projects that don't materialize. Nevertheless, on the whole, a good many projects are being reported as operational, including state and regional union catalogs, retrospective cataloging and recataloging, automated bibliographic networks, and other automation services. These may, like the NYSCAT project in New York state, be limited to one or two types of media,[23] or they may include the entire range of print and nonprint media materials held by the participants.

Experimentation in standardized cataloging, automation in standard forms, and omnimedia catalogs may be possible with help from cooperative partners, many of whom already have experience with any one or all of these. They may be limited to the particular group of participants or they may be tied into a national network service. In all cases, these are the ways libraries can make changes without spending more than their budgets allow. Sometimes the only help needed by local librarians is in obtaining the resources to develop a program to which participants are already committed in principle. Very often, higher level bodies have specialists with knowledge of available funding, ways to write proposals for grants, or other methods of creative financing for viable projects. In other instances, local institutions need to be encouraged to look beyond their immediate needs to the future.

Comparing practices in more recent surveys with those described in the 1955 ALA survey is both illuminating and interesting. The Connecticut state survey indicated dispersal of responsibility for media among librarians with all sorts of other primary tasks ranging from circulation to children's services. The ALA study also found librarians other than catalogers responsible for media cataloging. In academic libraries recently, this is not usually the case. Either media librarians or catalogers are selected to supervise media access. The school library survey probably assumed the individual school librarians were responsible for all services. This may also be true in many small public libraries and the Connecticut survey may only be reflecting this fact. Many of those who responded to the author's public library survey said they were responsible for both technical and public services and for both print and nonprint media materials.

The number of libraries doing standard style cataloging, except for school library reports which were indeterminate, has increased greatly over the ones who were using LC cards or rules in the 1950s (the equivalent of standard codes today). LC rules, which the ALA survey respondents thought would be an appropriate foundation for standards, have become just that through their incorporation into *AACR1* and later into *AACR2*. LC will probably continue to be a major influence through its control over the MARC formats, but its impact is shared with the bibliographic utilities who use the formats in their databases, as well as the committees of professional organizations empowered to make official changes to them. The popularity of LCSH for subject headings has remained steady over the years. In contrast, the relative popularity of Dewey classification for media seems to have waned, though it is still used often in two-year colleges. Nonstandard classification does not seem to have lost its appeal for arranging nonprint media materials despite the trend toward standardization of descriptive and subject cataloging.

Availability to the public of media cataloging is the major change revealed by comparison of the surveys. There is also a decrease in uncataloged collections over the span of years. Both of these findings—that most media collections are cataloged and that the cataloging is available for public use—implies changes in the ways media materials are used in libraries today. Early film collections in public libraries, at least, were to serve as resources for library-sponsored programs expected to attract large audiences. Today, however, films are borrowed by individuals for home use as often as they are used for library programs. Academic libraries also have as many individual borrowers as large-audience users, i.e., classes or campus groups, though the film medium will often be preferred for audiences over individual use and video will be preferred for individual or small group use. The ease with which media can be altered (tapes of films, photographs of slides, etc.) is another new element in the mix.

The University of Maryland is typical of innovative academic libraries with extensive holdings of videorecordings used primarily by students as individuals rather than in classes. Lower schools have similar needs, satisfying them with different kinds of media appropriate for individuals and groups. The point of these examples is that in virtually every case where individuals use media resources in the way books have been used for decades, the same need for bibliographic data arises, and libraries have responded in largely the same ways, providing similar catalogs for media materials. Some have integrated media information into the main catalog which would previously have listed only books.[24] Newer facilities which were always multimedia might never have had a single medium catalog limited to books, but most libraries established before the midpoint of the century would have had print holdings before they began to collect nonprint media, thus their catalogs would have been so limited. The ALA survey found few omnimedia catalogs; the national public library survey found a large minority of them overall, smaller libraries leading the way with 40 percent of their public catalogs integrated; and about half of Dale's two-year colleges had omnimedia catalogs. Bibliographic networks demonstrate that omnimedia listing online is both possible and desirable, allowing searchers to limit their inquiries to a specific medium or not. OCLC has not separated its union catalog into different databases for various kinds of media, but finds it more advantageous to combine all entries. Entries for each index are interfiled whether they are part of a record for a book, serial, or audiovisual item. RLIN, however, has chosen not to combine print and nonprint records, so each file is maintained separately and searchers enter separate commands for each. The dichotomy remains in new form.

There is a parallel between limitation of access to media catalogs in the 1950s and a similar limitation of access to the catalogs of the bibliographic utilities today in many places. The terminals of the utilities are, for the most part, for staff use only, just as the earlier media catalogs were. Perhaps we need to think about the value to patrons of having access to these tools, complex though they may be, as well as to public catalogs. It may be better to make available *more* information than before, even though it won't be used by every client, than to continue in the tradition that certain kinds of information are off limits to all but a few staff members. Information that is costly to prepare and maintain ought to have the widest possible audience, if only to enhance its cost-effectiveness. Even the public catalog is not used by all library patrons, some of whom prefer to do without materials unless they have personal assistance in finding them. The trend toward greater sophistication and more self-help on the part of patrons may increase use of such tools currently denied to the public.

The question about need for a manual of procedures for nonprint media, asked by the ALA survey long ago and resoundingly affirmed then, would probably elicit a positive reply if it were asked today. Despite the many excellent manuals produced in the last several decades by experts on cataloging and media, there remains a large area of confusion over the ways media should be handled ("ways" is purposely plural, since I do not believe in only one best way), not only in libraries but also in institutions whose practices are the result of long experience with relatively large collections and whose familiarity with standards is clearly above average. Not only have standards changed over the years, but media have changed, people using them have changed, and bibliographic methods have changed, too. Computers and their accompanying software are rapidly changing all the things librarians once thought were stable, including bibliographic standards, physical forms, cataloging methods, and people's ideas about information. Viable manuals of procedure for media and/or printed materials need to recognize the fact that previously-held notions of service probably won't do now and certainly won't do in the future.

Flexibility seems to be the safest attribute to build into systems, procedures, and services as well as catalogs, indexes, and bibliographies. Unfortunately, flexibility is an elusive characteristic and not one highly prized in catalogs. Librarians are much more at home with controlled vocabularies, elaborately constructed classifications that eliminate ambiguity, and labyrinths of cataloging rules. Administrators are even more cautious of the idea that collections need recataloging. Thus, new manuals of procedure have to emphasize the effects of particular methods and be explicit about changes that can be made.

SUMMARY

In this chapter several surveys adding knowledge of bibliographic practices in libraries of all kinds were explored. The 1955 ALA survey had data about treatment of nonprint media when there were few guidelines or audiovisual collections. It demonstrated that librarians were aware of the need for bibliographic information, that some of them followed extant guidelines and more wished to do so if suitable standards were constructed. Findings that many collections were not classified or open to public perusal is not at all remarkable for the time, when many libraries purchased films for in-house use only and even sound recordings were expensive and fragile compared to books. Among the distressingly familiar complaints the survey registered was the lack of adequate, accurate, and clearly-presented information on the items themselves. The lack of a uniform substitute or analog to a book's title page has always been a stumbling block to media cataloging. Others emerged concerning

LC cataloging: it was too little, too late, too complex, too simple, etc., and gives those who criticize LC today a link with the past that hasn't changed very much. In 1950, LC was the only game in town, and the only alternative was original cataloging, a most painful solution. Endorsement of the development of a manual of procedure for treating nonprint media was the last finding—one which remains perennially valid no matter how many manuals may be developed over the years.

The findings of three more current national surveys of nonpublic libraries were analyzed. These were conducted by various researchers between 1977 and 1981, covering the practices in school, academic, and two-year college libraries. They showed the different sectors of the library community as being, for the most part, at different points along a continuum stretching from unique treatment to standard practice. School libraries seemed the least concerned with standardizing bibliographic treatment, while colleges and universities conformed much more to nationally endorsed codes and rules than either schools or public libraries. Frequent use of computerized networks for cataloging media in academic libraries may have influenced their commitment to standards. Classification practices in college and university libraries continue to be highly individual, with many departures from general classifications used for books. The study of two-year colleges indicated, as did the ALA survey, that Dewey was the most popular standard scheme employed. Fewer than 10 percent of the academic libraries maintained uncataloged media collections. No similar statistic was developed for lower schools, but since they were the largest collectors of nonprint media presumably they would have to control collections somehow, no matter how far from standard practice the methods.

A 1974 survey of Ontario's public libraries conducted by Isabel McLean indicated increased integration of both bibliographic and physical treatment of nonprint media. Her study was performed at a time when the Ontario-based Canadian Library Association had published a manual of procedure designed to produce integrated catalogs and encourage integrated storage and use, which may have influenced the outcome.

Three statewide surveys of public libraries in the U.S., conducted in the late 1970s in Connecticut, Wisconsin, and California, confirmed the suspicions of media experts that collections were below the minimum level standards set by national professional organizations and that services, including cataloging, were far from adequate. They reflected the depressing statistics forcefully presented by Boyd Ladd in his 1975 needs assessment for NCLIS—namely that nowhere were resources equal to or in excess of minimum level standards; and, furthermore, the imbalances between those who possessed resources and those who did not were strikingly large. This was true of both print and nonprint resources. The state surveys found librarians' attitudes toward media were overwhelmingly positive, but estimations of achieving equal funding for media were totally negative.

A nationwide investigation by Brown of the use of newer media in public libraries, an evaluation of several media databases in the U.S. and Canada, and an international survey of cataloging by Ravilious in conjunction with work toward an ISBD for nonbook materials, were described. Brown, whose study covered more than two hundred libraries, concluded these efforts would grow despite continuation of financial pressure on libraries because of their unique and as yet unexploited value to larger numbers of older and more media-wise clients. The database survey, called Project Media Base and jointly sponsored by NCLIS and AECT, uncovered a divergence in cataloging by media organizations (as opposed to libraries) which could prove an insurmountable barrier to a marriage between the mediacentric and bibliocentric communities under a common set of standards. Their fears, though mitigated by the proliferation of media entries in the initially print-only bibliographic utilities, may still be valid concerning the possible loss, perhaps forever, of data for older materials produced before the utilities had nonprint formats. These data may only exist in systems incompatible with MARC-style library networks. Ravilious' IFLA study exemplifies how negative findings can be overcome by sheer force of will, provided people have the necessary will. He found there were not, at the time of his survey, enough media cataloging rules in use by national libraries which also matched existing ISBD guidelines to warrant going ahead with an international standard. Yet, evidence of willingness and desire to create such rules was sufficient that Ravilious' recommendation was positive. An ISBD(NBM) was published in 1977. (Although some experts believe bibliographic descriptions do not have to be identical for entries to be interfiled, but only headings must be compatible,[25] I believe that dissimilar descriptions are difficult to manipulate in a system, especially if it is automated, discouraging integration.) Absence of an ISBD(NBM) might eliminate inclusion of media from present and future tools tied to Universal Bibliographic Control, thus, the standard is welcome even if it isn't perfect.

The studies described in this chapter evidenced varying patterns in the control and retrieval of bibliographic data for nonprint media in different kinds of libraries. They imply continuation of real differences in the substance as well as the form of this information from sector to sector of the library world. A commitment to eliminate incompatible practices is important in order to provide better access to materials. Change is already a fact of life for most catalogers as they come to grips with automation. The prevailing unsettled environment could result in the integration of media into the mainstream of information services for the public. Reluctance toward changing traditional practice (even when it is less than satisfactory) seems to pervade the library profession, but manuals of procedure which emphasize flexibility may help to overcome it.

With this view of actual practice in mind, examination of attitudes follows. Attitudes, though intangible, are nonetheless an important factor in the ongoing determination of how libraries function. Chapter 5 details the results of the author's national public library survey concerning perceptions of the nature and uses of nonprint media as well as ideas about bibliographic services for the public.

NOTES

1. As previously noted, the work of this committee was reported in the Fall 1957 issue of *Library Resources & Technical Services*, pp. 180-97. All material in this chapter concerning the survey is based on this report, prepared by Frances Hamman.

2. Eunice Keen, *Manual for Use in the Cataloging and Classification of Audio-Visual Materials for a High School Library* (Lakeland, Fla.: The Author, 1955), p. 35.

3. JoAnn V. Rogers, "Nonprint Cataloging: A Call for Standardization," *American Libraries*, 10 (January 1979), pp. 46-48. All material in this chapter concerning the survey is based on this article, supplemented by conversations with the author. At the time of this writing, Rogers is attempting to resurvey the school library situation.

4. Nancy B. Olson, "Survey of Audiovisual Materials Collections in Academic Libraries," in *Cataloging of Audiovisual Materials; A Manual Based on AACR2* (Mankato, Minn.: Minnesota Scholarly Press, 1981), pp. 1-3.

5. Doris Cruger Dale, "Cataloging and Classification Practices in Com-

munity College Libraries," *College & Research Libraries*, 42 (July 1981), pp. 333-40.

6. JoAnn V. Rogers, p. 46.

7. Jean Thornton Johnson et al., *A V Cataloging and Processing Simplified* (Raleigh, N.C.: Audiovisual Catalogers, 1971).

8. Warren B. Hicks and Alma M. Tillin, *Developing Multi-Media Libraries* (New York: Bowker, 1970). A second edition was published in 1977, entitled *Managing Multi-Media Libraries*.

9. Judith L. Westhuis and Julia M. DeYoung, *Cataloging Manual for Nonbook Materials in Learning Centers and School Libraries*, rev. ed. (Ann Arbor, Mich.: Michigan Association of School Librarians, 1967).

10. Esther J. Piercy, *Commonsense Cataloging; A Manual for the Organization of Books and Other Materials in School and Small Public Libraries*, 2nd ed. (New York: Wilson, 1974).

11. These are LC's serial publications, *Films and Other Materials for Projection* and *Music, Books on Music and Sound Recordings*.

12. Doris Cruger Dale, p. 339.

13. Isabel K. McLean, *Non-Print Resources; A Study of Ontario Public and Regional Library Systems* (Ottawa: Canadian Library Association, 1975), p. 62.

14. Two of these surveys, California's and Connecticut's, were noted in Chapter 2; the Wisconsin study was reported by Kandy B. Brandt, "Audiovisuals in Public Libraries?" *Wisconsin Library Bulletin*, 74 (July-August 1978), pp. 175-78. Material in this chapter about these three surveys was based on these reports.

15. Boyd Ladd, *National Inventory of Library Needs, 1975; Resources Needed for Public and Academic Libraries and Public School Library/ Media Centers* (Washington: NCLIS, 1977).

16. Nancy B. Olson, p. 53.

17. These were *Guidelines for Audiovisual Materials and Services for Large Public Libraries* and *Recommendations for Audiovisual Materials and Services for Small and Medium-sized Public Libraries*, both published in 1975 by the Audiovisual Committee of the Public Library Association, a division of the ALA.

18. James W. Brown, *New Media in Public Libraries: A Survey of Current Practices* (Syracuse, N.Y.: Gaylord, 1976), p. 218.

19. *Problems in Bibliographic Access to Non-Print Materials; Project Media Base: Final Report* (Washington: NCLIS, 1979).

20. James W. Brown, *Nonprint Media Information Networking: Status and Potentials* (Stanford, Calif.: ERIC Clearinghouse on Information Resources, 1976), p. 60.

21. C. P. Ravilious, *A Survey of Existing Systems and Current Proposals for the Cataloguing and Description of Non-Book Materials* (Paris: UNESCO, 1975), p. 132.

22. *Ibid.*, p. 112.

23. The NYSCAT project is, as of this writing, an experimental project for the development of a computerized film and video catalog by the Mid-Hudson Library System, funded by a grant from the New York State Council on the Arts. The union listing includes the holdings of the state's public libraries.

24. In a description of the Library of Congress' nonprint optical disk experiment, contained in the September 12, 1983, issue of its *Information Bulletin*, one objective of the project is preparation of data for an integrated catalog (see page 313). It explains, "This goal may be understood as a desire to use a single locus—the Library's computerized catalog—to inform a researcher of all relevant holdings in the institution. The program's indirect contribution to this goal will be derived from the disks containing the Prints and Photographs Division collections, but the work may serve as a model for other special collections."

25. This appears to be the conclusion of experts in a variety of institutions who have, over the years, incorporated many different standards into one catalog by making their headings compatible, but leaving the bibliographic descriptions in whatever form they were originally made. This is also true of the bibliographic utilities. A recent article by Martha M. Yee, "Integration of Nonbook Materials in AACR2," *Cataloging & Classification Quarterly*, 3 (Summer 1983), pp. 1-18, seems to endorse this view.

RECOMMENDED READING

Chisholm, Margaret, ed. *Reader in Media, Technology and Libraries.* See especially Part XI: Media and Networking.

Dale, Doris Cruger. "The Community College Library in the Mid-1970's," *College & Research Libraries*, 38 (September, 1977), pp. 404-11.

Dennison, Lynn C. "The Organization of Library and Media Services in Community Colleges," *College & Research Libraries*, 39 (March 1978), pp. 123-29.

Grove, Pearce S., ed. *Nonprint Media in Academic Libraries.* Chicago: American Library Association, 1975.

Niles, Ann. "Bibliographic Access for Microform Collections," *College & Research Libraries,* 42 (November 1981), pp. 576-80.

Philos, Daphne. "Selection and Acquisition of Nonprint Media," *School Media Quarterly,* 6 (Spring 1978), pp. 179-87.

Truett, Carol. "AACR Who? The Case for Using the New Anglo-American Cataloguing Rules in the School Library Media Center," *School Media Quarterly,* 12 (Fall 1983), pp. 38-43.

Chapter 5

Attitudes of Public Librarians

IN the public library survey, two kinds of questions, which complemented one another, were devised to elicit attitudinal information. The first kind were statements with which the respondent indicated his or her level of agreement or disagreement on a five-point scale, from strongly agree to strongly disagree. The second type of question consisted of pairs of statements expressing alternatives for performing the same public services from which the person selected the choice they believed provided better public service. In the second type, extraneous issues such as relative cost, space requirements, and logistics of a decision were to be ignored, though these may be the deciding factors when such choices are made.

The following attitudes were investigated:

Desirability of equal bibliographic treatment for all materials. These questions explored the issues of an integrated catalog versus separate catalogs for media as well as the efficacy of descriptive cataloging rules and subject heading lists developed originally for books to be applied to all materials.

Desirability of equal physical access to all materials. These questions centered primarily on the use of classification schemes developed for books with media materials and on the value of open versus closed shelf access and the issues of intershelving print and nonprint media materials on the same shelves.

Perceptions of the cost of nonprint materials. The high cost of nonprint items compared to books has been cited as a barrier to their use; therefore, questions about the cost of both software and hardware were included. Librarians were also questioned about the value of increasing budget allocations for media materials and their cataloging.

Perceptions of the nature, content, and use of media materials in libraries. Here, questions covered both respondents' own ideas and their perceptions of clients' beliefs with regard to the inter-changeability of print and nonprint media for various purposes. Staff may behave in a manner contrary to their own attitudes if they believe client attitudes are significantly different.

Perceptions of the value of uniformity in cataloging. The issue of uniform versus customized cataloging in general, while not confined to the print-nonprint considerations of the study, has relevance for attitudes toward networking—a valuable source of bibliographic data and a source of materials through resource-sharing. There is an essential tension between desires for standardization and its benefits and treatments which may be superior for individual agencies or collections. National cataloging networks responded to this fundamental compromise by creating local fields, i.e., areas in the standardized entry format where data unique to the institution doing the cataloging may be entered.

While no one can predict with certainty that a particular opinion or attitude or belief will cause a person to act in only one way, authorities on the subject write about attitudes as predispositions to behave in a certain way.[1] Consider the alternative. If a professional librarian believes a particular procedure is providing poor service, is he or she going to change from some other procedure to implement it? Probably not, if the librarian has the power to make the choice. Other things being equal, one's attitude is a measure of willingness to change.

The following discussion is divided into five sections, covering each of the five attitudes enumerated above. A sixth section analyzes the implications of the findings and the conclusions that can be drawn from them.[2]

EQUAL BIBLIOGRAPHIC TREATMENT

Equality of treatment of materials in all physical media, bibliographically speaking, is a set of processes or procedures, not just a single decision to treat things equally. The most basic decision is whether to display all entries together in a single catalog file—an integrated catalog. If an integrated catalog is chosen, it is assumed it means catalogers will have to apply the same rules for bibliographic description, subject headings, and selection of access points. In addition, it assumes entries will be interfiled, with books, films, recordings, etc., of the same work appearing together in an uninterrupted series of entries. This may not necessarily be done in the field, e.g., one can envision a library having a catalog where entries for nonbook forms follow all the entries for books, or where the same rules are applied, but the entries are not displayed together. Therefore, several questions regarding equal treatment were asked, including some about the use of one cataloging code and subject heading list for print and nonprint materials as well as the main question of the person's opinion of an integrated catalog.

Two statements addressed the fundamental issue. One said, "I want to see entries for everything in the library in one catalog," while the other said, "Each information medium should have its own catalog." One would think these statements would elicit equal but opposite responses, but this was not the case. People felt more intensely positive about the first one than intensely negative about the second. Also, more people affirmed the first than opposed the second (disregarding the level of response) as can be seen in Figures 5-1 and 5-2. The largest numerical response to any statement at the stronger level of intensity was in (strong) agreement with integrated catalogs. A clear majority at both intensity levels favored inte-

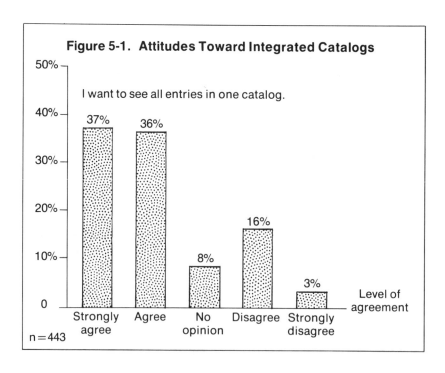

Figure 5-1. Attitudes Toward Integrated Catalogs

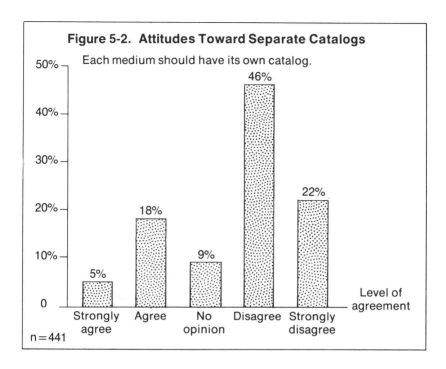

Figure 5-2. Attitudes Toward Separate Catalogs

grated catalogs and opposed separate catalogs. Also, the smallest number of "no opinion" replies was given for these statements. When asked to choose between putting all catalog records into one public catalog and maintaining separate catalogs for each information medium in order to serve the public better, the responses were more than three to one in favor of an integrated catalog.

Clearly, the overwhelming majority of librarians surveyed believed that integrating catalogs for the public provided better service than separate nonprint catalogs. This inevitably raises the question of why this preference is not translated into action more often, since far less than a majority of them had integrated public catalogs. One speculation is that, faced with a tradition of separate cataloging, it takes more than attitudes to initiate change.

One statement declared, "It is difficult to apply *AACR2* to nonprint materials"; another said, "The subject headings used for printed materials are inappropriate for nonprint materials"; and a third said, "*AACR2* is an improvement over previous cataloging codes." Each of these statements about applicability of rules commonly used for books with nonprint media was greeted with a large proportion of "no opinion" replies. Negative replies to the first two statements, indicating approval of applying one standard to all media, were in the majority (see Figures 5-3 and 5-4), but mostly at lower intensity levels. Responses to the statement evaluating *AACR2* and its predecessors, excluding the noncommittal ones, were overwhelmingly positive, but again, at lower intensity levels. This came as a surprise because the literature was still full of articles expressing either strong support for the new code or extreme displeasure with it—

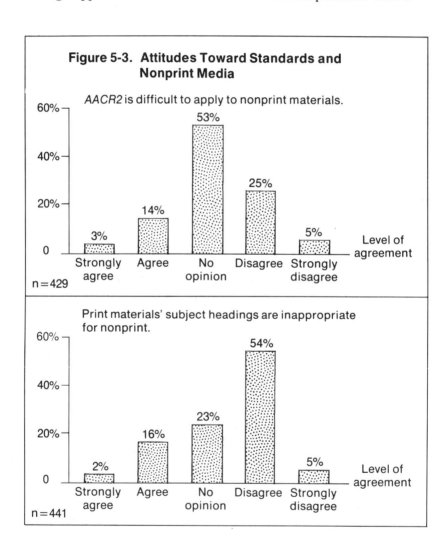

Figure 5-3. Attitudes Toward Standards and Nonprint Media

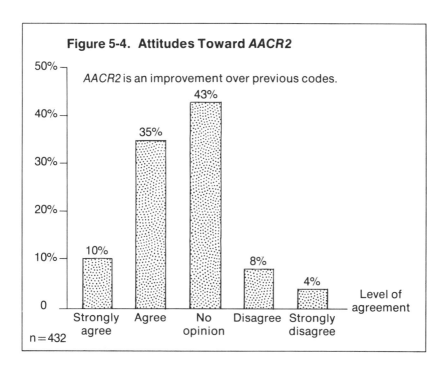

Figure 5-4. Attitudes Toward *AACR2*

AACR2 is an improvement over previous codes.

n = 432

though sometimes the anger was directed at its implementation rather than its contents. Apparently people in the field—at least those surveyed here—bore no such extreme warmth or hostility to *AACR2*. Feelings about *AACR2* explored (indirectly) agreement or disagreement with the idea of one code for all materials, since none of its predecessors covered all materials or had as their aim to produce integrable entries.

In general, replies to all of the statements and choices indicated perceptions that integrated cataloging provided better service, and that the same rules and standards were applicable to all materials. Interestingly, many people wrote comments in the margins of the questionnaire objecting to the notion that a library could not have both an integrated catalog and separate, media-specific catalogs. There is no question that offering several approaches to materials is desirable, but it is also, unfortunately, more costly than choosing between them. Until it is feasible to provide a variety of bibliographic products at low cost—as automated systems could—most libraries will still offer only one option to their clients.

EQUAL PHYSICAL ACCESS

In the area of physical access, bibliographic practices for print and nonprint materials were the farthest apart, with virtually universal use of the Dewey decimal classification for books and only one third of the libraries using it for nonbook media. Was this, like the minority of integrated catalogs, something professionals really did not believe was providing the best service? One statement said, "The classification used for printed materials is inappropriate for nonprint materials." Or did these public librarians think nonprint media should be classified and arranged on shelves differently from books? The response, far from what might have been expected, was almost equally divided between those who agreed and disagreed with it. (See Figure 5-5.) This result is difficult to interpret. It certainly does not support the status quo in any emphatic way, but it does not negate it either. The lack of a clear majority of people who believe one classification cannot be applied to both print and nonprint media indicates that current practice is not in harmony with prevailing attitudes on the subject, but neither is a strong opposition indicated.

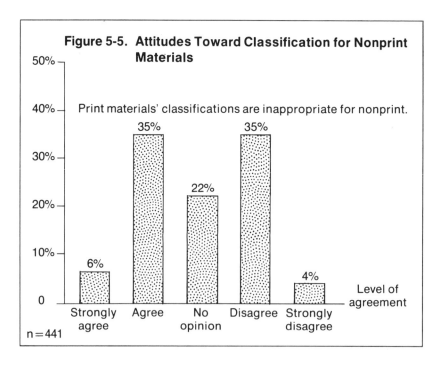

Figure 5-5. Attitudes Toward Classification for Nonprint Materials

Two pairs of statements regarding physical access gave clearer indications of attitudes about other aspects of shelving and use of materials. One pair offered a choice between intershelving books and nonbook media *and* furnishing reading areas with media hardware, too, and providing areas separate from book stacks and reading areas for shelving and using media materials. Responses were about two to one in favor of the latter choice. The second pair of statements asked for a choice between closed stacks for media with added staff to help people obtain desired materials and open stacks with more frequent replacement for damaged or stolen materials. The majority was in favor of open stacks with more frequent replacement and was almost two to one.

Clearly, public librarians expressed a commitment to open stacks for all materials quite in keeping with traditions established at a time when print materials were the only kind widely collected by public libraries. This belies current practices, which relegate at least some nonprint materials to closed stacks.

When libraries began collecting nonprint media, individual items in nonbook formats were more costly than books, and some media were delicate, breakable, or otherwise in need of special protection. Now, however, several trends have altered the situation radically. First, there has been a trend for some time in the direction of lower costs for many nonprint formats as well as for higher costs for books. The discrepancy between them has thus diminished. Librarians are also now aware that books are not the hardy, indestructible things they were thought to be. At the same time, some relatively fragile media, e.g., phonograph records, are produced in much sturdier forms and are easily duplicated for protection against permanent loss. Many nonprint media are now produced with the same kind of bibliographic information as books.

Equally clearly, librarians reject the notion of intershelving and multipurpose use and reading areas for the public. Further research might reveal the reasoning behind this posture. Separate storage and use areas may have to do with economy of space and the cost of repackaging some items so they can fit on book shelves, although respondents were asked to ignore these factors. Other determinants may be more closely related to the media themselves, e.g., differences in the audiences who use media and books; or differences in the environment provided for use of media and books, such as the need for electrical outlets to support hardware. Environmental problems are more expensive to address than repackaging and, in older buildings, may be easier to resolve by adding an entirely new section rather than redoing older ones. This tends to perpetuate separate use areas, with separate storage areas as natural adjuncts. In these cases, the result is the same: endorsement of the view that separate storage and use gives the public better service.

Equal physical access is perceived quite differently from equal bibliographic access. Most of the librarians polled believed in open shelves for all materials. In this respect, equality of treatment was unequivocally endorsed. Mainstreaming media storage by inter-shelving materials in all formats was seen negatively, however, and the efficacy of a scheme such as Dewey classification for nonprint media was approved and disapproved by approximately the same number of people. These very different reactions to various aspects of physical access to materials indicate it is a complex and multifaceted problem.

COST OF NONPRINT MATERIALS

When libraries began to collect nonprint materials following World War II, these costs were tied to different technologies than products being sold today. The *Public Library Inquiry* mentions the high cost of media as a deterrent to their acquisition by small and even medium-sized public libraries,[3] and other articles from that period reiterate that position. Twenty-five years later, when this author worked in a small public library, a record album (a long-playing, twelve-inch disk which is the equivalent, bibliographically, of a trade book) cost about eight dollars, though many records went for less. Ordinary novels were listing for about the same price. Since both kinds of items were purchased at substantial discounts, the actual cost to the library was about five dollars for either a hardcover novel or an LP album. This does not, of course, include the cost of processing. Just as some books cost a great deal more than five dollars, so did a great many record albums, including one multidisk album of all thirty-two of Beethoven's piano sonatas that retailed for about three hundred dollars and another set of language cassettes that went for about two hundred dollars. Run of the mill, single-disk recordings, whether of popular, classical, or spoken material, were all in line with the cost of hardcover books. Short films, also a product of new technologies since the 1950s, did not command the high prices of their feature-length counterparts of earlier decades, although there was no uniformity in the prices of films in general. Though feature-length films remained a high-price category, other educational films were about as costly as higher priced books. Videorecordings and computer software, all beginning to be collected by public libraries in the late 1970s and early 1980s, have become the high-priced end of the software scale and, by comparison, films and sound materials as well as filmstrips, transparencies, and other graphics are very reasonable. Music scores and maps, often collected by libraries, can vary in price from under five dollars for the same music recorded on the twelve-inch LP album, to quite expensive for a few pages of paperbound music or a few sheets of maps. It all depends on what the materials are and who produces them.

Cost factors have obviously changed between 1945 and 1981, when the survey was conducted. Many nonprint media are currently in more or less the same price range as books, although there is no doubt that some media materials are extremely expensive. There is also the consideration for the library of the purchase and maintenance of hardware for in-house use of materials. Even when hardware and software are not linked in the budget, the contrast between providing a chair and a lamp for the use of books and furnishing a sound station, viewing booth for films, microform reader, or television equipment for the use of various media is dramatic. Thus, survey participants were asked about both kinds of costs.

Two statements addressed the issue of software costs: "Nonprint materials cost too much for the library to afford"; and "Public libraries should spend more of their budget on nonprint materials." More than twice as many people replied negatively to the first statement than agreed with it, with three times as many disagreeing than agreeing at the higher intensity levels. The second statement elicited quite a different response, though slightly more people agreed with budget increases for software than disagreed with them. Another big difference between the two statements was a much larger number of noncommittal replies to the second. Perhaps this reflects innate resistance to the idea of changing allocations. The question was asked at a time when the real value of budget dollars was declining and a great many public library budgets were declining in absolute dollars as well; therefore, people may have been extremely sensitive to questions about increasing any kind of allocation. Still, a majority of respondents expressed a positive view of software costs, even for increased allocations. (See Figures 5-6 and 5-7.)

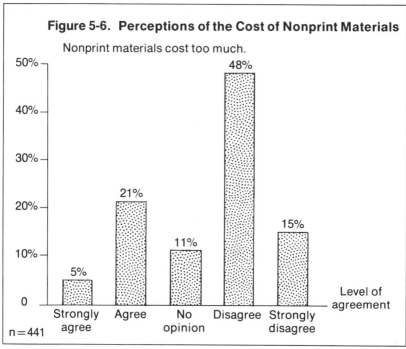

Figure 5-6. Perceptions of the Cost of Nonprint Materials

Nonprint materials cost too much.

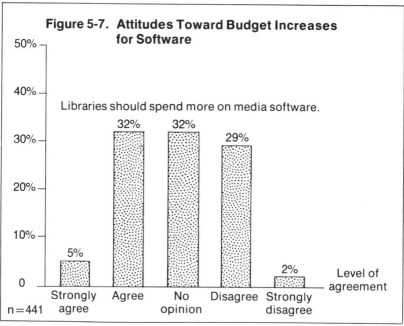

Figure 5-7. Attitudes Toward Budget Increases for Software

Libraries should spend more on media software.

The statement, "Public libraries should spend more of their budget on the equipment needed to use nonprint materials in-house," brought the same kind of response as the parallel statement for software. There were many "no opinion" replies and a slightly larger number in agreement than in disagreement overall. (See Figure 5-8.) The reason more people believed in additional spending for hardware, perhaps, is that many libraries have little or no equipment at all, and others who already own some hardware are aware of the difficulty of keeping it in good repair without expenditures of money.

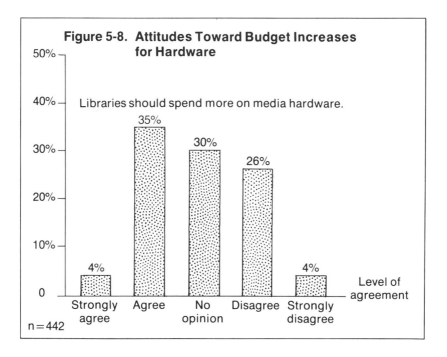

Figure 5-8. Attitudes Toward Budget Increases for Hardware

Libraries should spend more on media hardware.

n = 442

The survey reflects a change in librarians' perceptions of the cost of nonprint media as not too much for libraries to afford, in contrast to the opposite notion appearing years ago in such publications as the *Public Library Inquiry.* A slight majority also believed budget allocations should be increased for both software and hardware despite the bleak economic outlook at the time of the survey. Implications of this generally positive attitude are explored in more detail later in the chapter.

NATURE, CONTENT, AND USE OF NONPRINT MEDIA

There are often references in the library literature to the "unique" nature of nonprint media. True, looking at the images and hearing the sounds on a film or videotape is a different experience from reading a book, even though the words used in all media may be the same. Is this what is meant by unique nature? If so, what does the uniqueness imply? A popular image in libraries of nonprint media materials is that they are used only for recreation. When people think of library media, do they think of classical music or popular songs, recreational films or science materials, scholarly reference works or slides of paintings or computer games? When library professionals think of media, what are their gut reactions?

The other perception of media being investigated here was how they were used in public libraries. These ideas, like those about the contents of media materials, cannot be the same for all libraries. The uses of media depend on their contents, which vary.

Two statements addressed notions about the nature and contents of nonprint media. The first said, "When seeking information, public library users prefer using printed materials to nonprint forms." The overwhelming majority of replies agreed with this statement. The second statement said, "Public library users like using nonprint materials when they have equipment available," and even more

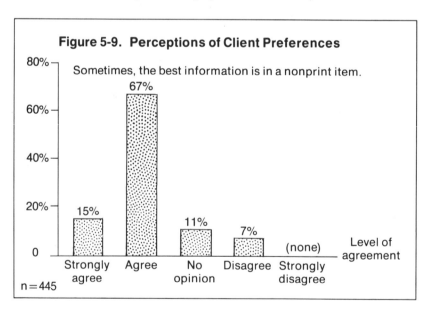

Figure 5-9. Perceptions of Client Preferences

Sometimes, the best information is in a nonprint item.

n = 445

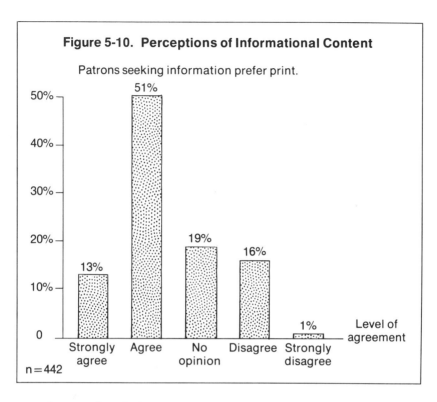

Figure 5-10. Perceptions of Informational Content

Patrons seeking information prefer print.

people agreed with this one. The key difference appears not to be the medium, but the contents. Yet, when asked to react to the statement, "Sometimes the best information is not in a book, but in a film or a recording or other nonprint item," even more librarians agreed than with the other two statements. (See Figures 5-9 and 5-10.) Finally, the issue was posed directly: "Nonprint materials are used primarily for recreation." At both intensity levels, a slight majority agreed. What they seem to be saying is, "Yes, we believe there is good information in nonprint materials; and yes, again, we believe people like using nonprint materials when we make it possible for them; but, nonetheless, we feel people prefer printed materials for information seeking and also, we believe they use nonprint materials for fun, not for serious business." This somewhat jumbled picture might be a result of the general lack of available hardware, or it might reflect the existence of largely recreational collections in public libraries—unlike those in academic institutions which tend to purchase only nonrecreational materials. Regardless of the explanation, the fact remains this is a commonly held belief with a serious implication for the future of media management in public libraries.

VALUE OF UNIFORM CATALOGING

There are arguments for and against uniformity in cataloging. Some librarians believe their collections and users are so distinctive that what they do must be different from any other library and that what other libraries do would be unusable for them, although most professionals do not take such an extreme view. The popularity of LC cards and, more recently, OCLC and other networks has shown that one person's meat not only is not poison to others, but is most welcome to the alternative of original cataloging. Despite the many complaints about the utilities, their thousands of users speak for the ability of librarians to use other people's work in their own catalogs.

One of the main objectives of *AACR2* was to promote uniformity in cataloging, and it achieved this in two ways: by establishing one structure for all entries cataloged using the code, and by conforming in the creation of the structure to international standards for bibliographic description. The value of uniformity was in facilitating exchange of bibliographic records within and between countries. It also made possible the use of one set of rules for all media.

As with any standard that tries to be all things to all people, many objections were raised to provisions of *AACR2*. When it was incorporated into the computerized format used by the bibliographic utilities, even more distress surfaced. The idea of cataloging with the MARC format raised a flurry of protest over the restrictions imposed on description and entry. Many of the loudest protests had to do with MARC formats for nonprint media. MARC, just like cataloging rules and subject headings, was designed with books in mind and adjusted at a later date for other media. In the minds of many media catalogers, the "adjustment" was neither complete nor sufficient. A great many more wrote, pragmatically, that it is better to disseminate more bibliographic information quickly and cheaply to a wider audience than to create every entry as perfectly as catalogers can make it, and have that same entry painstakingly recreated in every institution buying the particular item. These pragmatists pointed out that many catalogers do not create entries perfectly, and for many users of the catalogs it is not necessary anyway. Often what people want from the catalog is to know if the library has something and where it can be found; therefore, it is better to have *some* entry in the catalog than to have a great backlog of materials awaiting perfect cataloging.

On the whole, however, integrating the catalog requires the use of rules that are not equally advantageous for every item in every medium to which they must be applied, nor can they be equally tailored to the needs of every library. The survey addressed this issue with a pair of statements for respondents to choose between: "In order to serve the public better, (1) use *AACR2* for all cataloging, or (2) tailor cataloging rules to local use." Most of the replies were in favor of tailoring rules to local use. Catalogers still believe their institutions and users are different from the rest and should have catalogs designed to meet those differences. What are the implications of this belief and others expressed in the survey?

IMPLICATIONS OF LIBRARIANS' ATTITUDES

One of the clearest findings of the attitudinal survey was librarians' positive reaction to the idea of integrating catalogs for public use. They believe it provides better service. They also believe the same cataloging rules and subject heading lists are applicable to all media, and that *AACR2*, which permits this integration, is better than codes that preceded it. Other trends in the field are leading professionals to evaluate services provided by their catalogs. When decisions are made about what to enter into new automated systems, presumably nonprint media data will be included with bibliographic data for books. The computer system will be able to receive, store, manipulate, and present many more entries than manual systems could, with far less effort, time, or money. Even those librarians whose catalogs remain in manual modes may be inclined to add to the main catalog those records currently filed separately, simply because they believe it to be good service. The cost of integrating is justified by improvements in service that follow. The cost of separate cataloging and filing may not be much less than integration and may even be more.

As more libraries integrate their catalogs, the predisposition to follow them may become even stronger for several reasons: people will be used to this kind of catalog and will come to expect it as a normal bibliographic service; as more nonprint records become available in automated databases, librarians will realize they can achieve the same savings in time and effort by cataloging nonprint materials online they have had for years with book and serials cataloging; and they will be able to use archival tapes containing nonprint entries as the basis for various products including COM catalogs, online catalogs, printed indexes, or anything else desired by the library. Those people who wanted both integrated and medium-specific catalogs could produce both with the same machine-readable records.

Some libraries always serve diverse groups of clients with needs for different kinds of bibliographic tools. A dictionary card catalog might be preferred by persons who are intimidated by mechanical devices such as COM readers, though most people seem readily adaptable. A classified catalog might be preferred by some searchers; others might prefer dividing subject listings and author and title listings. Each possibility serves some users better than others. Media entries can be a part of all variations. Using an automated cataloging system for all of a library's cataloging work spreads the cost of the system over more entries than limiting its use to printed materials, making the library's initial investment more productive.

Libraries serving the largest populations and having the largest concentrations of nonprint media materials are not leading their colleagues in the move toward integration, however. The tail is wagging the dog, with the smallest libraries more likely to integrate cataloging in practice, according to the survey. Are larger libraries, with their large catalogs, more resistant to change in general—even change they believe to be beneficial? Is their investment in the status quo so enormous they cannot make changes without serious loss of money and function? Don't the large libraries have the most to gain from the integrated approach? They have the largest numbers of resources in all formats and the largest number of users with the greatest diversity of interests, backgrounds, and abilities. They are also most likely to conform to professional standards or lead in their creation. This disparity between attitudes and practice should be fertile territory for change.

In contrast to clearly defined findings about integrated catalogs, views on informational value of nonprint media were divided and conflicting. The idea of the library as essentially bibliocentric is a function not only of the relative size of collections, but also librarians' perceptions of their clients' information-seeking preferences. One of the most widely held views was that nonprint media sometimes contained the best information on a subject. Another was that people liked using nonprint media when equipment was available. In spite of these opinions, however, it was agreed that nonprint media are used mostly for recreation and that people prefer using printed materials for information. How can these attitudes be reconciled? Think, for a moment, about the most common information-seeking activities of daily life—obtaining up-to-date news of the world, the nation, the region or locality, the weather, sports, and so forth. How do most people learn these everyday facts affecting their lives either directly—e.g., the weather forecast, influencing the choice of clothes—or indirectly—e.g., world affairs? While millions read daily newspapers, it is a good bet that many more, including those who faithfully read newspapers, either watch television or listen to the radio to get their basic, life-directing information. Radio and television offer much faster communication of events than newspapers. They bring, in every gory detail, news of disasters *as they are happening*, not the next day. The list of live broadcasts—sports events, presidential news conferences, United Nations debates, political contests—is virtually endless. Yet, librarians believe these same people who get their weather forecasts from TV and traffic reports from car radios prefer to get their library information from books.

Sometimes an item may be "recreation" to one person and "information" to another. The same musical sound recordings borrowed by some clients of my library for a party or individual leisure time listening were used by a composer of serious music as background information for a score-in-progress. The list of nonrecreational uses to which a primarily recreational collection may be put is long. Studies of contemporary history and popular culture are based on comics and movies and all sorts of other nonbook materials.

Who can say what people prefer using for information when it so obviously depends on individual needs and interests and the pool of available materials? Libraries provide a much larger pool of information materials in book and periodical form than in nonbook forms. It may be accurate to say people use printed materials for information in libraries more frequently than they use their nonbook counterparts, but attributing it to preference is another issue. It makes one wonder how many times a public library user is offered both a print and nonprint version of some work and, assuming no lack of equipment for the nonprint item, the person chooses the printed item. The survey responses imply librarians see nonprint media as recreational and believe the public does, too. They view the library-as-information-center as essentially bibliocentric and believe the public does, too.

Perhaps librarians believe the recreational uses of materials should be given greater emphasis in public libraries when they agree with budget increases for software and hardware. The public library is both an educational institution and a provider of leisure-time materials and activities. Sometimes these functions are performed by the same items, e.g., preschoolers' picture books, educational toys and games or, for adults, fictional biographies, inspirational literature, etc. However, the informational and cultural purposes—the emphasis on including all points of view, on furnishing the material necessary for an informed citizenry, on the provision of the best literature—seem to be placed before pure pleasure as a worthy objective. The debates over purchasing popular versus "good" reading, or popular versus classical music, or computer games versus *VisiCalc* or *WordStar*, are really fueled by a difference among librarians over the different purposes of the library as a public institution. The idea that leisure-time materials should also be didactic or uplifting is not new, but critics of public library policies that provide only "good" reading, "serious" music, or educational games point out that free public education through the high school years satisfies most of society's needs for education. The library is not the only place where poor but deserving people can get civic, aesthetic, or cultural education. Librarians cannot believe seriously in the importance of the recreational objective if they feel materials must have educational value in addition to being wanted by the public. Naturally, materials perceived as primarily recreational must also be considered less valuable than those believed to have educational or informational value.

Another implication of the perception of nonprint media as primarily recreational relates to its bibliographic treatment. The ways nonfiction and fiction books are treated in public library catalogs are analogous to the way print and nonprint are treated. One of the chief differences is that fiction rarely, if ever, is assigned subject headings although the books might deal with subjects as diverse as medicine, espionage, psychoanalysis, politics, and crime. Few notes are made for fiction, and classification is often totally lacking. Some may attribute this to greater simplicity in bibliographic presentation by publishers, but I believe it is due to policy decisions to treat fiction differently from nonfiction. Those who espouse policies of simplification for fiction cataloging do so for logical reasons, including the notion that people who use fiction entries are only checking to see if a library owns something, not to find out whether the book has a bibliography or index, if it relates to other titles, etc. In view of the probable uses to which the entry will

be put, why put the same time, money and effort into adding information to it that will rarely be used? It is hard to argue.

On the other hand, fiction is not always false. Some fictional crea-
tions have been researched with greater accuracy and attention to
detail than some nonfiction works. It is said that truth is stranger
than fiction; it may also be said that fiction is sometimes more factual than books purporting to be true. Nonetheless, only in
children's fiction are subject headings commonly applied, because
teachers, parents, and librarians need them to find suitable reading,
e.g., a book about divorce or one about Egypt. If it is all right for
children to read fiction to learn about Egypt or divorce, why not
adults? Perhaps it is more insidious to give someone a nonfiction
book whose factual accuracy has not been verified. There have
always been books accepted as factual at first, only to be shown later
to be inaccurate. Designating a book as nonfiction does not
guarantee its informational value, but it does put it into a particular
class as far as cataloging is concerned. The cataloger will look much
more carefully at what additional kinds of data might be useful to
someone looking for it besides its author, title, publication, and
physical description. Hours may be spent on subject cataloging and
classification, all avoidable if the book is fiction and it will only be
read for pleasure.

The bibliographic survey showed that entries for media are also
likely to be simpler than those for printed works, a finding that supports the theory that media are recreational. Access to more complex items such as multiwork sound or videorecordings, films,
scores, micrographics, and computer software should be more detailed since they are often used to carry more than one intellectual
entity, whereas books usually comprise only one work. Only in the
last few years has money been made available to do detailed cataloging for micrographic sets purchased by research libraries—
cataloging which would have been done without question had the
individual titles been purchased in their original book forms. When
a microform set is purchased instead of books, or a videodisk instead
of a group of films or books, they are treated as a package, although
the original books or films would have been individually cataloged
had they been purchased. The difference is important, because people using libraries have come to expect there will be access to individual books, full-length films, or concerts, even if several of them
are grouped together in one complex physical unit such as a
videodisk. Though library clients can be retrained to look for books
or other comparable works through microform or video indexes just

as they have been trained to do for periodical articles or poems in anthologies, it won't happen overnight, and the question remains as to the propriety of shifting responsibility for access from the library in this way. It does not fulfill Cutter's object for the catalog to show what the library has by an author, or on a subject, or whether a particular title is owned.

Inadequate access to multiwork items is only one problem resulting from simplified cataloging for media. Media are also, because of the way they are produced, likely to have more complicated origins than books. It is unlikely that a videorecording, for example, will be written, produced, directed, and recorded by the same person or group, let alone also performed by them. In order to give the same kind of access to these kinds of works, much more information needs to be included in a catalog entry than for a one- or two-author book, even if it also has an illustrator or editor. Librarians do not make access points for the rest of the contributors and do not even create cast and credits notes with consistency. Any reference librarian who has tried to find all the materials in which a particular actor or singer appears, or on which a particular director worked, knows how difficult it is to use the catalog to satisfy the request. Even the rule whereby a four-author work will only be accessible by title or first author is questionable in this day of multi-authored works resulting from the team approach to research. Clearly, access will deteriorate if these practices continue in view of changing technologies and modes of authorship.

A question the survey did not ask, but should have, is what level of information a catalog should reflect. When only manual catalogs were possible, the idea of doing a massive job of creating analytics was beyond reason. Now, however, computer-produced and accessed analytics can furnish access to tables of contents with the same speed and convenience though, admittedly, not the same cost or initial effort, as to titles. Cutter's objects involved *books*. Books remained the unit of entry for catalogs from then on and the minor problem of periodicals was ignored. Films, filmstrips, sound recordings, and other early media forms were treated much like books. Now, there is a different situation, and these policies are less effective. Is a book in a microform set less of a book than if it were on paper? Is a performance of *My Fair Lady* on tape less of a complete work when it is part of a multiwork videodisk? At what point does an individual work demand representation? These implications remain to be explored. Thus far, studies of what catalog users would like to see in online catalogs seem to indicate a desire for more information, not less.[4]

The implication for nonprint media, in the public library sector at least, seems to be continued simplification unless their perception as recreational materials changes, or unless public libraries begin to view the recreational function as a truly important *raison d'etre*, equal to the educational and cultural functions. School and academic libraries should have less concern with this issue, since recreational materials are purchased in very limited numbers and nonbook media are just another form of instructional or research materials.

A far less equivocal finding of the survey was public librarians' belief that intershelving media with books and combining use areas was not good public service. Supporting this belief was the view that classifications intended for books and other printed materials were not equally applicable to nonprint media. The implications for the future are that nonbook materials will remain separate from books. There is no argument with the fact that it takes more planning and probably more money to combine storage and use of all materials. Intershelving has not been popular in public libraries,[5] so introducing it would involve different shelving and packaging of media and major changes in older buildings. It is possible that librarians believe intershelving is an impossible task, or that the results aren't worth the effort or cost. If separate shelving makes for better public service, separate use areas make sense, too. Why ask a client to take a film to the reading area of the library to view it when a viewing station could be put near the film stacks? Hyman points out one advantage to intershelving is that it introduces people new to the library collection to all the materials it contains.[6] For introductory or indoctrination purposes, then, intershelving may be of value. This could be interpreted to mean only children's collections have reason to be intershelved, but not adult collections.

Another explanation for librarians' attitudes is they believe media use is not compatible with reading. Media materials are often used by groups rather than individuals. Films, slides, videorecordings, and filmstrips are enjoyable by many people at once. Books are usually read by one person at a time. A combined use area would be difficult to arrange so as to accommodate individuals and groups of all sizes without sacrificing someone's convenience and comfort.

Media materials are often used by people who don't like to read. Such people might not be considerate of the needs of readers. Both of these problems existed in the combined use area for books and sound materials under my supervision. Individual adults, whether reading or listening, were disturbed by group listeners, especially if they were teenagers. Young persons were less concerned about what others were doing, however. Group listeners tended, regardless of age, to be noisier and more unsettled than individuals, talking with headsets on, humming or singing along with music, and responding more intensely than individuals to whatever they heard. Even individuals hummed and sang, laughed out loud, and otherwise reacted in a manner disturbing to someone trying to concentrate. Combining use areas doesn't mean a reader must sit next to a television monitor or alongside a phonograph. Space, even for combined use, can be divided into areas for one kind of activity or another without separating them with walls. Even reading areas, after all, attract groups working on a project or individuals who talk, react to what they are reading, and behave in a disturbing manner. These are user problems rather than material problems. On balance, the problems of intershelving and combining use areas seem to outweigh possible benefits of making all materials of an author or subject available in one place. It is unlikely future plans in public libraries will include methods for physical mainstreaming of nonprint materials.

Application of the same classification scheme to all materials, seen as appropriate and inappropriate by approximately the same number of people, might have been expected to be heavily weighted on the side of inappropriate. Nevertheless, a great many people are not convinced nonprint materials cannot be classified by Dewey or LC classification. After all, using the same classification does not require intershelving and has the great advantage of dealing with only one system for both the staff and public. Since no general scheme will ever treat a large, specialized collection with the same specificity as a system designed to do that, there is no reason Dewey or LC are not as useful as any other general classification for media.

It is a subjective judgment, after all, that a collection is so large and specialized it requires its own kind of classification. In public libraries, collections may run from a few thousand to millions of items. New York Public Library's collection of circulating sound recordings is satisfactorily classified by a far less specific kind of classification system than would be provided by Dewey or LC. Other libraries use more complicated schemes for smaller collections of the same sort. There is no clear pattern relating classifications used to the makeup of the collections they organize. The validity of using nonstandard schemes in general public libraries seems difficult to justify. One public library may believe its nonprint media are very specialized while another, with a similar collection, might not. Both size and content of collections are judged more in subjective or relative terms than in absolutes. Here is fertile territory for future change, with lack of confidence in nonbrowsable special schemes for nonprint media evident from survey responses. It would be useful to reclassify a small collection from an accession number scheme to Dewey to see if it enhances user access. If, as I suspect, it would, then it is logical to follow suit with larger collections. Nonprint media that encompass a variety of subject areas can be treated just like books on these subjects. It will not help a searcher who always obtains call numbers from the catalog before going to the shelves, but uniform classification will shortcut the process for those who can go directly to the shelves and browse until they find something suitable. The person who is accustomed to finding Shakespeare at 822.33 will be happy to see sound and video materials by or about him at the same number. After all, if a library collects heavily in literary criticism, it doesn't junk the 800s and establish an accession number scheme. By the same token, if it has many art slides, it doesn't have to junk the 700s and resort to esoteric schemes, especially those based on accession numbers.

An adjunct to these issues was the view of those polled on open versus closed stacks for nonprint media. The commitment to open stacks is traditional in U.S. public libraries, and one would think the choice would be obvious. More than one quarter opted for closed stacks—a sizable minority—although the majority took the opposite view. What happens when stacks are closed? Several advantages are obvious. Keeping people away from materials helps prevent careless or unnecessary handling, vandalism, and pilferage. It also prevents browsing. Materials will not need meaningful classification, just location identifiers. But, if public libraries continue to circulate their nonprint media, some of the advantages of closed stacks disappear. It will not put an end to damage and theft without also stopping circulation. it will, however, put an end to browsing. Catalog searches are then the only means of access. Some advantages of optimal storage environments are also negated by circulation, so if this is the library's highest priority, closing stacks is a wise choice. If this is the criterion on which the group of survey participants based their answers, however, they balanced it against the ability to browse, an interesting departure from a long-standing tradition in public librarianship. Perhaps there is a resurgence of the importance of the custodial function of librarianship in these times of limited budgets.

It is possible, although the question was not included on the survey, that people who preferred closed stacks for nonprint materials might also have preferred them for books and periodicals. Certainly the same factors are operative in keeping stacks open for print materials, too, i.e., damage from careless handling, theft, inefficient use of space, lack of a controlled environment, and the need to do time-consuming processing for patron access. Perhaps public librarians are rethinking the value of open stacks in view of what we know now about preservation of printed materials as well as the recent developments in the book trade which cause titles to go out of print so fast they cannot be replaced. Physical growth of collections may also affect these decisions—solutions to limited shelf space may include compact shelving and movable stacks operating on switches which might discourage browsers, or permitting browsers to operate the equipment. If this is true, the implication is that catalogs and indexes to collections will become more important than ever before.

Survey participants were also offered a choice between spending money to improve the cataloging of either printed materials or non-print materials. Quite a few people did not respond to this question, and comments written in the margins explained that the lack of reply was a protest rather than an oversight. The idea of spending money on cataloging outraged some who didn't have enough support for new materials or programs. Those who did reply, however, favored improving nonprint cataloging by a very slight margin. Apparently, many of these librarians believe cataloging for printed materials needs improvement, too, even though it is often more detailed and follows national standards more closely. The implication of these attitudes depends to some extent on whether they reflect dissatisfaction with all sorts of cataloging practice or with the principles of access on which they are based. The choice of bibliographic units has already been questioned. Others have examined the subject access furnished by library catalogs and found it does not give people what they want, i.e., access to more specific topics. Different levels of information for different uses is another frequently mentioned improvement, most easily provided by automated systems programmed to give a brief or more detailed entry according to the user's request. Elimination of backlogs is a basic improvement that should not be overlooked because it is less glamorous than some of the others. Brief listing is sometimes the antidote to backlogs that persist despite catalogers' best efforts to increase productivity. If this minimum amount of information is satisfactory for most user needs, administrators reason, why bother with full records? These arguments challenge some basic principles on which current rules are based. The use of new technologies in the creation and display of cataloging data invites a rethinking of the whole entry. Studies of how users search in online modes and what features would enhance access for them given the capabilities of computer systems go far beyond the addition of a few more subject headings or fuller title information for some items. The fact that almost three quarters of those surveyed believed cataloging needed improvement implies an area of future change.

Questions involving opinions on the cost of media software and hardware elicited reactions mildly in favor of increasing allocations for both and negating the notion that software costs too much. More people favored increasing the hardware budget than the software budget. Many, however, chose not to express any opinion about increased allocations, echoing the California study that found generally negative feelings about increased funding for media.[7] Present inadequate provisions for hardware may have influenced this reply, or it may reflect a new commitment to in-house use of materials. Some public libraries lend hardware just like software; and this kind of service may increase in the future. Trends toward lower costs and miniaturization for tape recorders, computers, projectors, etc., make them more attractive as lending materials. This area has potential for change.

SUMMARY

The results of the attitudinal survey of public librarians were clearly in favor of integrated bibliographic access, but against physical integration in the form of intershelving and combined use areas. Despite much criticism of *AACR2* in library literature, most of those surveyed were noncommittal about it, preferring "no opinion" replies to favoring or opposing statements evaluating the code. Most librarians believed one subject heading list was appropriate for all materials, but as many believed one classification was inappropriate for all materials as believed it was appropriate. Open stacks were affirmed by most people, but one quarter of the participants believed closed stacks provide better public service. Implications for the future indicated greater catalog integration.

The opinion that nonprint media materials are primarily recreational was affirmed by a small majority, but even more important was the widely held belief that clients prefer using printed materials for information. Still, majorities believed the best information could sometimes be found in nonprint materials and that clients liked using them when equipment was available. Implications of these somewhat conflicting attitudes include continued simplified cataloging for nonprint materials and continuing debate over the mission of public libraries. Should the recreational function be deemphasized in the future, it does not bode well for nonprint media collections.

Most participants believed that customized cataloging was preferable to strict conformity to standards. This finding implies future efforts to balance the advantages of uniformity, a high priority in computerized systems, with the needs of individual libraries. There may be more room for diversity as techniques to match different cataloging formats are developed for use in machine-based systems.

In general librarians surveyed believed the costs of nonprint materials were not too great for public libraries. A slim majority also believed in increased allocations for software and hardware, and on the improvement of media cataloging. Whether divided opinions on topics of such importance imply the encouragement of change in the future is questionable, to say the least. It appears nonprint media are more appealing in theory than on the bottom line.

It is assumed that integrated cataloging is both a reasonable and desirable goal. So, too, is enhancing the catalog's capacity for service through automation. Possibilities for achieving automated, integrated systems are explored. Whether or not the future of society will be paperless, as experts have predicted, or just less full of paper than bibliocentric librarians imagine, the key to library collections will still be a catalog, and its value will depend on its contents, organization, and accessibility.

NOTES

1. Fred N. Kerlinger, *Foundations of Behavioral Research*, 2nd ed. (New York: Holt, Rinehart & Winston, 1973), pp. 495-96. Kerlinger defines an attitude as "... an organized predisposition to think, feel, perceive, and behave toward a referent or cognitive object. It is an enduring structure of beliefs that predisposes the individual to behave selectively toward attitude referents...."

2. Sheila S. Intner, "Access to Media: An Investigation of Public Librarians' Bibliographic Practices and Attitudes Towards Access to Nonprint Materials" (DLS dissertation: Columbia University, 1982). The data used in this chapter are based on the results of the survey of public library catalogers contained in Chapter 5 of this dissertation. The survey questionnaire is reproduced in an Appendix.

3. Robert D. Leigh, *The Public Library in the United States: The General Report of the Public Library Inquiry* (New York: Columbia University Press, 1950).

4. See, for example, Carol A. Mandel, *Subject Access in the Online Catalog: A Report* (Washington: Council on Library Resources, 1981), p. 30, and Karen Markey, "Thus Spake the OPAC User," *Information Technology and Libraries*, 2 (December 1983), pp. 381-87.

5. More may have been done in physical intershelving of media in school libraries, although McLean and other Canadians reported trends in that direction on the part of public libraries, too, in studies done within the last decade. For a more recent examination of intershelving, see Richard Joseph Hyman, *Shelf Access in Libraries* (Chicago: ALA, 1982), p. 178 and Chapters 3-5.

6. *Ibid.*, 99.

7. Mary E. Bogan, "A Survey of Audiovisual Resources in Selected California Libraries and Library Systems," *California Librarian*, 37 (October 1976), p. 53.

RECOMMENDED READING

Davis, Bryan. "Sound Ideas—Books on Tape for the Smaller Library," *T*H*E   U*N*A*B*A*S*H*E*D   L*I*B*R*A*R*I*A*N*, 48 (1983), pp. 21-25.

Holley, Robert P. "Priority As a Factor in Technical Processing," *Journal of Academic Librarianship*, 9 (January 1984), pp. 345-48.

Intner, Sheila S. "Managing Media for Public Access," *Technicalities*, 3 (September 1983), pp. 7-9.

Kessler, Julia Boone. *Bibliographic Access to Audiovisual Materials: A Comparison Between Professional Recommendations and Regional Practice.* Washington: Educational Resources Information Center, 1981.

Politis, John. "Developing a Worthwhile Popular Music Collection," *T*H*E   U*N*A*B*A*S*H*E*D   L*I*B*R*A*R*I*A*N*, 39 (1981), pp. 13-16.

Part Two

A Rationale for Change

Chapter 6

Computer Applications for Bibliographic Data

In the years that followed World War II, the word "computer" conjured up visions of monstrous installations of incredibly complex equipment attended by armies of specialized workers. The likelihood of small and medium-sized libraries using computers to process bibliographic data for their collections seemed remote. But the quarter-century between 1945, which more or less marked the birth of those enormous first-generation computers, and 1970, when computer applications began to proliferate at the local library level, witnessed a remarkable series of technological advances which caused the hardware to be scaled down in size and cost while its computing power was increased. The development of the silicon chip in the 1960s enabled the hardware to shrink to a fraction of its former size—minicomputers may be the size of a large desk or filing cabinet and microcomputers are no larger than a portable typewriter. The trend toward miniaturization was important for libraries as well as for the rapid spread of computers in science, business, and industry, beginning in the 1960s.

Just as hardware improved, the design of software became more sophisticated, too. Programs for manipulating the kinds of information contained in bibliographic entries and for creating indexes for retrieving them became feasible in the 1960s. A few institutions like the Library of Congress, Stanford University, and Northwestern University began to explore the application of computer technology to bibliographic information during this period. The work done by the Library of Congress on formulating a standard entry format was quickly adopted by those early library systems designers who foresaw the impact of the technology and the importance of standardization in reaping its benefits. It also became the basis for lowering the costs of library applications in smaller institutions by enabling data from LC to be shared among many institutions and systems.

A brief review of some of the major bibliographic computer systems now in use in the information world will illustrate their diversity and technical capabilities. The first half of the review divides a selection of existing systems according to their primary function into reference and technical processing systems and describes them. The division is purely one of convenience, since reference systems have value for technical processing and vice versa. The second half of the review examines the functional attributes of computerized bibliographic systems to provide a foundation for understanding new methods of managing media information.

REFERENCE SYSTEMS

Three of the best known reference systems of bibliographic data online are DIALOG, ORBIT, and BRS (Bibliographic Retrieval Services). DIALOG and ORBIT are both privately owned, profit-making enterprises. Until early in 1982, DIALOG was part of the Lockheed Corporation. It is now a separate corporation. ORBIT is owned and operated by the System Development Corporation based in California. BRS, a nonprofit organization, is based in Albany, New York. The largest of the three is DIALOG and the smallest is BRS.

These reference systems are made up of a number of separate databases, each of which contains bibliographic information for the literature of a particular subject area, interdisciplinary group, or industry. Though much of the value of a database lies in its currency, some importance is also attached to the cumulation of citations permitting retrospective searching. In addition to the citations, the databases include abstracts of the articles and books which enable searchers to ascertain their scope and coverage and the ideas they contain. Individual databases may be the output of government agencies, abstracting and indexing services, publishers, or other organizations which organize such information for a particular constituency. Some of the databases in these three reference services include the Educational Resources Information Center (ERIC), the National Technical Information Service (NTIS), Chemical Abstracts, INFORM (covering business management literature), the Congressional Information Service index (CIS), the Public Affairs Information Service (PAIS), COMPENDEX (an index of engineering materials), and many others. These few examples simply serve to highlight the variety and diverse orientation of reference systems, brought together and delivered to a customer or subscriber by the three online services. Differences between the three purveyors are measured not only in terms of the number of different databases to which they give access, but also the methods of searching they provide and services and products that can be derived from their use.

The three reference services have a variety of searching capabilities and offer a multiplicity of services. Bibliographic citations can, first of all, be searched by author and title. They can be limited to desired publication dates and languages. Subject searching varies from one database to another, with some of them requiring the use of a prescribed set of terms, e.g., ERIC requires the use of the terms in the *Eric Thesaurus*[2] while others have indexes of key words. Another method of subject searching in online databases is "natural language searching," whereby the computer will locate any word or phrase anywhere in the database. This selection of words can be limited to a single sentence, a paragraph, or an entire segment of an entry. All of the services enable the searcher to combine subjects or qualify them through the use of Boolean operators, the words "and," "or," and "not" added to multiple subject terms to tell the computer exactly what is desired. For example, if you are interested in an item discussing Beethoven's piano sonatas, but not his violin sonatas, you might tell the computer to search BEETHOVEN *AND* PIANO SONATAS *NOT* VIOLIN SONATAS; or, if you were interested in a discussion of both, you may decide to ask for BEETHOVEN *AND* SONATAS *AND* (PIANO *OR* VIOLIN).

Other searching aids include the ability to put in portions of a word or name to retrieve all forms of the word. For example, if the searcher directs the system to search the term LIBR-, it will consider "librarian," "librarians," "libraries," "library" and any other word beginning with the right letters. In the same way, entering part of a name can retrieve all the names which contain the specified letters. This can be of great assistance in finding desired citations when full information is not available. Some systems allow the searcher to browse the indexes, i.e., to see the names or terms which immediately precede and follow a specified word.

Another valuable searching aid enables the user to set up a series of search commands to retrieve desired materials in one database and then save them so the same search can be executed using another database automatically, saving the time and effort of the searcher. Since charges for use of the systems are based primarily on the time one actually searches online, called connect time, every saving in time is money saved as well. The fact that the system reports how many entries, or "postings," satisfy a searcher's request also saves time by giving the user the choice of narrowing or broadening the search to retrieve a reasonable number of items. There are very few times one would wish to retrieve every item whose abstract contained the word "public," for example. If a reference system was queried for such a term, it might respond that several thousand or more postings were identified. If one proceeded to combine "public" and "school" and "library," the number might drop to several hundred. If the request were further qualified to include only items in French published since 1980, one would probably retrieve only a few items, if any. It saves the searcher both time and money to know how much material is available in order to decide whether it is appropriate to his or her needs before reviewing the material itself. This is similar to looking at the number of cards or drawers in a card catalog, or pages in a bibliography that satisfy your request before examining the individual entries one by one. The advantage of the computer over the other formats is that one can punch in an alternative command to winnow out less desirable material or add possibly relevant material and the machine does the rest. When searching in card files or books, it is not possible to reorganize the entries this way. Still another search aid is the ability to obtain several levels of information from a minimum of abbreviated citation to a maximum of a full citation and abstract or more. This, too, saves time (and therefore money), since a searcher does not always need to peruse the full entry to recognize desirable material. Sometimes a look at the abstract is all that is required for a searcher to satisfy an information need, without reading the document itself.

The most important service offered by these reference systems is the availability of large amounts of current literature in the databases. Many studies have shown that the newest material is in the greatest demand in libraries and other information agencies, and online reference services control this literature much faster and more comprehensively than any of their printed counterparts. Second is the multiplicity of databases contained in each of the three systems, even the smallest, BRS, which has eighty. The range of subjects and disciplines covered by the largest system, DIALOG, may well outstrip the print resources of even medium-sized general libraries. Certainly the flexibility of computer searching is a great advantage over manual methods and the search and its results may be printed immediately for the user to have as a permanent record, called a hard copy, of the screens viewed.

Even more important is the document delivery service provided to subscribers. When a search is completed, copies of the complete articles may be ordered by punching in appropriate commands. The subscribers are automatically billed and the documents sent in far less time than the interloan service provided by any traditional library. One of the complaints voiced by searchers in libraries is the inability of these local institutions to maintain sufficiently broad periodical resources to support the demand resulting from online searching. But the online service itself will, for a fee, provide the documents. Use of this service is a matter of dollars and cents, and for many libraries the logistics of payment are enough to warrant avoiding it.

For additional fees, the subscriber can create a personal file online into which private data can be stored and retrieved. Security of the personal file is protected by the system by means of authorized passwords. Through electronic mail service, provided for an additional fee, messages may be sent among subscribers. All of the added fee services create problems for public and college libraries whose own services are normally free to their constituencies. Not only does charging fees for services require libraries to make different fundamental philosophic choices about service policies, but it has a built-in structure of bookkeeping and billing which in itself creates new costs for the library. All the services provided by computerized reference systems rapidly make available large amounts of current literature in a wide spectrum of subject areas; they give users access to many separate databases at once; they offer flexible searching strategies and allow a printed copy of the search and entries found to be made immediately if the appropriate printing equipment is available; they also provide educational services to subscribers to learn to use the systems effectively either free of charge or for additional fees, and they provide automatic ordering of desired materials discovered by the search; they permit subscribers to create private files for their own data.

TECHNICAL SERVICE SYSTEMS

There are four distinct kinds of technical service systems with different structures and functions as well as services to be seen in this section. They are (1) bibliographic utilities; (2) vendor-based systems; (3) turnkey systems; and (4) microcomputer systems.

Bibliographic Utilities

There are currently four bibliographic utilities, or large, non-profit, shared cataloging database systems called bibliographic networks, too, operating in the United States: OCLC, the Online Computer Library Center, oldest and largest of the four networks, dating from 1967 with over 3,000 members and a database of over ten million records representing many media including books, serials, maps, printed music, sound recordings, films, videorecordings, graphics, three-dimensional representations, and kits; RLIN, the Research Libraries Information Network, a group of less than one hundred research libraries of which only about a quarter are full-fledged members, organized in 1978 as a development of Stanford University's own BALLOTS (Bibliographic Automation of Large Library Operations Using a Time-Sharing System) catalog system and containing somewhat fewer multimedia entries; WLN, the Washington Library Network, smaller still, with participants located primarily in Washington State and its environs and a database of still fewer records in fewer media; and UTLAS, the University of Toronto Libraries Automated System, an outgrowth of the Canadian university's own system and the newest arrival on the cataloging network scene in the U.S.

The concept of shared cataloging online, which began with OCLC, has been expanded considerably in recent years. It was, even in its most minimal form, an exciting improvement. From the beginning of online shared cataloging, the Library of Congress' contribution of its machine-readable MARC records prepared for its own database formed a nucleus of records in the databases of all the utilities and were standards of cataloging excellence. A MARC record for a work will supersede and replace any original cataloging done by a participating library. Indeed, in a large measure, the rapid building of the databases of all networks was assisted by the availability of LC's MARC distribution service which were dumped en masse into the systems.

As with many earlier cataloging innovations, OCLC began with book cataloging, always the bulk of general library materials which the newly formed Ohio College Library Center[3] was created to serve. LC did this, too, developing a MARC format, i.e., a method for coding and entering data, for monographs as its first priority, following it with a serials format and then other nonprint formats. Later, OCLC added its own nonbook formats based on MARC, which currently cover the wide variety of media enumerated above. The breakdown of entries in the OCLC database follows this order of priorities quite closely.

Perhaps because OCLC was, from its inception, both a trailblazer and a truly cooperative venture, less importance was attached to the quality of participants' original cataloging than to other matters. As a result, duplicate records, variant practices and errors began to build in the database along with truly amazing totals of bibliographic records. The computer world has several phrases to describe the situation: *Quick and dirty* is one; and *garbage in, garbage out* is another. It is possible to remove errors and duplicate entries from the OCLC system, but it is an uphill battle because of the size of the database, its constant expansion, and the rate of human error which is not eradicable. Nevertheless, some institutions are known to do less than acceptable cataloging and rather than accept their work, other participants spend the staff time and money to make the changes they deem necessary to a record before using it. Unfortunately, this results in a loss of the system's benefits for those fastidious librarians who do extensive editing. The chief benefits of OCLC and other bibliographic networks is the speed and cost savings with which cataloging may be done since original work is minimized. It also enables staff members without the training to do original cataloging to handle routine cataloging of materials found in the database, and these staff members are usually paid at a lower rate.

The OCLC database was not originally designed as a public catalog. Two characteristics of public catalogs are missing from the OCLC system: subject heading access and authority control. Authority control would have helped avoid some of the variation, duplication, and error in bibliographic entries mentioned above. However, it required far more complex and sophisticated programming than could be developed by OCLC's software specialists within their timeframe as well as their resources at the beginning of the project. Also, the primary purposes of OCLC's designers was to speed up the processes and pare down the costs for obtaining catalog cards for their traditional card catalogs, not to replace the card catalog. Thus, subject search capabilities were more or less superfluous for a system in which author and title were the main access points. Furthermore, libraries may have used different subject heading lists and still been quite within the bounds of professional propriety. Unless the subject vocabulary was totally uncontrolled (as with free text searching in online reference systems), establishing a subject authority would have required network participants to adhere to it. The same situation did not exist with rules for description and access. Only the *AACR* was acceptable by professional standards. There were other reasons for the lack of subject access, which are not necessary to review, primarily technical.

Some of the problems of quality control encountered in the OCLC system were recognized and addressed by the RLIN network. In many respects, it was also much easier for RLIN to exert control over its participants as well as its database. For one thing, it was developed first as the cataloging system of a single university rather than a group. For another, its participants are a small, relatively homogeneous group who emphasize high quality cataloging in order to serve the needs of their highly special patrons, scholarly researchers.

In the participants' schedule of fees, the more complete and detailed a record is, the lower are the charges for its entry as original cataloging. RLIN has invested much of its resources in developing the attributes required for becoming a true catalog, i.e., authority control and enhanced subject search capabilities. Problems with hardware in providing basic services have slowed down its development plans, but though the timetable may change, the goals are achievable within the framework of current knowledge and computing power.

The database of the RLIN network also contains a variety of different media, though it does not have a manuscripts format as does OCLC, and the proportion of nonbook records is not as large as in OCLC, reflecting its members' collecting patterns. Approximately 3 percent of its database is devoted to nonprint media.[5]

The Washington Library Network, designed with authority controls, has an editing capability built into the cataloging process which requires a human being to review members' original cataloging before it is added to the database. Unfortunately, the trade-off for this procedure is a time lag between the cataloging and the availability for use of a bibliographic record, reported to be as long as two weeks.[6] Originally part of the Washington State Library, its structure expanded, but it did not change radically and was thus under even tighter control than RLIN. Smaller than OCLC and RLIN, the database contained almost three million records as of this writing,[7] with a smaller variety of media included among them because music, sound recordings, and maps cannot be cataloged on the system.

The search capabilities of the WLN system have been called more powerful than either OCLC or RLIN;[8] they approach the flexibility of the reference databases. As for its use as an online public catalog, or to provide circulation control, WLN has preferred its members develop their own systems. Circulation control may be provided by their purchasing the DataPhase Circulation Control system at a member-discount, and public catalogs may be developed from WLN software. Both systems can be based on members' WLN data, but there is no direct service of this nature provided by the WLN system.

UTLAS, the Canadian-based utility, has over six hundred clients located primarily in its home country, although it has a growing group of users in the United States and other countries. Its database was reported to be more than twenty million bibliographic and authority records in 1983[9] and growing at the rate of over two million records a year. It enters data from British and Canadian sources and provides authority controls and file space within its system for each client, within which they can alter or edit records derived from the main database to suit local needs. The utility does not have to be concerned, as do OCLC and RLIN, about the quality of cataloging done by its participants, although members do contribute cataloging. UTLAS offers a variety of services, but not circulation or public online catalog functions on the same hardware and software. Users who want these services have the option to acquire an in-house minicomputer system which can be interfaced with the larger system. The variety of media for which bibliographic records are available in the UTLAS system include books, serials, audiovisuals, films, music, machine-readable materials, maps, and manuscripts. It will produce a variety of cataloging products for its users including COM as well as cards, magnetic tapes, and printed book catalogs. The commitment to distributed processing, a system in which all operations are not performed on central computing equipment, but in which individual computers are linked while supporting individual operations within an institution, allowed UTLAS to grow substantially in a short time without compromising service performance. It may, indeed, grow to rival its U.S. counterparts in their own country, but for the moment that has not occurred.

One of the most important features of a bibliographic utility, as with an online reference system, is the search capability it provides. The major differences between the utilities are the variety and character of available access points. Access points currently offered by one or more of the utilities include the following:

LC card number	Personal author
ISBN/ISSN	Corporate author
CODEN	Performer
Government document number	Title
Utility control number	Author/title combination
Recording label number	Series title
Call number	Conference name
Music publisher	Subject heading
	Keyword

The unique numbers assigned to published works by various authorities are extremely useful identifiers because one number describes only one item. The first six access points in the list above are unique identifiers. Only the CODEN is composed of letters instead of numbers, but it, too, has a one-to-one relationship with items in the database. Almost all of the other access points apply to many more than one item, particularly in a large database. (Just think how many items are described by either the author or subject heading UNITED STATES.) In some libraries, unique call numbers are assigned to each work cataloged and would function in the same fashion, but this is not universally the case. It is obvious that searching by means of a unique identifier is virtually foolproof as long as no errors are made in its entry. The value of these access points is limited by the fact that they are difficult to remember, and unless they are known it is virtually impossible to locate them by other means, unlike authors, titles, series titles, and so on, which often can be browsed with partial information to locate a desired item.

The balance of the access points listed are not unique for each entry, except coincidentally, and the possible search methodologies, the flexibility of the database, as well as the knowledge and experience of the searcher will affect the success with which it can be used, exactly as with the reference systems.

Of all these options, subject heading access is currently the one very desirable access point unavailable in the OCLC system, either by headings designated by a specific list such as the *Library of Congress Subject Heading* list or by keywords derived from titles. RLIN, WLN, and UTLAS all offer some form of subject searching, though they differ in what can be searched and how. Those many hundreds, if not thousands, of libraries that use OCLC to provide information to the public at their reference desks would find the addition of subject access most important.

As already noted, use of the OCLC system as a public catalog would certainly require the addition of subject heading access. Subject access in an online system is different than in a card catalog, however, because there are more approaches and methods of doing subject searches than finding the acceptable subject heading and looking under it. To begin with, that kind of search *can* be done in the other three utilities, just as in a traditional card catalog or printed bibliography. In addition, partial information may be entered in some systems (called truncation); keywords as well as full headings may be entered in some systems; and Boolean operators may be added in some systems.

One characteristic of the OCLC search options is that full information is not keyed in, but a specific portion of the element or combination of elements is designated as a code or search key[11] for the whole. Search keys, not full information, are used for the personal and corporate authors, performers, titles, series titles, conference names, and the author-title combination. One of the difficulties in using the OCLC system is the requirement that names and titles be translated into one or more of the search keys in order to locate them in the system. Beginning users, whether technical services or reference staff, and certainly patrons, have problems deciphering correct titles, dealing with multiple authors and corporate, conference, and series names to derive the proper key. It is time-consuming, too, to have to try several search keys before either locating an item or considering the search a failure. On the other hand, the search keys permit items to be coded into fewer characters than full names or titles would have to have keyed or typed in, and an experienced user becomes adept at selecting the best search key and translating accurately for a successful search on the first try. Also, the search key, while not a unique identifier, usually retrieves many fewer items than full-character author-only or subject searches would do.

The OCLC system does not have Boolean searching, but it does allow search requests to be limited by year of publication and by medium. When too many items satisfy a particular search key or when only specific media are desired, it saves the searcher time to employ these delimiters.

A printed record of the search and resulting entries may be made by adding printing equipment to the terminal of any of the utilities.

OCLC has only one print format, however, while RLIN has several. Some characters, such as diacritics, will not print as expected in the OCLC system. This may be disconcerting to someone unfamiliar with the system. RLIN's emphasis on more varied print formats is probably due to the importance its research libraries attach to nonstandard scripts since a great deal of their collecting is done in foreign language materials including those written in non-Roman alphabets.

It should be kept in mind that any utility's hardware can support only a limited amount of computing. Overloading the system may result in very slow response time or in periods when the system is inoperable or both. Each utility offers a range of services that it must support for all of its users. A desire to increase activity usually means accompanying increases in computer power must be made unless existing power is more than sufficient to satisfy these increased needs. Naturally, some activities require more computing time and more complex operations than others. Also, a utility like OCLC with thousands of members has a different level of increased activity if it adds a service than WLN, which has a much smaller group of users. All of these considerations must be weighed in any plan to provide additional services.

The basic service all bibliographic utilities offer is cataloging support, but even this can be provided in a number of ways. The size of the database and character of an individual library's acquisitions affect how many of these acquisitions will be found in the system and not require original cataloging. For example, when the University of Oregon compared OCLC, RLIN, and WLN, they estimated they would find 90 percent of their items if searched on OCLC, 70 percent to 90 percent on RLIN, and 50 percent to 70 percent on WLN.[12] They based their estimates on a search of one hundred items in the three utilities plus allowances they made based on reports from library literature and from comments of current users.

A second factor in the performance of a cataloging service is how much editing a library will require before accepting entries found online. A system like WLN, with its editorial review, would be attractive to an institution whose policy demanded only the highest quality cataloging in terms of accuracy and detail as well as authority work, while OCLC would seem the opposite. If, however, it was more important to do a minimum of original work and find the largest number of entries online, OCLC would be most attractive and WLN less so, particularly if the time lag for editing was considered an important liability.

A third factor is the length of time required to obtain the desired end product, whether it is catalog cards, computer tapes, or another format on which are recorded a library's cataloging transactions. Some of the utilities presort and alphabetize catalog cards before shipping, making it easier to file them. Shipments of cards, still the primary product, are usually made on a daily basis, but they may fall behind schedule for a variety of reasons, not the least of which is system failure. Part of the time span from cataloging to end product also relates to hours of service, speed of response time, and requirements of the system in the process. These elements should not be forgotten when the total speed of service is measured, though they affect the length of time it takes to catalog an item to which must be added the time for actually obtaining the cards. UTLAS offers a COM catalog as an end product, in addition to cards, magnetic tapes, etc. This eliminates having to take tapes or disks to another vendor or service to have the COM product produced, also a time-saver.

The utilities have other technical service applications as well as some important public service uses which capitalize on the availability of bibliographic data in easily manipulated machine-readable form. The technical service operations which can capitalize on the data entered by an individual library are its acquisition and circulation operations. The same core data, author, title, edition, imprint, and physical description used to describe an item in the catalog are also used to order the item and to identify it for circulation purposes. It is quite logical then that systems for using this core data would be devised, either within the utility itself or by means of an interface between the utility and another computer system. OCLC and WLN have operational acquisitions subsystems; RLIN has plans for a similar system, though it was not fully operational as of this writing. All of the utilities permit interfaces to be made with specially designed equipment between their systems and separate library circulation systems.

Another method of utilizing cataloging data for a circulation system is by using the individual library's transaction records (archival tapes) as the foundation for the circulation database. Each function of technical services requires its own particular set of function-specific data in addition to the core bibliographic information. Either programming and hardware for creating, storing, and manipulating the function-specific data has to be incorporated into the utility's own system—in which case it becomes a functional subsystem—or a second system has to provide it. OCLC is the first of the utilities to try to integrate all the functions based on the core bibliographic data into one system, although few of its subscribers have availed themselves of all subsystems. UTLAS and WLN have stated a preference for interfacing with separate circulation and on-line public catalog systems. RLIN also interfaces with individual circulation systems and does not envision its own circulation subsystem in the foreseeable future. RLIN has, however, participated in joint investigations of public catalog systems with OCLC and others, and has hopes of eventual service in this area.

Several services are specially designed to treat serials within the bibliographic utilities. The differences in handling technical service operations for serial publications is sufficient to warrant having separate serials departments in many libraries, so it is not surprising to find separate serials subsystems in some of the utilities. These subsystems not only have a separate format for bibliographic description but also provide for check-in of each issue as it arrives, automatic claiming of issues which do not arrive, automatic renewal or notice of impending renewal of subscriptions, fund accounting, and tracking of volume parts for binding. Holdings information for serials is difficult to standardize because title changes are common, and because publishers issue supplements or special issues erratically, or fail to number everything sequentially, or change the frequency with which they publish a title. As with monographs, subject access to serial titles, or, even better, to portions of them after the model of the online reference services, would be a great public service asset, though not currently available or planned by any of the utilities. An interface between a library's holdings data, contained in the utility database, and an online reference system such as DIALOG, ORBIT, or BRS, would provide the same desirable link.

If technical service is defined as behind-the-scenes service, the reporting services of the utilities can be subsumed under it. However, reports on library operations are usually classified as management support. Type of categorization aside, statistical reports on system activity, breakdowns and analyses of the activity, and financial reports are valuable services provided as a by-product of computing operations. They enable administrators to figure costs of various technical service functions, receive information for collection development programs, and plan personnel use based on activity. Perhaps the most important use of computer-generated management data is the factual underpinning it provides to justify changes in policy, budget, and operations.

In addition to technical services, the utilities also offer important public services, including reference support, interloan, and resource-sharing services. The terms interloan and resource-sharing are not used interchangeably here. All interloan may indeed be a form of resource-sharing, but all resource-sharing is not interloan. Here, interloan will be defined as the lending of one library's material to another library, while resource-sharing will be defined as any and all activities by which two or more libraries use one another's resources.

Just as the online reference services give access to information available in particular disciplines or industries, the bibliographic utilities give access to information available in particular libraries or groups of libraries. A major difference is that the unit of information to which the utilities give access is much larger—the book, serial title or issue, film, recording—while the online reference service gives access to articles, chapters, etc.—to the ideas contained within the works. The broader approach, to the information unit or package rather than to the information itself, may have drawbacks from the point of view of the idea-seeker, but it has an advantage for the patron who seeks known items, i.e., a book, a film, or whatever type of material for which author or title are known, as well as for the institution which needs more convenient units for control than ideas.

A merging of the two kinds of systems through interfaces between them or adding different kinds of access and information to existing utility systems would provide users with both approaches to information—the best of all possible worlds. In the meanwhile, the bibliographic utilities offer the same approach to information as the library's catalog, with several important enhancements. First, the online database is more current than any catalog format except an online catalog. Second, it contains the holdings of many libraries, a union listing. Third, it is easier to search than traditional catalogs for one who knows how to take advantage of all the search options. Fourth, it may also contain acquisition and circulation information. Thus, the terminal of the bibliographic utility is a valuable and flexible tool for helping the public locate desired materials. We have noted earlier that different utilities have different capabilities for reference support depending on the kinds of searching they permit. Other limiting factors are the size of the database, ability to access all subsystems, and performance of the utility, i.e., amount of time the system is in operation, known as uptime,[13] as well as response time during searching.

The other two public services, interlibrary loan or interloan (ILL) and resource-sharing are two sides of the same coin. The utility's database is a gigantic union list with location information for every entry. The OCLC system enables a searcher to obtain location information for a title by state, by region, or for the entire geographic area covered by its membership. Interloan requests may be handled online through a subsystem that automatically generates and delivers them to several libraries that hold the desired items. Each of the utilities provides some ILL support in the form of information contained in the database. OCLC and RLIN also have message-switching systems; UTLAS and WLN do not. WLN also provides its location information on microfiche, which is less easily searched. Interloan services consist of two facets: maintaining the union listings and generating and transmitting the requests. When both facets are within the functions of a bibliographic utility, requests made online are satisfied in less time and with less behind-the-scenes processing work than in a manual mode.[14]

Resource-sharing may be accomplished in other ways than ILL, which is necessarily a one-by-one request procedure. Collections may be shared among a group of participants with the utility performing the union listing function. The fact that many institutions are able to have immediate access to information that any one of them enters into the system, without waiting for any manual processes, is the key to the success of computer-assisted resource-sharing. Naturally, agreements to take advantage of the opportunity afforded by sharing the same database are necessary to implement resource-sharing projects. These agreements are not always easy to reach, and failure to negotiate them negates the possibility of expanding access to more materials than are owned by a single library.

Some members of the publishing industry believe that the utilities pose a real threat because of this potential for an explosion of resource-sharing.[15] Other observers believe publishers' fears are unfounded, because they point out a library's most used materials are not usually shared since they are in great demand at the home library, and that libraries will always spend all available funds for materials anyway, albeit on a different set of titles, if some less-used titles will be available from other sources. What may actually happen is that the materials in greatest demand will remain on everyone's purchasing list, even in multiple copies; and most libraries will purchase a selection from among the rest of the thousands of available works, but not the same ones. Resource-sharing would diffuse the selection among many more titles and tend to eliminate the overlap in the lower-demand areas of individual collections. The result, for the publishers and producers of various materials collected by libraries, would be to sell the same amount in dollars and cents, spread over many more items. This could present problems of a different sort, if too many titles have too few buyers to pay for their production. However, this has always been the case in information production. Some items, whether books, films, recordings, computer programs or whatever medium, are not sold in sufficient quantity to produce a profit. Their losses are offset by other titles with better sales. Although libraries are a large proportion of the marketplace for information materials, they are only a part. To attribute the demise of unborn titles to the activity of libraries would be too simplistic.

The bibliographic utilities have already realized great service benefits for libraries. They accumulate millions of entries for all kinds of materials into a single source, the database, which is immediately available to all members in their libraries. They provide a variety of search methods. Each utility has a series of subsystems derived from its central role of cataloging support, including some or all of the services required for acquisition, circulation, serials control, public catalog, interloan, reference support, and management information and planning support. The extent to which these functions are fulfilled automatically by the system differs from utility to utility, just as their search capabilities differ. No single utility does everything or has all search options. They are evolving, however, toward some kind of arrangement for libraries that need more services than any utility could provide alone.

All the utilities contain multimedia data, though the number of formats accepted in each varies. It is no surprise that print materials usually outnumber nonprint, since this mirrors typical collecting patterns in libraries. As the nonprint components expand in both size and variety, however, they have a larger impact on the entire network of member libraries. As bibliographic control of nonprint materials approaches the comprehensive character of print, it may provide added impetus for libraries to collect in nonprint formats on a broader basis.

Vendor-based Systems

Vendor-based systems are computer services that depend upon the computing power of an outside library vendor, not a bibliographic utility or other nonprofit bibliographic network. While this definition would include the online references services, in this section we are dealing only with technical service systems which provide support for acquisitions, cataloging, serials control, and/or circulation.

Vendors, like libraries, have to manage bibliographic information on a large scale. As a result, many vendors are experienced in online bibliographic systems, installed for their own purposes, but having additional benefits. In this context, two systems are described in which the individual institution has access to the vendor's database, either through a terminal accessing it directly, or by means of off-line processing of data produced on local systems and communicated to the vendor's processor, located at their headquarters.

Two systems representing two different kinds of local-remote relationships are not the only types of systems currently feasible, but they demonstrate a range of activity and service typical of this genre. The first is the Gaylord automated circulation control system; and the second is the Baker and Taylor acquisition system, called LIBRIS II.

In the Gaylord circulation system, a combination of online and offline processing is provided for the local agency through its distributed processing system. The library will have, in-house, a minicomputer to support its day-to-day services, including checkouts and check-ins, renewals and holds for materials as well as its transaction files up to the opening of each day's business, which can be searched for information on the online system. At the end of the day, however, that day's transactions must be transmitted to the main computing facility at Gaylord headquarters for additional processing and updating of the files, printing of reports and notices and additional searching. This distributed processing permits many more terminals and a high level of transaction activity to be supported by a single minicomputer at the local level. However, it also prevents all data from being available at once, online, and completely up-to-date.

Trade-offs such as this are not uncommon in automation. While we want the computer to do what we want it to do, we are rarely able to pay the high price for specially created systems that could fulfill our desires. In order to maximize automation benefits in an atmosphere of limited resources for investment, we must give up those things we feel we can do without. In vendor-based systems, total ownership and control of the system are given up for a much larger database than individual institutions usually have, and a structure that has been designed to serve the vendor's purposes. One immediately recognizable benefit for the library is that it will pay less for relatively sophisticated services. It is necessary, however, to understand exactly how much can be accomplished on in-house equipment, whether purchased or leased from the vendor or owned independently by the library, and how much can be done only with the help of the central computing facility.

The Gaylord system offers choices as to how much data are locally accessible online. Patron and title data may be provided on microfiche or, if the library prefers and is willing to pay for it, they may be made available online and searched by means of various search keys. An attractive feature of the Gaylord system is its support for interlibrary loan, in which the central computer, called the host, searches for requested titles in the files of all libraries in a system the night a request is made. This nightly ILL search is, for the local agency, performed offline; nevertheless, it is probably faster than alternative methods for systematic ILL searching, making it result in much swifter response to requests than previously possible. Printing of notices and reports offline by the host is also not necessarily slower than alternative methods; it is probably much faster than manual typing, collating, etc., and may also be as good as some online printing systems.

The second vendor-based system is LIBRIS II, an acquisitions system offered by Baker and Taylor. LIBRIS II operates much like the online reference services, where the individual library is connected by means of telephone lines, called dial-up access, to the Baker and Taylor computing system at its headquarters. Customers will have, in their library, a terminal for interaction with the mainframe as well as the option to add printing equipment for automatically preparing orders. They may purchase the hardware from Baker and Taylor, or use their own equipment if it is compatible with the host system. One advantage of the connection with Baker and Taylor's database is the information about the availability of particular titles, whether they are in print or out of print, and so forth. This information is entered and updated weekly by Baker and Taylor for their own and their customers' use. Three levels of service are offered with varying price tags, from a minimum of searching, ordering, and editing orders to a maximum of these three functions plus maintaining open order files which can be searched, fund accounting, automatic claiming and cancelling, reports, and direct receiving. Orders to Baker and Taylor can be delivered via electronic mail and processed within twenty-four hours. Orders to other vendors are created automatically but are still processed manually. The practical result would seem to be that libraries using the service will rely most heavily on Baker and Taylor as their primary vendor, if not their only vendor, which is undoubtedly among the motivations for provision of the LIBRIS II service in the first place. While this in itself may not be bad, it inhibits utilizing many vendors to maximize achievement of acquisitions objectives set independently by the library.

A similar acquisitions service is offered by Brodart, in which the local library dials up Brodart's database from leased or purchased equipment and orders may be placed online, etc. These services are a natural result of utilization of the computer first to control inventory and provide data to support vendor's own services and second to extend those services to the customer. Nevertheless, one must not lose sight of the fact that ownership and control of the database and central computing system, the heart of the total system, reside with the vendor and not with the library. As a result, the participants' priorities may not coincide, and the library must be careful in evaluating the system's costs and benefits without being lulled into accepting whatever is offered because it appears more convenient.

Turnkey Systems

Another kind of individual library system is purchased as a package from a vendor who takes responsibility for design of the system, selection of the hardware, and creation of the software as well as all or part of the hardware installation, staff training, implementation support, and maintenance of the system. This kind of system is referred to as a turnkey system, presumably because all that is necessary to utilize it is to turn the key that turns it on. Of course, a turnkey system is not so simple, though it is far simpler than a self-designed system.

Turnkey systems may perform only one library function or several. They are usually based on minicomputers; some are designed around microcomputers. Some vendors have several designs with varying capabilities and price tags to match, and they are prepared to create new designs to suit customers with special needs. Others prefer to market a system with limited variations, capitalizing on the cost savings they achieve in this way.

The first turnkey system, a circulation system, was introduced by a company known as CLSI in the early 1970s. It consisted of a minicomputer, devices for communicating with it known as terminals, software, installation of the equipment, some training and general assistance with implementation, and ongoing maintenance. The system package sold for about $91,000[16] and permitted purchasers to maintain total control over every item entered into the database. The system was originally designed to accept an abbreviated form of bibliographic identification, not the complete information used in catalogs, or even all that appeared in printed bibliographies, because of the added cost and space that would have been consumed by fuller entries.[17] An immediate success, the CLSI system was improved and enhanced with new features as rapidly as technology and internal company research and development allowed. CLSI also began to offer a variety of systems depending on the needs of individual libraries. Within a decade, CLSI sold more than three hundred circulation systems, some of which performed the functions of materials booking, acquisitions, and an online public catalog as well. Later systems were designed to accept fuller bibliographic information without taking up more physical space or costing as much as previous ones. CLSI was quickly joined by other vendors who used different arrangements and brands of hardware, created different programs and supplied differing amounts of support services. Among the better known turnkey vendors are DataPhase, GEAC, Systems Control, Inc., and Universal Library Systems, Inc.

While the principal advantages of turnkey systems were their affordability, the speed with which they could be obtained and implemented, and the minimal expertise in computer technology they required from the purchasers, they had disadvantages as well. First, they were standardized to a greater or lesser degree, depending on the vendor's internal flexibility and the customer's willingness to pay more to get more. Thus, turnkey systems did not always do what each individual customer wanted them to do, and tailoring them to individual needs, if a vendor was willing and able to do so, was frightfully expensive—nearly as much as creating one's own system from scratch. Second, individual customers were limited in how the turnkey system could be altered to suit particular needs, e.g., CLSI software is written in a company-controlled software language and held in escrow for the customer and cannot be changed or redesigned by the customer without incurring penalties specified in the customer's contract. Third, not all turnkey systems could be expanded to perform additional functions or made to interface with other computer systems that did in order to achieve an integrated system of technical services for a library. Indeed, some of them could not even be expanded, and users were forced to purchase new systems. Fourth, lack of knowledgeable technical staff and control of the system made the customer dependent for its maintenance on others. Sometimes this was left to the vendor; at other times it was handled by manufacturers of the various components; and sometimes it was a combination of the two. Fifth, vendors had to divide their attention and resources between continuing service to old customers and attracting new ones. This inevitably created a tension between these groups in allocation of vendors' staff and funds.

Nevertheless, for numerous reasons libraries may decide to select turnkey systems rather than join networks or develop their own in-house systems for automating one or more technical service functions. If they do, they have more control over what bibliographic data are entered into the database than if they joined a network, but less than if they design their own system. The choices that can be made may include the format of the data, sometimes limited by system design, and which of the library's materials are included in the system, limited by the total size of the database that can be accommodated. Important decisions have to be made by the purchaser of a turnkey system.

The database being built by an individual institution ought to have lasting value, beyond the life of the hardware or software of the turnkey system. Building the database is an expensive prerequisite to using the system fully. Some libraries make every entry manually, working from a shelflist or from the materials themselves, doing some of the items off the shelf and others as they circulate. Some libraries put machine-readable labels in their materials and purchase the use of an existing database with a similar content and expect to match labels and entries as materials are handled for processing or use. Still others have existing machine-readable data which can be converted for use in the turnkey system. Some libraries pay to have their machine-readable records created for them. No matter what process is used to convert the information into a turnkey database, its value will ultimately lie in how much of the library's materials are thus converted as well as how long they can be used. Computer technology changes so rapidly that specific items of hardware may be rendered obsolete in only a few years. But the database should not become obsolete and should be transferable as a library moves from one system to another or finds new uses for given systems.[18] The more of a library's holdings are entered into an ongoing, transferable database, the more useful it is. Many libraries enter their reference collections into circulation databases even though these materials do not normally circulate. The reason is twofold: Reference materials are occasionally lent and can be controlled by the system; and the database is often used for reference support, and inclusion of these materials makes it unnecessary to search a separate reference catalog. The entry format most likely to have lasting value and be useful in a variety of systems is that which conforms to standards that exist in the field, i.e., the MARC formats. Unique entry formats designed for specific purposes or systems require modification before they can be used in other situations if, indeed, they can be used at all. Even when the modification process is very inexpensive per record, databases containing thousands of entries are costly to change and it may take valuable time to process them. In the long run, it may prove penny-wise and pound-foolish to accept nonstandard entry formats in a turnkey system which becomes difficult and costly to transfer.

Microcomputer Systems

The newest computer systems for storing, manipulating, and retrieving bibliographic data are based on very small "personal-sized" computers known as microcomputers or micros. These machines are usually the size of portable typewriters and look very much like them since their dominant feature is a typewriter-like keyboard. The system requires some kind of additional equipment to store and communicate information to the user, most often in the form of small units known as disk drives designed to hold 5¼-inch, 8-inch, 11-inch, or other sizes of recording devices called floppy diskettes or floppies and a TV monitor for visual communication, a printer for written communication, or both. Micros are much smaller than minicomputers and mainframes, but they are really alike except for their size. This limits the amount of data that can be dealt with at any time to what can be stored or written on one diskette or, with added disk drives, up to the maximum a system can take. This makes it possible, for example, to maintain all of a very small number of records, or part of a larger collection of data. Suppose you want to control the circulation of a very small library. You might not need to maintain records on materials that are on the shelf, but only those in circulation, i.e., an absence system. Also, you might not require a full bibliographic entry to identify items, but only some minimal information like author, title, and perhaps a unique control number adding up to a total of, say, forty characters in all. With current micro systems, including space for programming required and access by the control number and an author-title key, you could handle a circulation of more than a thousand transactions with an ordinary system configuration.

Some of the turnkey vendors whose systems were originally designed for minicomputer storage and processing have developed smaller designs based on micros to attract small libraries as customers, or for special purposes. Among the special purposes to which a micro could be put is backing up a minicomputer-based system. As everyone is aware, machinery can stop operating either because something has gone wrong or because it has been stopped deliberately. At those times in the life of a library with one or more functions performed by a turnkey system, or indeed any computer system, it is enormously helpful to have a micro backup instead of having to resort to manual operations which are usually even slower and more cumbersome to perform than whatever kind of procedure preceded the turnkey system. Indeed, one vendor of both micro- and mini-based circulation systems, CTI, Inc., of Utah, began as a producer-vendor of a micro backup for the CLSI LIBS 100 minicomputer circulation-control system. In the wake of CTI's success came the realization, on the part of turnkey system producers as well as customers, that backup plans were an important addition to the packages they provided and could be made to be a marketing asset, too. Micros, while not the only form of backup developed, were certainly important ones.

New vendors have sprung up whose automation packages are based on microcomputers rather than minis. Like other vended packages based on minicomputers, they may provide support for one or more functions such as circulation, acquisition, or serials control. Vendor-produced packages are not the only kind of micro systems in use in libraries today. Librarians can buy only the software to use with hardware they purchase themselves or, still more individually-controlled and designed, they can do the programming themselves or adapt existing software packages intended for general use, not specifically for libraries, to do what they want their computer systems to do. It is not difficult to learn to write programs and, once started, there is a great deal of help available for the amateur programmer in the form of online tutorials, books, media packages, periodicals, clubs, and professional associations, as well as classes in local schools, colleges, and universities or their computer centers. It is also easy to obtain maintenance for the hardware in cities and towns all over the country as the manufacturers develop markets among small-business people, private individuals, and school-age children.

The main advantages to micros in libraries are their versatility (they can be adapted and programmed for a myriad of uses); their economy (the basic computer, minidisk drive and monitor hardware package costs under $2,500 and additions to the hardware or purchases of software packages are usually in increments of well under five hundred dollars and often even less); their portability and economy of space consumption; their ability to be individually controlled by their owners; and their proven track record of reliable performance. Such an impressive list of advantages hardly deserves to be spoiled by reminders of micros' disadvantages, but they, too, need to be enumerated. Perhaps the most important disadvantage is that their small size limits the size of the database that can be maintained online and also makes it quite senseless to use up more space than is absolutely necessary for individual entries. Thus, to use a micro to maximum advantage, programmers rarely consider identifying bibliographic items by more than a minimum of necessary information, and this is often drastically abbreviated by traditional catalog entry standards. While this feature in itself is not bad or incorrect, the resulting database tends to be useful only within the limited sphere of the institution that creates it and for the particular tasks for which the program is designed. It is of little importance to the information community at large as a method of sharing bibliographic information. It is not a method of building a lasting, transferable database of bibliographic information for the institution, either. It does, however, serve specific purposes for a library with great ease and economy. If it cannot be shared, at least it can easily be copied and adapted. A small database is appropriate for a variety of situations, e.g., a small school or public library, a special collection in a larger library, or support of a special service such as maintenance of bibliographies, bookmobile circulation, referral services available in the community, administrative records, and so on. Micros have been used to replace small files of all sorts with smashing success, but larger files with the need for longer strings of data per entry are another story.

A second disadvantage of micros is the lack of uniformity among the products of different manufacturers. Apple, Radio Shack, and Atari are household words, but IBM and others are also producing powerful and versatile micros to compete with them. These are not interchangeable, and the software that can be run on one brand or model may not always be transferred to another. There is always a risk that a particular brand will be phased out or superseded before you are ready to purchase another system. Also, no matter what system is chosen, all commercially available software will not be compatible with it. If you are not prepared to write your own programs and expect to use software currently being marketed, it is important to determine whether or not it can be used with the hardware you expect to purchase. Not all microcomputer software will run on any micro. It is analogous to buying a sound recording on a cassette and finding your equipment will only play back cartridges.

Although these problems should not deter anyone from using micros for bibliographic data manipulation, bear in mind that micros do not have exactly the same applications as minis, and librarians cannot expect them to perform the same job in the same way. When a company such as CLSI offers both mini- and micro-based circulation control systems, they are not capable of performing the same tasks in the same way for the same collection. Some libraries use micros together with mini-based systems. Obviously they do not store identical data or handle it identically. Designs for microcomputer systems should not be expected either to contain the same data in the same organizational structure as would a minicomputer or mainframe, or to support the same services. In some cases, a micro is the right tool for a job; in others it may force data to be abbreviated to the point where it cannot perform a task adequately for users. The selection of a system requires careful matching of its potential for storing and organizing information with the needs of the job it is expected to do. Microcomputer systems are only beginning to be exploited in libraries. Creative librarians make new and valuable discoveries of how to use this versatile tool every day.

Electronic Media: Video and Computer Software

To the user of a computer system, the differences between the data and its organizational structures, its manipulation and its transmission, are invisible. It is all contained somewhere within the screen (or printer) which accepts our requests and responds to them with the information we seek. The same instantaneous communication between the user and the material contained "inside" the screen is an attribute of television, though everything on a TV screen may not be a live transmission, but simply a playback of previously recorded material. It is possible to have a two-way transmission between an ordinary television screen and a broadcasting center with computer links as part of the complex of communication structures facilitating the interaction. This is telecommunication. The electronic media associated with telecommunication networks differ from books, periodicals, films, and other library materials because they combine as an integral part of their existence as information materials the communication medium which connects them to the user. This dual nature of computer and video materials and transmissions is what Marshall McLuhan perceived as the essential and distinct characteristic which set them apart from all earlier communication forms. The amount of information which could be packaged into a book is limited, and the time it takes for a book to be written, published, read, and absorbed by a user (reader) is considerable. The leap ahead in the amount of material which could be packaged and the almost total elimination of a time lag made possible by new technologies is simply boggling. For these media, the information *is* the communication; the medium is the message.

Suppose your local public library has an online catalog and offers to permit anyone with a home computer and the necessary additional equipment or with a television set enhanced with telecommunications equipment to access it. Suppose also that the online catalog contains the library's order files, in-process files, and circulation files as subsystems of an integrated system of technical services. You could sit at your home computer or television set and find out instantly if a book you wanted was available, on order, or on loan to another person. With an interactive system, you could type a request for an item you wanted that was on the shelf and the system would instantly "flag" it and inform a staff member of your request. (Interactive means that two-way communication takes place, unlike ordinary television broadcasting, in which viewers receive programs on their TV sets but cannot transmit messages back to the broadcaster.) There are already networks of such systems in England in which library patrons can communicate from their homes with their local libraries as well as in Canada, and, on an experimental basis, here in the United States. They involve both computer and video technology to provide instantaneous two-way links between distant points. In this country there are several private firms marketing these services for profit, notably The Source and Dow-Jones. The possibilities of the media seem limitless, and there is little doubt they are already having a profound effect on information transfer and the nature and character of information itself.

Go back to the home-and-library-connection scenario for a moment and imagine that all of the materials in the library's holdings were recorded in a giant database in toto, not just their catalog entries. Now if you want articles, films, or books, they can be viewed directly on your home screen, with no delay while a library staff member receives and processes your request from the computer and sends you the desired material. Of course, one could certainly opt to have the book in hand, so to speak, for the pleasure of reading print on paper or being able to take it along wherever you might go. Even sound recordings could be transmitted, however, and who knows how a creative librarian could fill your screen with visual delights to accompany the recording. The attraction of this direct link between information in machine-readable form and users does not imply that people would not want to handle actual documents, as mentioned, or go to their library in person. It does mean that they would not have to do so in order to obtain the content of library materials. It also means that having books on shelves accessible to a single user per item could become far less important than having them in a database accessible to many viewers at once. To a generation of people growing up getting their daily news from a television screen, learning mathematics or spelling or languages from an educational computer program and playing Pac-Man in video arcades, it is hard to imagine the library of the future lacking a strong computer/video component. Furthermore, no amount of resistance is likely to prevent computer/video information from ascending in importance because of its inherent qualities of currency, speed, and economy, and, because of its continuing significance, from having an effect on all information transfer.

To appreciate the qualities of computerized information a bit more, let us review them quickly: (1) A computer system stores and manipulates much more information than a single book, or group of books, or whole libraries of materials; (2) It does more than play back a prerecorded set of signals by organizing its data in a variety of ways so they can be retrieved and used to satisfy different needs; (3) The computer and the person using it can "converse" or interact with one another to achieve incredible flexibility; (4) The computer not only has information in its database, much like a library has books on its shelves, but it transmits it to a user at a distance directly, which the library has never done, though libraries could use the computer to assist them in doing it now; (5) Many things done by computer can be completed more rapidly than if they were done manually, such as sorting, editing, transmitting, etc., provided the software is available to direct the computer's activities.

Video software has some of the same dual qualities of information storage and retrieval because of the videodisk's enormous capacity for information storage and the fact that video hardware can also be made to transmit over distances very cheaply and instantaneously. The combination of computer and video technologies with the established global telecommunication network makes it hard to accept the idea of very limited access to published or produced information. Whether the limits are in the number of available works, or the speed with which they can be delivered to a user, more and more people are changing their willingness to tolerate a lack of flexibility and individualized service satisfaction from their local libraries.

DESIRABLE CHARACTERISTICS OF COMPUTERIZED CATALOGS

What were the qualities of book and card catalogs that made them valuable formats in their day? No one would suggest giving up any of their advantages for a new format that does not improve upon them. The book catalog, which seems to have grown quite naturally out of the medieval manuscript inventory or list of acquisitions, was the most prevalent form of catalog before 1900 in the United States. It was used by such eminent institutions as Harvard, Yale, and Princeton Universities to attract donors as well as serving as a key to their collections. Book catalogs could be distributed widely and even sold as reference tools. They were difficult to update, however, and were out of date even as they went to press. It was costly and time-consuming to produce new editions. When the Library of Congress began selling its printed catalog cards, the book catalog was quickly replaced by the new format. Card catalogs had the advantage of being almost infinitely hospitable to new entries, easy to update, and cheap to maintain compared to book catalogs. Cards cost only pennies for the highest quality cataloging available from LC. Thus, to match the attributes of book and card catalogs, a new format would have to be available in many locations at once, easily and economically updated, hospitable to new entries, and able to provide the highest quality cataloging. And if they could also be used to interest philanthropists in supporting the institutions, that would be an added virtue. Do online computer catalogs have these characteristics?

First, online computer catalogs can be made available in many locations at once; however, only a finite number of terminals can be supported by any individual computer. With the proper equipment systems, the database can be extended to such a large number of locations, as with DIALOG and OCLC, that they could be considered virtually infinite. New ways of interfacing with systems allow for expansion to serve more users at once, and it is possible that advances in telecommunications technology will offer still greater opportunities. A single institution could certainly support many more catalog sites than with a card file, and hard copy printouts of desired subsets of the entire database could provide still greater flexibility within departments, for specific audiences, or for particular collections.

An online catalog is always current. The computer's ability to sort data with great speed is one of its basic capabilities. Updating a computer database requires only entering the new data and identifying the access points correctly for the programming to assign them to their indexes. Under normal operating conditions, the computer will not make any errors in executing these programs. Errors may occur under unusual weather conditions, for example, and also when data are not entered accurately. When human beings make mistakes, computers may compound them many times over. Thus, though updating an online catalog may be swift and easy, and though automatic machine filing is more accurate than human filing, no system is absolutely foolproof.

Computerized catalogs may or may not be more economical to maintain than the manual systems they would replace. It all depends on the amount of information to be handled and the service objectives to be satisfied. In very large libraries, manual systems break down in a variety of ways. Huge cataloging and filing backlogs build up; card catalogs become problematic as collections grow and space becomes too precious to devote to the hundreds of drawers required. The cards themselves deteriorate, too, with years of handling. Adding new editions or volumes of a set requires altering entire sets of cards, while changes in cataloging rules, subject headings, or classification schedules require corresponding amendments to whole sections of the catalog. The financial investment to convert card catalogs to machine-readable form may run to hundreds of thousands of dollars or more. Nevertheless, it may prove more economical to operate than card or book formats as salaries rise.

The fourth characteristic, that an online catalog be hospitable to new entries, is eminently satisfied by a machine that is designed to alphabetize, sort, and file according to programmed rules. It is not, however, able to hold an infinite amount of data with the same hardware. Thus, though OCLC has almost ten million bibliographic records in its database, it still has limits with its present hardware. It is wise to understand that any equipment or programs purchased now are not going to last forever. As technology and system objectives change, the online catalog will change, too.

Online computer catalogs are as likely to contain high quality cataloging as card or book catalogs were up to this time. It all depends on what is put into their systems. In the bibliographic utilities, Library of Congress MARC records supersede the entries of other libraries. Perhaps one should look at how much of the output of information is cataloged by LC and then determine whether the balance, cataloged in some other way, would be superior to what is available online. There is no requirement to subscribe to a bibliographic utility in order to have an online catalog. A library could buy a computer system and catalog and enter every item without outside intervention at all. Practically speaking, though, it does not make sense to ignore various kinds of cataloging assistance available.

It is fair to conclude that online catalogs can do all the things book and card catalogs have been able to do. Now we must ask what else they can do to make them more attractive than these alternatives.

First of all, they can give more searching flexibility than book, card, or computer-assisted COM catalogs. An online catalog has all the access points of traditional catalogs, i.e., author, title, and subject, and it can have several more, e.g., call number, date, language, keyword, ISBN/ISSN, and other unique identifiers. Not only can the online form have more access points for less expense than alternative formats, but they can be combined in several ways using Boolean operators to give catalog users great power in refining their searches to obtain what they want more quickly and easily. For a staff member verifying a particular item, using the LC number of ISBN/ISSN is much faster than finding an entry first by author and title and then checking the identifier. It is also more accurate, since the number only has to be read correctly once to be typed into the machine.

The second advantage of the online format is that it can be interfaced with acquisition and circulation systems or subsystems to give status information from the moment a title is entered as an order. Usually, searchers are interested in more than whether or not an item is listed in the catalog. They want to know, if they are patrons, whether the item is available to them; and, if they are staff members, if the item has been ordered, or is in process, or if it is in circulation and when it is due back, or if it has been overdue for a year and should be considered lost. Having status information along with bibliographic information saves time for staff and public alike, eliminates the frustration of looking for things that are not to be found, and allows greater control over collections.

Other advantages of an online catalog are its ability to be attached to printing equipment that provides users with hard copies of the information they find on the terminal for future reference or later analysis, depending on the reason for the search. It can be programmed to produce statistical reports for use in future planning as well as monitoring activity. Perhaps the greatest of its advantages is its ability to provide individualized service, i.e., for each query, responding with an individually-tailored bibliography of citations that fulfill criteria set by the user. If the online catalog can be programmed, like DIALOG, to index chapters, articles, poems, songs— in other words, to give access to smaller portions of works—and to deliver the document or item itself as well as provide abstracts, evaluations, and reviews, it would, indeed, be a new kind of wonder tool.

The use of computer systems should allow institutions to control all of their holdings bibliographically, not just some of them. There should be no reason to eliminate whole collections from the public's primary access tool, and the additional benefits for the user would accrue from having their catalog represent all holdings in all formats with the ability to limit their searches to films or sound materials or books published after 1980 if that is their need. The high-school student whose classmates have emptied the shelves of all copies of *Macbeth* the night before an exam might do even better learning the play from a videotape or sound recording. It certainly seems an improvement over turning away a disappointed patron. There are many similar service opportunities, in all information areas, which are allowed to go unsatisfied for want of the correct information.

NOTES

1. DIALOG Information Services, Inc., became a separate, wholly-owned subsidiary corporation of Lockheed in 1981. Announcements of the change in corporate status were made throughout the library press, including *Online*, 5 (July 1981), p. 9.

2. Educational Resources Information Center, *Thesaurus of ERIC Descriptors*, 9th ed. (Phoenix: Oryx Press, 1982), p. 569.

3. There are currently several excellent histories of the early years of

OCLC, including Albert F. Maruskin's *OCLC* (New York: Marcel Dekker, 1980), Chapter 2.

4. A December 1982 information sheet published by OCLC claimed that the breakdown of records into their format components for the whole database was as follows: 85.16% books; 6.37% serials; 2.31% films (AV); 2.57% sound recordings; 2.01% music scores; 1.21% maps; 0.37% manuscripts.

5. In October 1983, the RLIN system contained the following breakdown: books: 10,942,097 (ca. 87%); serials: 1,284,045 (ca. 10%); scores: 107,929 (ca. 1%); recordings: 48,599 (ca. .4%); films: 71,613 (ca. .6%); maps: 88,655 (ca. .7%).

6. Though dated, this information was included in an evaluation of the three U.S. bibliographic utilities performed by the University of Oregon Library and reported in *Journal of Library Automation*, 14 (September 1981), p. 226. Even if the time lag has been reduced, it is still a factor in the overall production of a usable bibliographic record.

7. Bristah Pam, "WLN, RLIN, UTLAS, and OCLC." (Unpublished term paper, Columbia University, 1984).

8. This is attributable to its authority control system, as well as the ability to search using Boolean operators and truncated entries.

9. This estimate was made in a letter from UTLAS' Marketing Representative Bob Eastman to Dean Terry Belanger of Columbia University School of Library Service, dated 12 October 1983.

10 A CODEN is a unique designation for a serial title containing six characters.

11. In addition to the letters composing portions of names and titles used for the search keys, punctuation of a particular kind enables the computer to interpret the data and select the appropriate index to be searched.

12. University of Oregon Library, "A Comparison of OCLC, RLG/RLIN, and WLN," *Journal of Library Automation*, 14 (September 1981), p. 225.

13. Twenty-four-hour, seven-day-a-week service is not typical for a variety of reasons, some of which have to do with the need to have round-the-clock staffing, but also due to the housekeeping operations which must be done daily and require a limitation of activity by users. Thus, the computer may actually not be shut down, but access is not permitted for operations by individual libraries.

14. It is not unusual for someone to wait three to four weeks for an interlibrary loan to be completed in a manual system. By comparison, online interlibrary loans may only take two days or less, especially when libraries also are provided with delivery services. Even when there are

no such delivery advantages, an online interlibrary loan takes less than a week, on average.

15. Articles and letters about this possibility from time to time appear in such journals as *Publishers Weekly*. But publishers are not alone in this opinion. See, for instance, Ronald Rayman's "Interlibrary Loans: A New Burden?" in *Publishers Weekly*, 221 (January 22, 1982), pp. 25-26. Rayman, a librarian and teacher, warns: "Widespread borrowing and lending of new and in-print books does not bode well for publishers of popular and general-interest books. I suggest it is an issue they would do well to address without delay."

16. This figure is, of course, only a rough estimate for a basic system including two terminals, two disk drives, a minicomputer, operator console, and two printers, described in detail in an overview of automated circulation systems in several issues of *Library Technology Reports* appearing in the summer and fall of 1975. At this time, the company was in its second year of installing systems. The acronym CLSI stood, at that time, for Computer Library Services, Inc., but it has since been changed, more than once.

17. The cost of storage space has since decreased, but even so, when small increases are multiplied by the thousands of records normally held in a medium-sized library, the amount of added storage is formidable, indeed.

18. Many libraries that had opted for drastically abbreviated entries for circulation systems discovered that, despite the lack of data, they were being used as finding lists, i.e., catalogs. Had the data been more complete, this use would have been facilitated at little additional cost.

RECOMMENDED READING

Information about databases used in reference services may be found in the following sources:

Database: The Magazine of Database Reference and Review. Weston, Conn.: Online, Inc., 1978-

Katz, Bill, and Anne Clifford, eds. *Reference and Online Services Handbook: Guidelines, Policies, and Procedures for Libraries*. New York: Neal-Schuman, 1982.

Nitecki, Danuta A., ed. "Databases," *RQ*. Chicago: RASD/ALA. (Column in quarterly journal of the Reference & Adult Services Division of the American Library Association.)

Online Review: The International Journal of Online Information Systems. Oxford: Learned Information, 1977- (Originally titled *On-Line Review*.)

Online: The Magazine of Online Information Systems. Weston, Conn.: Online, Inc., 1977- (First issue has a valuable supplement titled, "On-line Information Retrieval Bibliography, 1965-1967," by Donald T. Hawkins.)

Information about technical services databases and online catalogs is found in various articles in the following journals:

Information Technology & Libraries. Chicago: LITA/ALA, 1982- (Quarterly journal of the Library & Information Technology Association of the American Library Association.)

Journal of Library Automation. Chicago: LITA/ALA, 1969-1981. (Quarterly journal of LITA, previously known as the Information Science and Automation Division. Continued by *Information Technology & Libraries.*)

Library Resources & Technical Services. Chicago: RTSD/ALA, 1955- (Quarterly journal of the Resources & Technical Services Division of the American Library Association.)

Library Systems Newsletter. Chicago: LTR/ALA, 1981-

Library Technology Reports. Chicago: ALA, 1965- (Certain issues pertain to various computer-based systems for the technical services.)

Microcomputer Systems

Chen, Ching-chih, and Stacey E. Bressler. *Microcomputers in Libraries.* New York: Neal-Schuman, 1982.

Librarian's Guide to Microcomputer Technology and Applications. White Plains, N.Y.: Knowledge Industry Publications for the American Society for Information Science, 1983.

Miller, Inabeth. *Microcomputers in School Library Media Centers.* New York: Neal-Schuman, 1983.

Rorvig, Mark E. *Microcomputers and Libraries: A Guide to Technology, Products and Applications.* White Plains, N.Y.: Knowledge Industry Publications, 1981.

Useful information may also be found in marketing literature prepared by vendors of library systems for the technical services, and in the newsletters of the bibliographic utilities:

OCLC (Online Computer Library Center; Dublin, Ohio)

RLIN (Research Libraries Information Network; Palo Alto, Calif.)

WLN (Washington Library Network; Olympia, Wash.)

UTLAS (University of Toronto Libraries Automated System; Toronto)

Chapter 7

Skills for the Implementation of Automated, Integrated Catalogs in Libraries

A good understanding needs to be cultivated among staff members for a library to implement an automated system with the greatest ease and success. People can feel manipulated and dehumanized to have changes imposed without interacting with the forces of change. Resistance to changes may arise for many reasons, but fear and anger are sure to induce staff to resist the introduction of an automated, integrated catalog in their library. It is essential that staff understand the reasons for its initiation and see its benefits for themselves as well as for their patrons. Even if staff input is not in itself valuable, participation in the project gives staff members a stake in its success, as well as a feeling of control over the development of their own jobs.

COMPUTER LITERACY

A computer system is simply an operation involving a computer; or, more narrowly defined, it is merely a computer with its necessary parts for operation. The part of a computer system that does the actual computing is termed the processor. More formally it may be called the central processing unit (CPU). Distributed processing means having more than one unit processing data for the system, i.e., one in a central facility or headquarters and one in the local library. Hence the processing is distributed among several units. A bibliographic utility, with all its members, staff, equipment, products, etc., is a computer system in the broadest sense; while in the narrowest sense, it is only the equipment and its software. Even that, in a large utility like OCLC, represents thousands of items of equipment and lines of programming, and yet it is only part of the whole cataloging system.

This chapter will outline and describe the following skills or competencies that would facilitate a computer system's establishment: (1) computer literacy; (2) system literacy, i.e., understanding the tradeoffs between network and individual library-based systems; (3) organizational changes likely to be made; and (4) bibliographic rules and standards. A discussion of methods for acquiring the skills and plans for implementing them is included, at the end of the chapter.

A computer system must include: a processor; storage; devices for communicating with the processor; communication lines; software; people to operate and maintain everything; and an environment in which all can perform their tasks. If you purchase a computer and software, you have not done enough to obtain an operable system in the larger sense. You still need the rest of the components. Describing them one by one will expand the definition a little more.

Processor/Central Processing Unit/CPU

This is the heart of every computing system, the point at which data are actually manipulated according to the instructions of the user. Bear in mind that a computer cannot add two and two if its programs do not tell it how to perform the addition. When you search for a record in a sophisticated system like DIALOG, the programs first direct the system to connect you to a selected database and then have each entry in the designated indexes matched against the parameters you selected. Though it may appear to work almost instantaneously, it is actually performing a series of matches very quickly against the thousands or millions of entries in one or more of its indexes to satisfy the request. The speed, thoroughness, and accuracy with which it can do this makes it seem smart, particularly when users see it doing something that would take many hours, days, or longer to do themselves. In reality, however, the processor simply recognizes a series of signals and proceeds to one or another subsequent step according to whether they do or do not match. Every operation computers can do must be broken down to this fundamental process of comparing two signals and proceeding to another step after making that determination.

Storage

The processor does the work, but it cannot, by itself, hold a great deal more information than that with which it is working. In order to perform complex operations with large amounts of data, the processor needs to store the data it is not using at the moment. This place is called storage or memory. Storage may take several forms, including open reels of magnetic tape, disks of varying sizes in single or multiple units, and cartridges or cassettes containing magnetic tape in wholly enclosed containers. Computer cards and paper tape are also forms of storage for machine-readable data, but they have to be entered into the processing unit's memory before they can be utilized. Online storage has to be in a form that the processor can access more or less directly. Storage units called disk drives hold the disks and keep them spinning while they are "read" or "written on" by heads, designed for that purpose. Reels operate somewhat differently, but the principle is similar in that the data on them may be read or scanned by a head and can be written on or re-recorded as desired.

Input/Output Devices

The different kinds of equipment used to communicate with the processor are called input/output devices. The most familiar ones used in online systems are the television-like screens called cathode-ray tubes or CRTs, keyboards, and printers. There are various other devices by which we can communicate with the processor, some of which are offline, e.g., the keypunched cards which used to be synonymous with the word computer, and some of which are online, e.g., bar-code scanners in the form of lightpens resembling pencil-sized flashlights or laser beams.

Communication Links

Input/output devices have to be linked to the processor. This can be done in two ways, depending on which is more practical and economical: hard-wiring or modem-assisted telephone access. Hard-wiring means that the link is in the form of a cable which runs, uninterrupted, between the processor and the terminal. Hard-wiring tends to be limited by distance and location of the linked equipment within a single building or a wholly-owned property. The alternative, not limited by distance or jurisdiction, is modem-assisted telephone access, also known as dial-up access. In this type of link, the computer is wired by a cable to a telephone line and the modem, short for modulator-demodulator, translates between the computer signal and the telephone signal at both ends of the link. The signal translation is the assistance provided by the modem. Remote signals can thus be transmitted over media other than phone lines, but phone lines already connect virtually all of the country, ready to link any two locations together. Other types of transmission, over other cable networks, may become more important in the future because they can handle many more communications simultaneously.

Software

To define software as the instructions that tell the computer how to operate is not inaccurate, but it is simplistic. There are many sets of instructions, all of which must interrelate smoothly for the computer to perform. This relatively simple operation is broken down into all of the minuscule suboperations required for its performance; and each suboperation is programmed into the overall design. Each step of the task can contain only one decision point, i.e., a match or no-match, or a yes-no, on-off option. One of the difficulties of software design is figuring out how to break down complex operations into their parts and, still harder, to build up the parts to form a multi-operational system. In software design, though speeding up operations by minimizing the number of steps is considered, other factors have greater priority, such as maintaining the security of the data within and between operations and insuring an unambiguous progression of computations so the computer does not become trapped in an endless series of fruitless searches for unobtainable data. Try, for example, to describe making a known-item search in a card catalog in this kind of step-by-step manner as if you were communicating the information to someone with no understanding of the vocabulary involved and you will have an appreciation of what programmers must do. Computers are as "knowledgeable" as their programming, complete with thousands of definitions and predefined reference points, can make them; but they have no inherent human understanding.

Operations Staff

Today's computers do not require armies of technicians to attend to them, but they do require staff trained in operating them, maintaining them, and utilizing them in serving the public's information needs. Varying levels and types of knowledge are part of each distinctive job, but a general understanding of what the computer does and how it relates to the services performed—the end product of most library or information provision activity—should be the common frame of reference among all staff in an agency with computer systems. Some staff will need to learn only to type data into the terminal or identify the data that are already part of the database, say, for verifying orders or checking acquisitions requests. They must be able to operate the terminals, but they may not have to know a great deal more. For libraries with their own in-house processor, some staff will have to learn how to operate it, its disk drives or other storage devices, etc. in order to turn it on and off, make copies of the database, do regular maintenance routines, and whatever other tasks are required for day-to-day hardware supervision. Supplies such as paper, printing equipment, and spare parts may need to be maintained, too. Even for libraries without their own computing equipment, maintenance of the terminals may be an ongoing responsibility requiring special knowledge about their make-up and operation. Microcomputers and minicomputers also may require knowledge of programming, a specialized kind of knowledge affecting the kinds of computing that can be done by a particular machine as well as the structure and contents of the database. Managers, either those responsible directly for the computerized systems, or indirectly, for general services, production or planning, will need to know how the computer fits into functional systems, how inputs and outputs flow, and what the computer can and cannot do. They will need to plan systems of operation utilizing the computer effectively, budgets which include ongoing costs of operation and development, services which the computer can support and personnel training and deployment which takes account of the foregoing. They should be aware of their computer's reporting capabilities and how they can be incorporated into the higher level planning processes. Each staff member, from data entry operator to director and including part-time shelvers, volunteers, and/or maintenance staff, should understand what the computer is supposed to do, and, in general, how it serves the agency's goals. All staff members seem to be able to understand what a card catalog is supposed to do and, in general, how it serves a library's organizational goals. They are all capable of using a card catalog when they assume the role of patron in local libraries, even though they may not be able to catalog materials themselves. Why then should they be less informed about their library's computer systems which perform similar or related services, even if they cannot program it or enter and manipulate data themselves? What should be clear throughout the agency is the computer's role in the overall picture.

The Environment

The term environment can be defined in two ways, both of which have importance in this context. First it can describe the physical environment essential to the functioning of the computer equipment. Computers require electricity and also react to sudden losses of power, sometimes by losing pieces of information that were involved in computations at the moment. Thus, an uninterrupted flow of electricity is essential. Computers are sensitive to extremes in temperature and humidity, dust and other air pollutants, and static electricity. The best policy is to establish whatever physical environment is necessary to effect optimum operation, counting its cost as part of the purchase price. Micro-computers are less sensitive to physical environmental factors than minicomputers, and terminals are usually the least sensitive. Remember that terminals with dial-up connections to remotely located computers require telephones and other terminals may have permanent, or dedicated, telephone links with their hosts.

The second definition of the word environment is broader, referring to the general atmosphere or ambience in which the computer system is to be used. If it is one in which territorial boundaries are rigid or communications among departments, staff, and administration are limited and difficult, the computer system may become the focus of criticism. Computer systems cause change, cutting across departmental lines and engendering new organizational plans. All of these things necessitate communication flowing in all directions. Flexibility is a virtue, and lack of it can result in problems, if not failure to realize the system's potential.

SYSTEM LITERACY

System literacy, in this context, refers to the capabilities of two different types of computer systems: the institutionally-individual system and the network system. They differ in several ways, not only in the number of institutions which participate in them, but also in their capabilities, the services they can perform, their uniformity or diversity, their management and control, and their flexibility.

Except for the largest public and academic libraries, institutionally-individual computer systems are based on minicomputers and/or microcomputers. Very few individual libraries can afford large mainframes or need the enormous storage space and computing power they provide. A microcomputer is unlikely to be able to hold sufficient data online to do the job of a catalog.

How much data will be entered? In an institutionally-individual system working with a minicomputer, several hundreds of thousands of short records or somewhat fewer longer records can be maintained easily. Two questions need to be answered: (1) Will all items be entered fully? (2) What standards will be followed? Despite their many limitations, nationally promulgated standards provide the only answer to the second question insuring that the resulting database will have any extension beyond the life of this specific system. Nonstandard records can be entered by institutions that own and control their own systems, but when that system is obsolete, the database may be useless for other purposes. Thus, it pays in the long run to opt for standard data formats and entry of at least a minimally acceptable bibliographic record for each item entered.

In designing one's own data system, the elements required for identification may be kept flexible, and more attention can be paid to those which serve the institution's public. This cannot be done in a network, where standards must apply to all participants regardless of their needs. Within the framework of nationally endorsed standards for data format and entry, there is much greater flexibility for the individually owned system. The important thing to remember is that the standard framework must be observed. In addition, the first time an item is entered into a system, it should receive the fullest treatment it will have, because later conversion to fuller forms of cataloging are likely to be even more costly as well as more inconvenient. The second limit imposed by the choice of an individual or network system is the data format and entry, which will be more flexible in an individual system than in a network system.

How may software differ in individual and network systems? Software design controlled by an individual library is limited by its budget, needs, and imagination as well as the talent of its programmers. It is not limited by some of the things networks must face, e.g., a need to satisfy differing and sometimes conflicting needs; and it does not have the organizational distance between the programmers and the users of the system. In very large networks is is difficult to achieve any easily executed system of communication between designers and users.

Environmental factors tend to be more important for the individual system, while network systems usually involve less equipment on-site and, therefore, less responsibility for its operation. The type of hardware design, or the configuration as it is called, will determine the amount of physical preparation and ongoing environmental controls necessary. If only one of them is designated the host for the entire network, that library will have the whole responsibility. If, on the other hand, several participants act as "nodes" or centers for information processing and distribution, the burden would be shared among them.

In general, networks will tend to have more titles and more volumes or volume equivalents, grow more rapidly, and display more diversity in their collection characteristics than individual databases. Networks will also tend to cover larger jurisdictions containing more diverse populations. They may be composed of different types of libraries that are related by geographic proximity or similar subject orientations, or they may have only one type of library as participants, e.g., public library participants, college or university library participants, etc. The network may be a natural outgrowth of previous cooperative activities, such as centralized cataloging and processing, buying, and resource sharing; or it may be the participants' first venture into cooperation with one another. As improvements in new communication systems develop and lower costs for their services continue to be realized, they will become more commonplace, encouraging the range of network members, both geographically and in other respects, to broaden. What must be understood are the trade-offs between standardization, costs, and potential size and diversity available in a network or an individual computer system.

ORGANIZATIONAL CHANGE

Implementing automated systems in libraries that are divided into technical and public service operations tends to expose the often ignored relationships between them. One reason for this recognition is the emerging interdependence on rapid access to bibliographic information provided by an automated system. Whether the automated system supports acquisitions, cataloging, or circulation, or some combination of these functions, it will provide rapid access to much of the same data needed by all of them as well as by reference and reader services, management, and the general public. Depending on the amount and type of data in the system, the searching flexibility available, and the special training needed to use it, almost everyone in the agency will have some bibliographic data need the system could fulfill faster than traditional channels. Two examples of this will illustrate further.

In the first case, a medium-sized public library implemented an online, minicomputer-based circulation control system to replace photocharging systems used for at least ten years. Immediately, technical services personnel were affected by the intrusion of the minicomputer, which was located in an enclosed room adjoining the technical services area. The identification of materials and conversion of bibliographic data to machine-readable form required consultation of the order files, shelflist, and bibliographic tools located in the technical services department. It soon became apparent that the conversion of new materials could be expedited by integrating it into the cataloging and shelf-preparation process. Thus, the technical services staff was soon drawn into the data entry process, learning to operate the equipment and make decisions on search keys even before the circulation department gained such expertise.

Other public service staff members working with reserved materials, interloan, and the readers' advisory service were affected, too. Reserves or requests for titles, normally a part of circulation desk work, began to shift to the reference department as the importance of its effect on collection development became clear. The library's policy to attempt to satisfy virtually all requests, free of charge, now handled automatically by the circulation system and including automatic generation of purchase notices, encouraged an explosion of requests from the public. This led to the purchase of more best sellers to maintain a constant ratio between the number of unfilled requests and the copies of a title either owned or on order. The reference staff, responsible in part for collection development, began to view responsibility for reserves in a new light. Eventually, a separate reserve department under reference control was created to handle the flow of requests, monitor the effects of acquisitions, and oversee the logistics of loans between the main library and its branches. Interloan, always handled by reference assistants, was now dependent on searching the circulation control database for actual status information on titles. In addition, requests for items listed in the catalog but not in the database or on the shelf could be presumed lost and either immediately replaced or the request forwarded to another library. Interloan became both more efficient and effective, thanks to the circulation control system.

Another link in the chain which became visible was the dependence of the reference and readers' advisory departments on the bibliographic contents of the circulation database. They preferred it to the card catalog for ascertaining the availability of individual copies of titles which the catalog could not do, and it pointed up the role of bibliographic information in performing reference services.

Within a short time, the circulation control system became an essential factor in the work of the acquisitions department—which entered its titles on order so that reserve requests could be placed against them—the catalog department—for which the database became a more accurate shelflist than the card file—and the reference and readers' advisory departments, the interloan department, and the reserve department. Naturally, it was central to the work of the circulation department, which was forced to share terminals originally intended only for circulation work with all the other departments. The final link in the chain was the involvement of the central administration in using the reports generated by the system in planning for collections, programs, and services.

The second example was the introduction of an OCLC terminal into a small college library. Initially, the purpose of the terminal was only to assist in cataloging, and the terminal was placed in a relatively inaccessible area within the library's technical services department. Within a few months, however, the value of the terminal for verification of titles for acquisition and for aid in answering reference questions created a staff-initiated campaign to move the terminal to a more accessible location, as well as to permit its use by reference desk personnel. The library's director, surprised but pleased by the unforeseen turn of events, agreed to have the terminal moved to the front of the technical services department and to allow public service staff to use it provided their use did not interfere with the higher priority work of technical services staff. The next move by the staff was to urge purchase of an automated circulation system to further enhance the integration of functions into the automated mode as well as to utilize the existing machine-readable data for circulation. In this library, introduction of the OCLC system brought together for the first time the public and technical services staffs in the common goal of obtaining faster and easier access to more information used in their jobs. The director had no idea that the OCLC terminal would lead to such a situation.

Both of these examples occurred in small to medium-sized libraries that had well-defined organizational patterns. Very little interaction between public and technical services staff occurred until the introduction of a computer system and, in both cases, the mutually beneficial overlapping of their use of the computer was totally unplanned. In both libraries, adjustments were made to accommodate more effective use of the database, and old organizational patterns became less and less distinct.

Introduction of a computerized catalog for public as well as staff use is likely to make larger administrative concerns apparent. One of these concerns is planning for the future: collection development, program planning based on collections, and service patterns. Computer catalogs can be available to many remote locations at once, even to people's homes. They have the potential to alter document delivery systems radically by enabling people to use them without going to the library. Within the library, they will be used by all staff in some way, with no real distinction between public and technical services staff in the knowledge and facility in computer searching required.

Planning for the computer catalog should include some forecasting of what services will change and how staff can support the changes. Administration of the catalog cannot rest with any one department, but must be flexibly administered by all. One way public service staff can contribute to effective use of the catalog is by developing new service methods, tools, and packages and by working with technical services staff to realize them. Another is to discuss public service goals and objectives and jointly determine desired service levels and patterns. Input by technical services staff into the process can help identify problem areas before they foul up new projects. Creating solutions to public service problems can be as much a concern of behind-the-scenes personnel as those on the firing line.

Two steps can address the problems arising both from lack of communication between departments and from conflicting goals. The first step is to create an interdepartmental planning team with membership from all departments including administration. The planning team, which could become an ongoing steering committee, would have major responsibility for developing and modifying the computer system's goals and objectives as well as new services based upon them. Methods for working out conflicts to mutual satisfaction and promoting creative uses of the system would be high on the list of priorities. While administration should participate, the planning or steering committee cannot be simply a director's tool. Administration's participation needs to be equal to that of other areas in order to foster a really useful balance of power. Consensus on goals and commitment to service programs are important prerequisites to any truly effective program of automation. Interdepartmental commitments become necessary to support the success of any individual departmental programs, because the computer system is part of every department's operations. Thus, the need for interdepartmental cooperation and structure to insure it is essential.

The second step is to open communication channels throughout the library. The interdepartmental planning/steering committee is one important way to promote communication. Others can include newsletters, memoranda, formal and informal meetings, exchanges of all kinds between departments, and discussion of important short- and long-range goals of the library which the computer system is to serve.

It would seem self-defeating to ignore the impact of changing library services on the public and the contribution to the planning process which could be made by the public. Public library boards and Friends of the Library groups are made up of ordinary citizens and, in large measure, these people are the institution's contact with the public at large. School and academic libraries sometimes have advisory committees in which students and faculty participate. All kinds of libraries could benefit from frank and open interchange of ideas with more than just their board members or fund raisers, and open a dialogue with the public on a broader basis. Furthermore, all new and modified services have to be communicated to the public. How much more useful would it be to have public participation in the planning process when a new system is implemented?

CATALOGING STANDARDS AND STANDARDS-MAKING BODIES

One factor in creating computerized catalogs, which everyone but catalogers generally ignores, is the set of standards affecting the record format. Even catalogers are frequently fuzzy about the relationships of the various standards and standards-making bodies. Three interrelated codes affect record format: *AACR2*, ISBD, and MARC. Each of these standards is a factor in the design and building of an online catalog database. Each is the product of a different group, yet the memberships of the groups overlap and have common interests. This confusing picture must be sorted out to provide an understanding of what the standards cover and how, as well as who makes up the organizations that govern them.

National Standards—*AACR2*

AACR2 is the code governing the descriptive cataloging of all library materials. It is the first code in which books and all nonbook formats were treated together according to the same entry structure. It established that idiosyncracies of medium were not sufficient to warrant altering this structure, but rather that the structure needed to be flexible enough to accommodate all media. It was also designed to incorporate the ISBD structure after which it was patterned for the most part.

AACR2 tells catalogers how to select and record bibliographic data from the various sources available to them. The preferred sources of information for all materials are the items themselves, but alternatives are suggested which include "any source"[1] except for certain of the elements. *AACR2* also covers the selection of access points relating to the bibliographic description. No mention is made of subject access in the current edition of *AACR* or its predecessors, *AACR1* (1967), *ALA Rules* (1949), or the *AA Rules* (1908). The inclusion of all media in the rules is only one of many innovations. Separation of the rules for description from those for selecting access points is another, one that represents a fundamental departure from previous codes. The language of the code is a compromise between American and British usage. Conflicts over usage was one of the reasons there were two texts of the first edition published in 1967, one for North America and one for the British. Thus, we will find the words "full stop" instead of "period," and "catalog" is spelled "catalogue" in the British mode. Nevertheless, the spirit of compromise does not extend to the lists of terms used to identify various media if a library chooses the option of doing so. Two lists of terms for naming the media appear in *AACR2* and they do not match those recommended by the ISBD for nonbook materials.[2]

AACR2 prescribes eight areas or elements for bibliographic description: (1) Title and Statement of Responsibility; (2) Edition; (3) Material Specific or Mathematical Details, used only for serials and cartographic (map and map-related) materials; (4) Publication, Distribution Information; (5) Physical Description; (6) Series; (7) Notes; and (8) Standard Numbers and Terms of Availability. The first chapter sets forth general rules applicable to all materials, while the next ten chapters give additional rules for dealing with specific kinds of media from books to microforms. Additional rules for cataloging serial publications are to be used in conjunction with the rules for the medium, which take precedence over other considerations including the publication pattern, reproduction of a work in another medium, etc. This created grave differences in creation of bibliographic entries for microform copies of books, other printed monographs, and manuscripts under the new rules as contrasted with the first edition of *AACR*. The Library of Congress, OCLC, and the Association of Research Libraries decided not to follow the new rules and waged a successful campaign to get professional organization backing for a proposal to return to the old rules, whereby copies were described in terms of the original works. The ultimate resolution of this issue may have to wait until *AACR3*, but meanwhile, the rule stands and is not being followed by most of the library community. In contrast, the rest of the code appears to have been adopted by all major cataloging agencies in the United States, including the Library of Congress, the bibliographic utilities, and all processing centers dependent upon them.

International Rules—ISBD

AACR2 was designed to coordinate with and integrate into its structure the International Standard Bibliographic Description (ISBD) sponsored by IFLA. ISBD also prescribes eight elements of an entry and organizes them in the same order. It adds to this a distinctive punctuation for each element and sub-element, included in *AACR2*, which identifies them regardless of the language of the entry or even the alphabet in which it is written. The purpose of prescribing the entry elements and their order was to facilitate international exchange of information with the hope of eventually creating Universal Bibliographic Control (UBC) over the world's production of information. This grand vision may not be realized yet, but its success is technically possible with the tools available now. The fact that *AACR2* incorporated virtually all of ISBD's prescriptions is part of the many factors on which UBC's success depends.

Computer Protocols—MARC

The third standard related to *AACR2* and ISBD is the Library of Congress' machine-readable cataloging (MARC) format. This format prescribes the structure and identification for entering and transmitting bibliographic data in a computer database. While MARC has been a de facto standard since its development by LC in 1965, it was approved as an official standard by the American National Standards Institute in 1969 and thus acquired a measure of *de jure* status.[3]

MARC formats devised by LC exist for books and other printed monographs, printed music, manuscripts, films, serials, and maps. Additional formats for sound recordings and audiovisual media have been created for use in OCLC, based on LC's MARC. Each bibliographic utility has adapted MARC to its own purposes and uses subsets of LC's version of the standard. In a reverse kind of modification of a standard, LC's policy decisions on application of the rules of *AACR2* within the library constitute a subset of *AACR2* and are followed for the most part by cataloging agencies all over the nation. These decisions are not changes in the rules of the code, but merely rule "interpretations" which LC will follow; nevertheless, they take on the force of the rules themselves because so much local cataloging is actually based on LC practice as found in their own products—MARC tapes, fiche, CIP, the *National Union Catalog,* etc.—or created by the bibliographic utilities.

Responsible Authorities

An understanding of how standards are made is a first step in keeping ahead of current standards, becoming aware of impending changes before they are made and, even more important, influencing the direction of the changes.

The international standards are the responsibility of various committees or working groups whose members are selected by leaders of IFLA. There is usually a balance of nations and interests maintained on the working groups, though their composition has been criticized.[4] One of the problems of membership on such a committee is the need for extensive travel, since IFLA meetings are held all over the world. Generally, the drafts of specific ISBDs are circulated among some professionals in the field, but neither widely nor at the grassroots level. IFLA tends to rely on each nation's national library or equivalent agency and, perhaps, one or more national professional organizations to respond to requests for input on behalf of their entire information community. At the same time, IFLA is dependent on national agencies to implement the standards within their borders, adding to the burden they bear for all. The ISBDs have been undergoing reviews periodically, and some of them have been revised extensively, indicating IFLA's willingness to respond. The ISBD for nonbook media (NBM) was reviewed in 1982, five years after publication, and several suggestions for revision are currently under development.

ISBDs can only be implemented through their incorporation into national standards. We have two standards governing bibliographic description, *AACR2*—itself an international standard—and MARC. One of the objectives of *AACR2* was to facilitate the international exchange of data by prescribing the same elements in entries, in the same order, and using the ISBD style of punctuation for identifying them. By doing this as early as 1974, with a pre-revision of part of *AACR1*, adherents to the *AACR* demonstrated their commitment to broad international cooperation. The second edition follows almost all the provisions of ISBD—no mean feat considering that most of their formats were in an unfinished state during the very period that final decisions on the code were being made.

AACR2 is the result of international deliberations, too, but not on such a universal scale. Included on the Joint Steering Committee for the revision of *AACR* (JSCAACR) were representatives of five organizations in three English-speaking countries: Canada, the United Kingdom, and the United States. Three delegates came from national professional associations in their respective nations; the other two members were from the British Library and the Library of Congress. Each member body also had a deputy representative, making ten in all on the committee. Finally, the two men chosen as editors of the new work and a secretary brought the total involved in the work of the JSCAACR to thirteen people. This is the group who brought us *AACR2* in 1978. They still meet on an ongoing basis to consider changes, corrections, and amendments to the text. In their meetings rests the future of descriptive cataloging for all of us in the U.S. as well as for all other countries whose bibliographic fortunes are tied to ours. Naturally, the JSCAACR representatives are guided in their deliberations not only by their personal expertise, but also by the needs of their constituencies as expressed in the cataloging bodies of their associations or libraries. These bodies encourage participation from practitioners directly (in the associations) or indirectly (in the national libraries' requests for feedback). Thus, in effect, all practitioners have the ability to be heard if they will make personal efforts to speak within their organizations.

At the same time, the MARC formats for machine encoding of the data resulting from application of *AACR2* had to be able to treat the punctuation and other changes from old-style cataloging mandated by the new rules. These formats, though developed by LC and modified by users such as OCLC and RLIN, are not governed only by these individual bodies on a unilateral basis. They are also under the authority of an American Library Association committee with three-way sponsorship by the Resources and Technical Services

Division (RTSD), the Library and Information Technology Association (LITA), and the Reference and Adult Services Division (RASD). The name of this committee is the Committee on Representation in Machine-Readable Form of Bibliographic Information (MARBI). It is made up of representatives of the three divisions, LC, and the National Library of Canada. Changes to the MARC formats are considered at every Annual and Midwinter Conference of ALA, during which MARBI meets almost daily for several hours, and twice more during the year.

SUMMARY OF THE STANDARDS

ISBD prescribes the elements of bibliographic description, their order and punctuation. ISBDs for specific kinds of material go to IFLA's Committee on Cataloguing or the appropriate Working Group. The one for Non-Book Materials (NBM) is chaired by Christopher Ravilious.

AACR2 prescribes how bibliographic descriptions are made, following ISBD in the choice of elements, their order, and punctuation. It adds, too, what data should be put into each of the elements and how it should be derived and transcribed, as well as what access points should be drawn from the resulting description. *AACR2* is governed by representatives of the American, Canadian, and British Library Associations and the national libraries of the United States and the United Kingdom, who form a committee known as JSCAACR. Within each country, the Associations' cataloging committee consider recommending changes to *AACR2* based on proposals from all sources. In the United States, the committee in question is the RTSD CC:DA—the Committee on Cataloging: Description and Access. It has a membership of nine voting representatives and thirty-one nonvoting liaisons, including persons from ALA divisions and outside groups.[5] Thus, rule changes go through two committees: First the appropriate ALA committee; and then, if successful, the JSCAACR.

While *AACR2* can be applied without computer involvement, in the largest group of agencies producing cataloging copy used by others, i.e., LC and the bibliographic utilities, cataloging data is encoded into machine-readable form via the MARC formats. This means that the MARC formats must be able to accommodate the rules of *AACR2* and, indirectly, the ISBD's. The MARC formats, while ostensibly under the authority of LC, are really governed by a committee of professionals including representatives of LC and the bibliographic utilities among others—MARBI. Rule changes must be approved by MARBI first, and then be implemented by the utilities and LC, who govern the use of the formats.

LC has one further contribution to this complex of committees and responsibilities: It provides, for this country at least, interpretations of *AACR2*. These rule interpretations do not have the force of rules, but because most major cataloging agencies follow LC's lead, they acquire virtually the same status. LC, under no obligation to heed the community of catalogers, nevertheless does listen to proposals for alternative interpretations from all sources. In the final analysis, however, the Office for Descriptive Cataloging Policy must serve LC. The rest of us are free to differ and depart from its practice.

Standards must be understood by all professionals, not only the ones who sit on the committees or implement the decisions. All professionals are affected by these decisions, directly or indirectly, yet few of them make an effort to participate in the processes or even to make themselves aware of what is happening. The successful battle waged by the research libraries over microform cataloging should be ample demonstration of the possible successes that concerted efforts can bring to a determined, cohesive group with leverage within the standards establishment. If you do not choose to enter the game, you can still be a knowledgeable observer, prepared for upcoming moves by following the meetings of these standards-making bodies. You can be a kibitzer, as it were, of cataloging evolution.

ACQUIRING THE SKILLS FOR AN AUTOMATED INTEGRATED CATALOG ENVIRONMENT

This chapter has outlined four kinds of skills needed for adopting an automated, integrated catalog: computer literacy, system literacy, understanding of the dynamics of publicand technical service operations and management, and appreciation of the application and ongoing development of *AACR2*, MARC, and ISBD. How shall members of library staffs acquire them, without dropping their work responsibilities and going back to school? First, it should be recognized that for some staff members, going back to school part-time might be the best way to obtain the high levels of these skills necessary for planning and executing an automated catalog project without outside help. Not everyone, however, needs to be a programmer or a system designer in order to understand, evaluate, and work comfortably and effectively with computers. There are a number of ways such educational programs can be organized in addition to the traditional college or university course work, including in-house training, *ad hoc* workshops or institutes, personnel exchanges, and training programs sponsored by hardware and software vendors as well as special minicourses at local institutions, designed for non-matriculants desiring specific knowledge. How may each method contribute to a total effort to acquire the skills needed for working with available systems?

In-House Training

Many libraries use in-house training as a means of satisfying calls for staff development or transmitting news about new policies or equipment. This is usually nothing more than a meeting or demonstration. But in-house training is also a way to develop new skills that are not used immediately in a particular job, as well as a way to encourage interest in aspects of the library outside of one's own department. Both of these things—new skills and interest in other departments—are important attributes in implementing automated, integrated catalogs. In-house training, if it is appropriately planned, scheduled, and directed, can accomplish a great deal.

Library-wide programs with speakers from within the staff or from outside can be used to teach general theoretical concepts in much the same way they are taught in a university lecture. Topics handled well in this manner include overall objectives of the library and policy statements designed to implement them, computer literacy, standards for bibliographic access and the process of standards development, an overview of the bibliographic utilities and other computer systems for bibliographic access, and the structure of the catalog and cataloging rules. Follow-ups in various forms reinforce the lecture experience: applying what one has learned in actual situations; discussing what has been covered in smaller groups; or explaining the concepts taught to someone else. Departmental discussion groups can reinforce the larger lecture experience, and so can a newsletter or other publication summarizing information contained in the lectures.

In-house training can provide a base of theoretical knowledge and general information necessary for understanding the purposes of the institution, its general policies, what computers are and how they work, general cataloging theory, cataloging standards, and the local catalog as an access tool. Once everyone has acquired this common base of knowledge, they are ready to move to more individualized and pragmatic types of learning experiences to which workshops, institutes, or similar one-shot, hands-on experiences are well-adapted.

Ad-hoc Workshops and Institutes

One-time workshops and institutes can provide hands-on experience in which participants can experiment in a controlled situation with the use of a particular set of procedures or equipment, under the guidance of teaching personnel. Such workshops are ideal for "trying out" computers, cataloging unfamiliar materials, or problem-solving techniques. Guidance can be quite individualized without requiring a one-to-one teacher/pupil ratio. Some of these processes, while describable in a larger lecture typical of in-house training sessions, are better understood when actually performed in a workshop situation, and repeated several times to familiarize participants with common problems likely to be encountered in a real situation.

Naturally, workshops in computer operation should be attended by all library personnel, while those concentrating on topics such as problem-solving might be attended by supervisory staff and others on cataloging might be limited to professional staff or professionals plus all technical services staff. Some staff members will need to develop all skills, while others may need only certain skills.

Workshops can be conducted by knowledgeable members of any library's staff or by outside teachers from academia, industry, or other libraries. The important things are that the objectives of each workshop must be clearly set by the receiving library, not the instructor, and the teaching skills of the instructor must be suited to the job. Sometimes system vendors, manufacturers, and nonprofit services have excellent teaching programs adaptable to the needs outlined here. Since they are likely to receive the rewards of future market development and establish good will, they may be less costly than other alternatives. Sometimes it is less effective to employ your own staff as instructors simply because they are too familiar to their colleagues. However the workshop is organized and no matter who the instructors are, the following steps should be observed:

1. Set the goals of the workshop clearly and make sure the instructors are aware of them.

2. Don't try to cover more than one subject, procedure, or operation in each workshop.

3. Ask the instructors for an outline of their teaching plan, handouts, and problems, and make sure these match your objectives.

4. Provide adequate space and time for each workshop.

5. Have enough equipment available—especially if this is a hands-on computer workshop. If you are working on cataloging, you will need copies of *AACR2*, MARC formats, etc.; for each topic, there will be a set of "props" which contribute to the learning experience.

6. Make sure the atmosphere is comfortable enough for people to ask questions without feeling threatened and that their questions are answered fully.

7. Evaluate each workshop, getting feedback from participants which is useful for designing future workshops.

Workshops and institutes offer a means of obtaining a practical application of skills in a controlled setting, far more individualized than lectures. Even workshops, however, are not sufficient to provide mastery of a skill; that requires more practice than a one-time workshop can provide. In order to master skills, a third training method, personnel exchanges, can be employed.

Personnel Exchanges

There is no substitute for practical experience with any new system to make that system become part of a person's own knowledge. Since individual libraries cannot bring in and operate various kinds of systems simply to permit their staff to become familiar with them, the next best alternative is to send one's staff members to other institutions in which the systems are already operating. As of this writing, there are few states or regions in which computer systems of various hardware and software configurations are not within reach. In some cases an exchange of personnel or a brief apprenticeship might be arranged for a period of one or two weeks to minimize the cost and time involved, provided all parties to the arrangement were willing to participate in the project on this basis. Ideally, two institutions would both send and receive staff, who would spend sufficient time in the exchange library to learn a procedure or skill already part of its normal services. If such an even exchange is not feasible, some mutually beneficial arrangement should be worked out. Receiving libraries have much to gain from personnel exchanges, even if they are made with libraries that are not as advanced technically. Teaching has rewards of its own, not the least of which can be a careful study of one's own operations as seen through the eyes of an unindoctrinated colleague.

If no exchange can be arranged, there is always the possibility of straight reimbursement or other type of payment in service, resources, or both. Sometimes state library services include training coordination and can be employed in the effort. If no other method presents itself, special grants can be sought to underwrite the program of personnel exchange for libraries willing to participate.

So far we have been discussing personnel exchanges between libraries, but frequently we do not have to go that far to find opportunities to become skilled with unfamiliar systems and procedures. Sometimes other departments in the library, university, school system, company, or municipality can provide the teaching environment sought. Naturally, the most advantageous exchange involves the least sacrifice, inconvenience, and extra work on the part of the departments or institutions that cooperate together in this effort, and provides the broadest exposure to an operating system or set of procedures to be learned.

Formal Course Work

Traditional courses taken in a local institution have several advantages. They are usually taught by competent persons, they offer a structured learning experience designed to accomplish specific goals described in the program's literature, and they may lead to an additional degree or certificate. Some people enjoy the traditional learning environment and interaction with fellow students and teachers. Traditional courses cannot teach everything, but, properly designed and executed, they can help a great deal. Here, as with other kinds of learning methods, the goals of the courses must match the goals of the students and their sponsoring agencies.

Librarians are supposed to accept an obligation to continue their professional education, just as lawyers, physicians, and other professionals do. This commitment may be overlooked by some who consider themselves overworked and underpaid. In general, however, librarians are enthusiastic about taking part in the broad range of ongoing educational experiences, which often include attendance at conferences, professional reading, and discussion with colleagues. The prospect of acquiring new skills is a powerful motivation for professionals. It is important to remember that nonprofessionals or paraprofessionals are also dedicated to their libraries and that they will be an integral part of new systems and procedures, requiring many of the same skills as their degree-holding co-workers. Thus, the discussion of course work is applicable to all library personnel.

STAFF TRAINING PROGRAMS: THREE ALTERNATIVES

What is the minimum level of expertise a staff needs to plan and implement an automated, integrated system of bibliographic access?

Every member of the staff, including the pages and maintenance personnel, needs to acquire what we have called computer literacy. They need to develop an understanding in general terms of what computers are, how they operate, and the terminology used to work with them. They need to see what computers look and sound like and the various devices whereby people communicate with them. Every member of the staff who works with the catalog, circulation, or acquisition files in the manual system needs to understand what kind of information is contained in automated systems, how it appears, and the options available for access, display, and entry. Professionals, public and technical service support staff, need to learn about cataloging standards, local, and network bibliographic data systems. All staff should know basic library goals and policies and should have practical, hands-on experience with operating computers.

The simplest way to implement such an educational program is to maximize the number of skills that can be taught in a lecture-type mode and minimize those that require smaller groups and lengthier sessions. The skills that are best taught through large lectures are computer literacy in general, general information about automating bibliographic data, cataloging standards, and local and network systems, as well as basic library goals and policies. To minimize the cost in both time and personnel, these skills could be taught by library personnel at in-house lecture sessions. If follow-ups are necessary to reinforce and elaborate on what is covered in the lectures, they could take the form of discussion groups and, even more useful because they teach still another skill, online educational packages. If a microcomputer system can be made available to the staff members who are taking part in the program, they can practice what they learn directly on the system.

Some skills, especially the hands-on experience with operating computers and knowledge of applications to bibliographic information, must be gained in workshops, or by having the opportunity to work with real systems. Some help is available from professional associations, which often schedule such workshops, and local colleges or universities, which may make such workshops available, but the least expensive way to obtain such expertise is to arrange for personnel exchanges with other institutions or departments which have already implemented computer technology in their operations. One useful method which minimizes costs is to teach a nucleus of persons who can then teach another group, continuing the process until everyone has learned first-hand how to work with an operating computer system. The system can be a microcomputer or minicomputer-based system, and may deal with any kind of data, provided it is manipulated in the same fashion as bibliographic data.

A more elaborate plan would include establishing a staff planning committee to coordinate the training program, establishing the objectives, setting up the schedules of lectures, workshops, exchanges, etc., and evaluating each part of the project. Lectures would be kept to a minimum, with interdepartmental discussion groups covering such topics as library goals and policies. Some supervisory personnel might be selected to take courses at local colleges or universities in management, computer design, programming, and applications to library operations. Several computer systems might be purchased to be used to teach computer operation, which later could be integrated into whatever systems were eventually implemented.

An ideal staff training program would include publication of a staff training newsletter, development of computer game tournaments to teach operation of the machinery, establishing leisure-time, informal communications between administration, professional, and nonprofessional staff members in addition to the planning committee, and maximizing the number of staff exchanges that could be arranged. Workshops involving travel could be subsidized, and as many staff members as possible from all levels and departments would be encouraged and supported in attending conferences, institutes, and workshops on relevant subjects.

Ideally, the public should be drawn into the automation project at the beginning of the planning process, since feedback from members of the public as well as educating them about library goals and objectives can affect the design of the systems themselves. It might be important for the library to learn what the people who use the library's bibliographic tools actually think about them. While user studies are rarely the most important component in the design of a new bibliographic access system, they certainly ought to be part of the ideas on which a design is based. And while interaction with members of the public is not strictly staff-training, for many members of the staff it can prove illuminating.

Naturally, each individual library must tailor any staff training plan to its own people, resources, budgets, and needs. Ideally, everyone in the library should be able to understand the entire operation of every system it employs. At a minimum, no technology used should be totally incomprehensible to any staff member expected to interact with it.

The impact of computers is interdepartmental. Instead of merely expediting the work of the one department for which it is being used, e.g., acquisitions, cataloging, or circulation, it can expedite the work of all departments. In libraries, there are few departments or sections which do not use bibliographic data in their daily tasks. Automating this data, therefore, can affect its use in all areas of the library. The library that anticipates the many changes possible with computers can realize much more of their potential value than the library that assumes the computer is only a substitute—faster and more sophisticated to be sure—for the manual procedure it replaces. Computers not only handle more data more quickly and more cheaply than the manual files they replace, they do it in a different way—so that anyone with the proper equipment can have access to it instantly, with all of its versatility and comprehensiveness.

In contrast to other technical improvements, which tend to do a specific task more efficiently, computers can be interfaced with other systems to increase their already enormous service potential. Connecting them to video systems, telephone systems, local or remote printing systems, etc., enables them to do jobs that were previously unimaginable. Though conversion to computer technology requires a large investment in planning, equipment, and implementation, it can pay off in the accomplishment of much more than manual alternatives, and new capabilities are continually being developed. Thus, automation challenges traditional concepts of service even while it executes them with new speed and accuracy.

In order to use automation to support traditional services as well as to develop new services, library staff members need a broader and deeper base of knowledge than ever before. They need to have a clear picture of what they are trying to accomplish and how the systems are supposed to help them do it. They also need to have imagination, flexibility, and adaptability to take advantage of their system's potential. All of these take time, effort, and money to develop, but can provide great benefits to the public in the long run.

NOTES

1. "Any source" in cataloger's terms usually refers to accompanying materials such as nonintegral packages, data sheets from producers, distributors, etc., or information from reference tools.

2. IFLA, *ISBD(NBM): International Standard Bibliographic Description for Non-Book Materials* (London: IFLA International Office for UBC, 1977), pp. 54-55.

3. "USA Standard for a Format for Bibliographic Information Interchange on Magnetic Tape," *Journal of Library Automation*, 2 (June 1969), pp. 53-65 plus two Appendixes, pp. 66-95.

4. Michael Gorman, "International Standard Bibliographic Description and the New ISBDs," *Journal of Librarianship*, 10 (April 1978), pp. 132-33.

5. Among the outside groups permitted to have a formal relationship to CC:DA are special interest groups such as those for law, theology, art, Asian studies, recorded sound, research libraries, social sciences, medicine, Middle Eastern studies, music, nonbook materials, and archives, as well as such general and/or national organizations as the bibliographic utilities (only OCLC and RLIN), the Library of Congress, and the Special Libraries Association. This listing is not exhaustive.

RECOMMENDED READING

Bibliographic Rules and Standards

Alley, Brian, and Jennifer Cargill, "Getting Hooked on Standards," *Technicalities*, 4 (January 1984), p. 1.

Attig, John C. "The Concept of a MARC Format," *Information Technology & Libraries*, 2 (March 1983), pp. 7-17.

Hagler, Ronald, and Peter Simmons. *The Bibliographic Record and Information Technology*. Chicago: American Library Association, 1982.

Intner, Sheila S. "Reader's Soapbox: On Being Prepared," *Technicalities*, 4 (January 1984), pp. 13-14.

Computers and Computer Literacy

Aveney, Brian. "Online Catalogs: The Transformation Continues," *Wilson Library Bulletin*, 58 (February 1984), pp. 406-10.

Fayen, Emily G. *The Online Catalog: Improving Public Access to Library Materials.* White Plains, N.Y.: Knowledge Industry Publications, 1983.

Lancaster, F.W. *Libraries and Librarians in an Age of Electronics.* Arlington, Va.: Information Resources Press, 1982.

Magrath, Lynn L. "Computers in the Library: The Human Element," *Information Technology & Libraries,* 1 (September 1983), pp. 266-70.

Saffady, William. *Introduction to Automation for Librarians.* Chicago: American Library Association, 1983.

System Literacy

Boss, Richard W. *The Library Manager's Guide to Automation,* 2nd ed. White Plains, N.Y.: Knowledge Industry Publications, 1983.

Corbin, John. *Developing Computer-Based Library Systems* Phoenix: Oryx Press, 1981.

Durbin, Hugh. "Going On-Line With a Computerized Library Network," *The Book Report,* 1 (September-October 1982), pp. 34-36.

Epstein, Susan Baerg. "Systems, Automation and Libraries," *Library Journal,* 108 (January 1983-).

Genaway, David C. *Integrated Online Library Systems: Principles, Planning & Implementation.* White Plains, N.Y.: Knowledge Industry Publications, 1984.

Matthews, Joseph R. *A Reader on Choosing an Automated Library System.* Chicago: American Library Association, 1983.

Organizational Change

Bearman, Toni Carbo. "The Changing Role of the Information Professional and Its Implications for Library and Information Science Education," *Education for Information Management: Directions for the Future,* ed. Eric H. Boehm and Michael K. Buckland. Santa Barbara, Calif.: International Academy at Santa Barbara, 1983, pp. 19-22.

Conroy, Barbara. *Library Staff Development and Continuing Education: Principles and Practices.* Littleton, Colo.: Libraries Unlimited, 1978.

———. "People Networks: A System for Library Change?" *Journal of Library Administration*, 4 (Summer 1983), pp. 75-88.

Dowlin, Kenneth. *The Electronic Library: The Promise and the Process.* New York: Neal-Schuman, 1983.

Person, Ruth J., ed. *The Management Process: A Selection of Readings for Librarians.* Chicago: American Library Association, 1983.

Chapter 8

Integrating Catalogs

THE steps necessary for integrating the public catalog will vary, depending on the physical form of the catalog itself. Catalogs may be manually prepared and maintained,[1] e.g., card catalogs in which the cards are obtained through in-house original cataloging and/or Library of Congress printed catalog cards; computer-assisted catalogs, i.e., card catalogs where the cataloging is done on an OCLC terminal but the cataloging product is still a card filed manually into a card catalog; and online catalogs. COM catalogs are an unusual hybrid, being both computer-assisted and computer-maintained, but not online. As offline systems, COM catalogs will be included in the section on computer assisted catalogs rather than with online, interactive systems.

Products of the various systems will then be considered. For computer-based catalogs, these products represent opportunities for added services to staff and users, as well as methods of increasing the visibility of bibliographic services to the library's public as a justification for the added expenditures that these changes will inevitably cost. No one reading this book should contemplate automation as a way to accomplish services identical to those their manual systems currently provide. On the other hand, one cannot ignore the possibility for new and increased service available even without automating the catalog.

The ideas presented here are not exhaustive, but rather are intended to outline the kinds of new directions, services, and products that become possible and cost-effective with integrated catalogs. Readers will certainly find their own uses for the information and will invent products to solve their own particular problems or needs. The assumption with which this chapter begins is that a commitment has been made to include *all* holdings of the agency in one public catalog, regardless of its form.

ADMINISTRATIVE DECISIONS

A number of administrative decisions must be made prior to any change in procedures. Each agency must make the choices suitable for its situation, based on an assessment of the number of items it holds, its annual budget, and the size and knowledge level of its staff.

A basic decision is whether old records for items already held will be altered or updated, or whether the integration will apply only to new items added to the collections. One of the factors that should govern the decision is the rate of turnover of the collections. If, for example, much of the nonprint material is likely to remain in the agency's holdings for many years, e.g. if they are oral history tapes, well-protected musical or literary recordings, films, local history photographs, videodisks, or other materials of lasting value which the library expects to restore or replace as necessary, then new records should be made for the integrated catalog representing these items. If, on the other hand, most of the material is of current interest only, e.g. popular records or laboratory slides geared to a particular syllabus, it might be less important to recatalog these items. Also, children's circulating collections often have a rapid rate of turnover so that within a few years all new items fill the shelves. In such a case, changing the catalog records for the old items might be avoided.

It would be a mistake, however, not to convert to the new bibliographic format records for items that are likely both to remain in the collections for long periods and to relate to new materials being cataloged in the integrated format. Thus, if a library has a collection of documentary films on American presidents and begins cataloging the new acquisitions for the integrated public catalog, it would be a grave error not to update the cataloging for the rest of the films so records for all of the series, subject, or genre could be found in one catalog. Lest someone suggest as an alternative that the new items continue to be treated in the old way, it should be emphasized that these are precisely the kinds of materials for which access should be improved and made fast and easy, not the reverse.

The decision to convert cataloging for materials already held will depend, then, on what the materials are, whether or not they may be expected to remain on the shelves, and whether or not they are part of a developing collection to which improved access would be desirable. Furthermore, if the nonprint collections currently held are not very large, it may be easier to convert the whole nonprint catalog than to try to maintain two systems. Indeed, as a rule of thumb, it is more costly to maintain two systems with different rules and procedures than to integrate processes. For one thing, staff must learn both systems, which often requires two searches instead of one. Secondly, the more rules people have to remember, the more likely they are to make errors. Thirdly, as time passes, the old system becomes more troublesome to maintain as well as to use.

The second administrative decision to be made is the application of any or all GMDs in the cataloging records. One method of identifying nonprint materials is to use GMDs for all records except those for books and printed serials. It is far superior to color coding, using alphanumeric codes in the call number or similar methods for alerting users quickly as to the nature of the material being represented by the card (or book entry) they are looking at. The limits of color-coding make it unsuitable for collections with many varieties of media. *AACR2* lists 24 GMDs, making quite a rainbow if all of them are collected. Another drawback to color-coding is the possibility that it will be done in a less than professional manner, with less than professional looks and quality controls.

GMDs are also better than alpha, numeric, or alphanumerically coded call numbers. Call numbers are hard enough to remember, with many Dewey and LC numbers containing six or more characters. Nonstandard classification systems are even more confusing. The amount of space allotted to call numbers in most entries, whether in card or book formats, is not really well adapted to nine- or ten-character words like microfiche or videotape, and microcomputer software would simply be out of the question whether you opted for "machine-readable data file" à la *AACR2* or some shorter version such as "machine-readable" or "computer software."

Using GMDs also has the advantage of conforming to *AACR2* and MARC format standards, so that if and when conversion to machine-readable records becomes feasible, no added translation is required. The GMD can be encoded along with all the other elements of the bibliographic description, demanding no special attention. When patrons use the entry, they will read the medium immediately after the title, e.g. "Swan Lake [sound recording]" or "Swan Lake [music]" or "Swan Lake [videorecording]," enabling them to select the medium that suits their needs. If GMDs are not used, there is certainly more chance for confusion and frustration when patrons discover and decipher the color code, call number code, or less obvious physical description information.

Although there is something to be said for using the GMD "text" in book and printed serial entries, too, the addition of this GMD in the majority of traditional libraries where the great bulk of collections consist of books and periodicals would add much more keystroking without giving much more service. In most traditional libraries, patrons expect to find books on shelves and catalog entries for books in the catalog. They tend to be surprised at finding other kinds of materials in different media. Libraries and media centers whose collections contain less book stock and more media, however, might have much to gain from applying "text" to catalog entries for books and journals. In fact, it might well be that print items were the isolates, not their nonprint counterparts, and they are the entries that need integrating with the rest of the holdings. In any case, the GMD should be employed to alert users to the kind of material they have found and if they expect only films or tapes they may be frustrated if they are met with a book. If, however, the collections follow more traditional, print-biased paths, and books are expected, then films and tapes, etc., need to be identified.

Another administrative judgment governs the choice of classification and shelf arrangement given to nonprint items. There is no need to follow the same shelving system employed for books, to which many venerable catalogs containing both Dewey and LC classification numbers will testify. However, the call number must fit into the physical and intellectual format allotted for it. Accession number schemes might become unwieldy. Lack of any call numbers for nonprint might confuse them with fiction, which also often lacks call numbers and is shelved in alphabetical order by author's last name. To be sure, many libraries use "Fic" or "F" to designate fiction, preferring this to the number for current fiction from the classification scheme used, but many more simply have no indication of the location at all. In the library where I worked for seven years, fiction had no call numbers, while sound recordings were given either modified Dewey numbers (if they contained spoken material) or a unique modification of the M schedule in LC classification (if they contained music). Few patrons could understand or remember either scheme, and a great deal of explaining was necessary for people who thought scores were libretti, or recordings, or books.

Subject headings and main and added entries for nonprint materials will have to conform to the standards set for books. This is not a matter of choice, but necessity. The choice may be made on how to establish and control the conformity. Libraries which may have used nonstandard subject headings or omitted subject headings for media will have to change to standard subject heading lists or thesauri. It would certainly be a mistake to continue omitting subject headings for "nonfiction" media, though a case could be made for treating "popular" music as if it were fiction. The Library of Congress subject heading for popular vocal music, "Music, Popular (Songs, etc.)" seems about as useful as "Fiction" for novels. The fact that little retrospective recataloging is done in manual catalogs would also imply that even as LC is creating new and better headings it might be years before they made an impact on users. Indeed, eventually the old items would probably never be accessed by the earlier subject heading once the new headings were well-established. Whether or not "Music, Popular (Songs, etc.)" is used in the integrated catalog, the library will need to adapt its subject authority system for such decisions to include documentation for nonprint forms. Name authority files will also need attention and expansion to include personal and corporate name headings for nonprint media. Some libraries have been avoiding the issue, relying on their cataloging source for authority work. While they may still do this, their trust may be ill-placed, even for printed works only.

It would seem a matter of urgency in every case for individual libraries to maintain their own authority files and a method of documenting subject heading list decisions. Since local libraries often do not follow LC's changes or decide to follow local or regional practices, it would seem more important for them to keep track of what they are doing than it does for libraries which elect to follow national standards quite strictly and can rely on published sources for resolution of problems.

Administrative planning for the integrated catalog needs to include a review of how current separate cataloging is budgeted and accomplished; and funds need to be reallocated to reflect and support new integrated procedures. It would certainly seem counterproductive to continue obtaining cataloging from two different sources or departments and leave the job of integrating them to the unlucky filer or someone else who cannot control the creation of bibliographic records. For institutions where cataloging is all generated centrally and simply displayed separately, this will not be a problem, but in most cases the origin of records as well as their disposition tends to be separated. This will be discussed at greater length later in this chapter.

Finally, some attention should be paid to the kind of end products the institution wants to create in both the long and short run. Will they be satisfied with a single, centralized catalog or do they wish to have many catalog units available in multiple locations? If there are no funds for automating immediately, how much preparatory work might be done for the future as records are processed for an integrated catalog? If the current public catalog contains several kinds of catalog treatments, how much uniformity could be achieved? In other words, how much work is required to create a standard uniform catalog now, and what percentage of this work can be addressed while integrating the nonprint collections into it? What kinds of catalogs would be desirable in the future and how much preparatory work could be incorporated with the integration project? Here is an opportunity to review what needs to be done and, possibly, kill two (or more) birds with one stone.

Manual catalogs, and how they can be integrated, will be examined first.

INTEGRATING MANUAL CATALOGS

Today, most of our manual public catalogs are in card form, with book catalogs a very small minority. Totally manual card catalogs, i.e., those that do not obtain their cataloging from OCLC or another network or utility, have a limited number of options for obtaining cards. They may produce them themselves and undoubtedly do this for at least some items; they may purchase materials with catalog cards from a commercial or nonprofit source; or they may purchase cards separately from a commercial or nonprofit source. For new materials, the library might simply continue its traditional method of obtaining cards but obtain them for its nonprint materials as well as its print materials. If the card source produces standardized uniform cataloging according to current rules and standards, the number of items for which cataloging would have to be created "from scratch" would probably be relatively small. Some items, such as computer software packages, are not cataloged by the Library of Congress or any of the bibliographic utilities. Such cataloging as might be produced for them is nonstandard at the time of this writing. Standards are being developed, however, so the situation will change for the better in the very near future.

For materials already held and cataloged in nonstandard ways, new entries will have to be created. A library might opt to change only the access points, leaving the bibliographic descriptions as they were. If the previous nonprint cataloging was in card form, some proportion of the entries will not need to be transcribed onto cards, but access points—subject headings, main and added entries—may need to be added, altered, or deleted.

Calculating the magnitude of the task from a sampling of cards should be the first step of the project. If the previous cataloging was not in card form, the sample of entries will require addition of the estimates of the transcription to cards needed in addition to new cataloging. A random sample of existing cataloging for items in each medium, collection, and possibly even in each subject area, totalling no more than five percent of the holdings, should provide a relatively accurate guess of the number of new entries and/or new cards needed. This figure, in turn, has to be translated into a total amount in dollars and staff hours needed to produce this number of cards. Even though the dollar and time figures derived from the sample may be startling, they should not be disheartening. There is no need to do the retrospective conversion overnight. It is necessary, however, to consider methods of allocating funds and personnel over a short planning period, perhaps two or three years and certainly not more than five years, during which the bulk of the job can be accomplished for those parts of the collections which are expected to remain active. In this endeavor, even the least resource-rich have options:

1. Newer, standardized cataloging may be available for these titles from the Library of Congress.

2. Newer, standardized cataloging may be available from currently active commercial vendors or such nonprofit centers as the National Information Center for Educational Media in California for a fee.

3. Regional networks or other local groups may be able to provide the cataloging through regional catalogs.

4. Local groups may be interested in joining together to obtain cataloging for themselves, too, from an outside source.

5. A state library may be able to provide assistance through statewide union catalogs or state-level networking.

6. Local, i.e., countywide or statewide professional associations may be interested in assisting or coordinating a "from scratch" project, if other avenues fail to turn up sources of existing acceptable cataloging at reasonable fees.

An important point to remember is that no library is so small or isolated that it cannot successfully avail itself of the many opportunities for cooperative action to achieve its ends; nor is any library so large that a rational plan cannot be drawn to accomplish desired objectives if they are clearly justified and accorded appropriate priorities. Small libraries may believe they have so little money and so few trained staff that they cannot undertake to upgrade their catalogs. Large libraries often feel that the size of their collections precludes doing anything about them. Both ideas are faulty. Small libraries may, indeed, have to create liaisons with others who can benefit, too, from their joint activity. They will have to reach out of isolation and communicate with their local, regional, and state colleagues. They may have to work more slowly, perhaps, because of their limited resources, but they can console themselves that the task is not so formidable. Large libraries, on the other hand, usually have more and better-trained staff as well as larger overall budgets which can provide greater flexibility for absorbing the costs and labor of such a job. They often have more contact with and are located nearer to more information agencies as well as more professional resources and people, making cooperative activity much easier. Furthermore, they often have access to or justification for having more sources of standardized cataloging and need to review the disposition of material coming from these sources, rather than having to develop standardized sources from nothing.

Each library, having sampled its existing records and calculated the work to be done, must create a viable plan for obtaining standard cataloging and transferring the information onto usable cards. These may turn out to be a single operation, or they may require two steps, depending on the sources. At the same time, the supply of standard catalog cards for new purchases will have to be figured into the task of maintaining the integrated public card catalog. Of course, there will no longer be a need to maintain separate AV or nonprint catalogs, releasing the resources previously devoted to it for the integrated catalog.

The next step is to review existing procedures which supported maintenance of two or more catalogs and decide on the changes to be made for maintenance of an integrated catalog. If the library has a written manual of procedures, it will need to be analyzed and revised; if not, this may be an opportunity to start such a manual. In either case, new procedures should be designed and codified with the participation and assistance of all appropriate staff. As mentioned earlier, imposing new job responsibilities without fostering a spirit of participation and cooperation can result in resentment or even deliberate or accidental sabotage. In my experience, the level of tension between professional, paraprofessional, and clerical staff, and administrative, supervisory and nonmanagerial staff depends upon the organizational structure and personalities within each institution. These relationships contain the potential for facilitating or undermining change in the institution. I would recommend an investment in participatory management regarding the implementation of integrated cataloging procedures.

Every institution, large or small, will need to evaluate the new procedures fairly soon after implementation to insure that they are working smoothly and are not creating unforeseen problems in other departments. If problems do exist within the new catalog maintenance operation they will need resolution. If the new procedures create problems with other operations, i.e., at the interfaces with other departments or functions, then a somewhat larger effort may be necessary to address the problems. Needless to say, interdepartmental tensions, like interpersonal or interprofessional tensions, have the potential to confound change and require consideration in plans for change.

Some differences in the process of integrating the catalog should be considered if the manual public catalog is in book form rather than card form. Book catalogs may be prepared in-house, or by sending library-prepared cataloging to an outside printer, or by using an outside service for obtaining both the bibliographic information and the book itself. If the book is prepared entirely in-house, procedures for its production will need to be changed to include the larger job of adding nonprint entries. A large factor will be the kind of nonprint cataloging previously provided, e.g., if it, too, was produced in book form by the same process, or if it was in a different display format. If retrospective conversion of old, nonintegrated cataloging is done at once, this may simply be a one-time extraordinary effort, after which incorporation of all entries for all media will proceed with relatively minor changes to the process. If, however, retrospective conversion is done piecemeal, the task will have to be analyzed in terms of reorganizing book production schedules over time, adding a portion of nonprint holdings each time a new edition is produced. Whatever disposition is made of cataloging for works added to the holdings between editions of the book catalog—whether in the form of supplements, accession lists, card files, or whatever—it, too, will need to be expanded to include nonprint materials.

Depending on the process employed for producing the book and previous nonprint catalogs, the job of interfiling new entries may be relatively easier or more difficult, and may require redoing the entire book, page by page, or only part of it. If a book is assembled on the model of *Phonolog*, for example, where space for future entries or expansion of particular areas is built into the work, not all existing pages would need to be changed, though new pages would need to be inserted while others would need to be redone. If, however, the book follows the model of *National Union Catalog*, every single page would have to be redone. This estimate of relative effort depends on more than the production process, because it would also be affected by the relative number of book and nonprint entries and the organization of the book into a single alphabet or sections for authors, titles, and subjects.

Assuming the book catalog is produced outside the library, similar factors will govern the work involved in and therefore the cost of creating an integrated book catalog:

1. the production process

2. the organization of the book into one alphabet or several

3. the relative number of print and nonprint entries

4. the previous nonprint cataloging

One can imagine a scenario in which an externally produced book catalog for all media together would be less costly than several media-specific book catalogs, because everything can be done in a single run, and price is geared to the total number of entries or pages involved. This might also be true of an internally produced book catalog.

The source of standardized print and nonprint bibliographic data and whether it has been the responsibility of the library or someone else, such as a vendor who produces the book for the library, to prepare it, is much the same problem for book catalogs as for card catalogs. If the previous nonprint cataloging was nonstandard, upgrading is necessary and, for book catalogs, might require more than changing access points.

If a vendor supplies all information and it is all standard, the library could face lower costs or, at least, fewer headaches. The library could opt to continue getting separate catalogs *and add a unified integrated catalog* at slightly greater cost, since bibliographic service to patrons would be much more flexible this way. If an either-or choice has to be made, this author is clearly in favor of the integrated catalog. Depending on the relative sizes of the tomes, an integrated catalog plus *some* spinoff single-medium catalogs might be made for media other than books which attract special users, e.g., films, slides, computer software, etc.

If the previous cataloging was library-prepared and standardized, except for headings, a minimum of alteration would be required, but a systematic estimate of the work involved and plans to do it must be made as for upgrading cards. If the library is responsible for the data and retrospective conversion is necessary, sources of standardized data, estimates of the magnitude of the job, and plans for its execution must be made.

The last possibility is that the existing data are nonstandard and vendor-supplied. In this instance, if the vendor cannot provide standardized data, it is best to seek one that can. There are a great many vendors that can produce a standard product, and there are state and regional networks and district or county processing centers that are committed to existing cataloging standards. If you cannot switch, then consider fighting with your source to adopt standards and mobilize the vendor's other customers to demand the same quality. If the only saving you get from this vendor is received at the expense of standardized cataloging, it is a small saving indeed. It may well prove to be much more costly in terms of the limits on cooperative activity it places on your library and your ability to serve your public through interloan and other resource-sharing programs. Eventually, if you wish to become part of any machine-based network or program, your cataloging will have to be upgraded to standard quality in order for the data to be made accessible.

INTEGRATING COMPUTER-ASSISTED MANUAL CATALOGS

Computer-assisted manual catalogs are defined here as card, book, and/or COM catalogs that are either manually maintained or, even if they are maintained through machine manipulation, are offline and whose users are not interactive with a realtime processing system. In effect, to the catalog user, the computer is not a visible part of the system. Users still search for cards in drawers or pages in a book or images on fiche or film. Perhaps a clearer definition would be catalogs which are not accessed by means of a computer, differentiating them from online interactive catalog systems.

The differences in integrating a computer-assisted catalog are closely related to methods for creating machine-readable databases and have less emphasis on the quality (or lack of it) in the original records. Of far greater importance is whether or not these records can be converted to machine-readable form with ease. One factor in this determination is the type of computer assistance the catalog employs. The most frequently encountered is the card catalog whose cards are obtained through a bibliographic utility, e.g. OCLC. A library in this situation can obtain cards of equal quality to its entries for books by matching its old records or, if they are problematic to work with, the items in their holdings, with the nonprint entries in the OCLC or other utility's database in the same manner as any other retrospective conversion of holdings in print form. (OCLC even offers a special rate for retrospective conversion.) Entries that can be found in the database are presumed to be cataloged accurately and need only be edited for minor variations such as local call numbers, access points, and local notes. Entries that do not already exist in the database will require manual entry into the system and, for this group of items, the previous cataloging will have to be upgraded to *AACR2*-MARC format. Once again, a sampling of the holdings and estimate of how many are found online, how much editing they need to be acceptable, and how many items are not online and require full original cataloging, is important to determine the size of the job to be done. One approach might be to integrate immediately those holdings for which entries already exist and to recatalog over time those not found in the database. Though there are several studies by libraries of the proportion of entries found online in various bibliographic utilities, they are focused on newer materials and limited to books. Thus, no helpful hints can be gleaned from previous experiences in retrospective conversion to be applied to older, nonprint materials.

If the computer-assisted book or COM catalog is produced entirely by the library itself and there is no larger database from which existing nonprint cataloging can be derived, all existing non-machine-readable records will have to be converted to the format and quality of the library's choice. Integration of the nonprint entries with others in final form, whether book or COM, will have to be delayed until a cumulation of additions is made. A sampling of the holdings is necessary to estimate what kind of work is involved in the conversion and whether it can be done all at once or in smaller segments.

It is likely that the library contracts with an outside supplier to produce a computer-assisted book or COM catalog. The library may be responsible for providing the cataloging to the COM vendor or book publisher, though there are many vendors who supply the cataloging as well. A library responsible for giving the bibliographic data to a vendor or publisher needs to consider the magnitude of the recataloging project exactly as those with totally manual catalogs do. Others who purchase both cataloging data and the final product for its display may be able to purchase cataloging for any nonprint materials available in the vendor's database; while conversion of items not in the vendor's database may be obtained only at a much higher cost. The question of cost might well dissuade a library from including older materials in the integrated catalog at all, although it would certainly depend on the vendor, the materials, and the library. The point is that the library has little control over the decision, though it may choose to seek other vendors to accommodate its needs. Otherwise, they may have to settle for continuing with only a partially integrated catalog. Libraries may find vendors willing to perform retrospective conversions relatively cheaply using previous cataloging. The price for such a job should be carefully considered against the cost of doing it "from scratch" or doing without the data in the main catalog.

INTEGRATING ONLINE CATALOGS

There are, as of this writing, very few online public access catalogs in operation in libraries across the nation. Those that do exist represent a fairly broad range of systems, making it difficult to generalize about integrating them. One advantage of the online mode is that unlike other machine-assisted catalog formats, once the cataloging data have been converted to machine-readable form, the job is done. The computer can be expected to perform other operations necessary to create and reorganize end products desired, the first and foremost being, of course, the database itself.

A library has two basic choices in converting cataloging to machine-readable form: doing it manually, i.e., keying in all the data for each entry one at a time, or finding a way to employ another automated system to capture the data all at once and transfer it directly to its own database. If the online catalog is based on archival magnetic tapes such as those derived from OCLC, then the OCLC database can be the source of a proportion of machine-readable cataloging for the nonprint holdings. Even if the online catalog database was originally created entirely by keying in entries one by one, it does not mean that new programs couldn't be used to enter the nonprint data another way. The nonprint cataloging could be purchased in machine-readable form from a vendor or other cataloging service and dumped automatically into the online catalog by means of an interfacing program. If the Library of Congress MARC tapes for audiovisual materials and sound recordings contain a sizable proportion of entries for the library's holdings, they could be purchased and loaded into the system to be matched against previous catalog records for nonprint. Unused entries could be stripped off after the conversion was complete. Remaining holdings would then need to be keyed in manually.

In this mode, as in all others, a sampling of the nonprint holdings should be used to estimate the amount of work to be done in recataloging and conversion, particularly to test the value of outside sources of machine-readable cataloging for the nonprint items to be converted. If one hundred randomly selected items are matched against two different source databases and fifty items match in the first, while in the second seventy-five items match, the second database would appear to be the best selection, unless there was another reason for choosing the first.

Manual keying of nonprint entries, while likely to be more expensive than automated methods, is also an option. Once again, enlisting the support of other libraries that may contemplate moving to an integrated online catalog, too, is always a means to distribute either the cost or the work (or both) of such a project. It could serve as a focal point for efforts to share materials or form a local network. Other institutions in the area may have machine-readable databases used for circulation or reference functions which already contain bibliographic records for nonprint materials and could be used to facilitate the conversion. A word of caution, however, in the use of databases not designed for use as catalogs or cataloging support: Conversion to nonstandard entry formats, while putting the data into machine-readable form, may not serve the purpose of the library using the database as a public catalog. Thus, before "borrowing" a database to use as a source for conversion purposes, the entry format should be carefully scrutinized to be sure larger problems of nonstandard cataloging are not created.

Each library must evaluate both the state of its previous print and nonprint cataloging and its plans for the future when contemplating integration of several public catalogs into a single display with newly purchased materials. Such a change requires a careful analysis of the time and money as well as the processes and work flow employed in cataloging print and nonprint separately and, with the aid of all staff members concerned, devising an appropriate method of incorporating them into one unit. If the print cataloging is the larger, more standardized process, it should become the model for the integrated cataloging system. In the less likely event that the nonprint cataloging operation is the larger or more standard one, then that should be the model for the integrated system. If neither system produces standard quality cataloging, than a totally new process that would provide standard entries for print, too, should be established.

Retrospective conversion is more difficult to perform, especially if the collections are already quite large; if the previous cataloging is seriously substandard; if the library does not have control over the production of its catalog; and if the lack of budget or staff does not permit enough flexibility to work off the backlog with ease. Exchange of staff, reallocation of funds, retraining staff, and restructuring procedures are not simple, but they do not require the same kind of measures called for in undertaking a large retrospective recataloging. When all the factors contributing to a greater or lesser problem with retrospective conversion are negative, it might be best to accept partial conversion unless sufficient resources can be mustered to tackle the job properly and produce a catalog of standard quality.

In order to plan for integrated cataloging, a review of the current situation is in order. Is cataloging for print and nonprint materials done by different staff members? Do different departments have authority over and responsibility for cataloging different media? Are different media cataloged by different rules? Is a different kind of catalog produced for print and nonprint materials? If the answer to any of these questions is yes, a restructuring is necessary to unify the cataloging process for all materials. It is not necessarily bad for different staff members to catalog different media, but they must use the same rules and tools to produce integrable products. Authority over all cataloging should reside in a single department and in all but the largest of libraries it would be difficult to make a case for specialization to such a degree that it cannot be united. Administrative reorganization would have to unite fragmented authority and responsibility, prescribe one set of rules based on one set of tools, and produce the same kind of bibliographic product for all materials. A careful look at budget allocations by department and by medium will enable identification to be made of the dollars spent on separate cataloging processes, staff, and resources. A similar study of departmental staff deployment should permit similar identification of person-hours spent in the separate processes. Planners and administrators need to create a unified structure for the integration of all cataloging and an appropriate reallocation of funds.

PRODUCTS OF INTEGRATED SYSTEMS

The principal product of an integrated cataloging system is the new public catalog containing entries for all holdings in all media filed together in a single display. When a library user approaches such a display, there is no need to choose what type of work is desired. All works of an author, editions of a title, and works on a subject are collocated as well as identified in the catalog. There is no need to wonder if nonprint versions of works originally issued as books or other printed items are owned by the library but not indicated in the public catalog, or to make several trips to various different catalogs to locate all the information on a desired topic which might be available in the library. Whether the multimedia approach is intended or not, the catalog has the information to satisfy inquiries of all types, with the GMD providing a means to file identical titles in different media by logical means. If no GMD is used for books or other printed versions of a work, these would file first, preceding all nontextual media. Thus, the person seeking only books would not need to look beyond the first set of entries without GMDs to determine desired holdings. If any version of a work could satisfy a patron's inquiry, the catalog would present all possibilities, not only books.

The catalog is the most important tool the library creates for its public. It is not the only one, however, and one can imagine a number of spinoff products that the integration of print and nonprint cataloging would enable libraries to provide. The following section explores a number of possibilities but is by no means exhaustive. Although many of these products could be created from manual catalogs, computer-assisted or online catalogs enable them to be realized with minimal cost or effort. Computer assistance in the cataloging process may be a prerequisite for them.

Bibliographies. It should not be difficult to program a computerized catalog system to produce a series of individualized bibliographies for patrons. If an online catalog is augmented by a printer and/or a CRT terminal, whatever appears on the screen can be printed out simultaneously to produce whatever list of entries the patron has requested. One of the time-consuming parts of a manual search in a card or book catalog is the laborious copying of all relevant materials retrieved—even if the information is abbreviated. An online catalog with printer attached would allow all entries retrieved to be printed, with call numbers and full or partial bibliographic information depending on the request and capabilities of the system. The hard copy could then be taken to the stacks by the patron for reference or used for consultation after leaving the library. If materials of different media were not intershelved, which is the most common library practice, patrons could use the printout/bibliography of relevant citations in *all* media to compare each item actually found on the shelves with other possibilities in other stack areas, buildings, or departments. The importance of such a "mini"-bibliography in hard copy for patron use cannot be overemphasized. Individualized subject bibliographies, especially of materials available from the library's own holdings, could aid staff as well as patrons.

Larger bibliographies, more time-consuming to print even from a computer, might be prepared for special uses or special audiences, e.g., for distribution to schools, senior citizen centers, other community organizations, businesses, etc. Printouts of large-type holdings plus recorded literature could be useful to those with impaired vision. Teachers might want to direct students to specific nonprint items that coordinate with plays or novels they are studying. Consumer education groups might want listings of consumer information in periodicals, on videotape, or in recorded broadcasts, or any other form. The multimedia approach eliminates the need to search in many places for material on a particular subject and does not prevent fulfilling media-specific requests.

Acquisition lists. A list of the newest additions to the library's holdings could easily become a spinoff product of a computerized integrated catalog. With proper programming, the list could be permuted by author, subject, medium, audience level, or other desired elements. Acquisition lists can be sent to faculty in school and academic libraries as well as being prominently displayed in public libraries or other outlets. It is a common practice to notify selectors in academic libraries that materials they requested have arrived, but all types of libraries could provide a useful service by informing patrons of newly acquired materials in their special interest areas, i.e., selective dissemination of information (SDI). Public libraries have done little in this area, perhaps assuming that their users are too diverse to be served in this manner. Specialized lists, by subject, literary genre, medium, or audience level would certainly give more useful information to many patrons of college or public libraries. To these lists might be added a request form for desired items and other information, saving time and expediting the processes of document delivery. Having all media integrated into acquisition lists enables someone interested in opera, or architecture, or cell biology to be informed of the extremely important nonbook materials related to their field—musical scores, sound recordings, drawings, photographs, slides, videotapes, and so on.

Reference staff, usually well-informed about current book acquisitions, are often unaware of other new materials acquired, even if they pass through the same ordering and cataloging processes. Integrated acquisition lists would provide familiarity with these holdings, too, especially if they are not shelved with books. Subject specialists would not have to check in several places to discover what new holdings had been added in their field and might be made more aware of alternatives to books for their work with the public. Library users, once introduced to media collections, may discover new dimensions of information and enjoyment. The computer-produced integrated acquisition lists can serve reference staff, too, as instant bibliographies of the newest items in various fields.

Flexible catalogs. With an integrated bibliographic database, every department of a library could offer several public catalogs to their users, saving them the time required to use the whole file for every catalog search. In an online reference system, selection of the appropriate file or files to be searched is usually part of the request. For example, in OCLC searching, the format of the search key indicates to the system whether a title, author-title combination, author, or one of the unique identifier files is being requested. In RLIN searching, the user must specify the desired file—find pn Dewey, Melvil, where "pn" means "personal name." When a searcher knows which medium or date is wanted from among the various possibilities, e.g., a sound recording of Beethoven's Fifth Symphony rather than a musical score, or a recent publication of Shakespeare's works rather than an earlier edition, the computer will oblige by searching only those files or entries that satisfy the request. Just as it takes a person less time to search a smaller file, it takes the computer less time, too, and fewer duplicates will be turned up in the smaller search. In effect, the computer is ignoring the files or entries that do not satisfy the search request. An online catalog can be designed to produce all entries on a topic, or only those published/produced since 1980, or only those whose audience level is young adult, or only those on videorecordings. An online catalog, thus, can actually have many smaller, individual catalogs programmed into the public display.

It is also true, however, that the many individual catalogs together in one display constitute a "union" list of all holdings for searching. In some libraries, only the works contained in a particular department are included in that department's catalog. A patron who wants a book from the children's department, an adult book, and a microfilm might have to go to three different card files in a traditional manual card catalog; but with an integrated, online catalog, the three searches could be done at terminals in the children's department, in the adult book stacks, or in the microfilm area with equal ease. In the same way, library systems consisting of a main library and branches often have catalogs in the branches which contain only that unit's holdings. Changing to an online catalog expands information available to branch library users in such situations quite dramatically. With very little added investment in terminals and wiring, terminals can be installed within library buildings in stack areas, lounges, office areas, and other places where immediate access to bibliographic information could be extremely useful. Furthermore, including entries for materials in all media causes every use of the catalog to be more productive and each view of the holdings as "seen" through the catalog to be more unified.

Interfacing systems. As more and more people purchase home computers or have computers available where they work, the probability grows that they may be able to use the library's online catalog from their homes or offices. Schools are likely to be the prime beneficiaries of such remote access systems enabling students and teachers to search catalogs of local libraries and print bibliographies for their own purposes. Since integrating the catalog offers searchers the broadest range of materials, they are more likely to find what they want and be provided with opportunities for creative study. The catalog itself becomes the product in such a system.

Libraries in this country have been marketing their catalogs as reference products for many years, from huge, general catalogs such as the *National Union Catalog* and catalogs of great institutions such as Harvard University and the New York Public Library, to smaller, more specialized lists of resources such as the catalogs of the University of Michigan's Clements Library of Americana to 1860 and Columbia University's Avery Architectural Library.

These catalogs represent great collections, in many cases the most comprehensive or the most unusual. Catalogs of ordinary collections in most institutions are rarely thought to be of interest to anyone outside the library's patrons and staff. Nevertheless, local catalogs represent a valuable resource with the special advantage of containing materials that are readily available. If users could access the library's catalog from home cable TV sets, they might wish to subscribe to document delivery services, bibliographic services, or SDI services. Schools, public libraries, and local colleges or universities could have much to gain from the sharing of resources in the immediate vicinity, provided searching is as easy as adjusting a television set or dialing up a database.

System costs. On the surface, it would appear that it should cost no more to integrate nonprint cataloging in the main public catalog than to maintain it in separate catalogs, and once new procedures are established that may very well be true. What adds cost to the process of integrating the catalog are the planning and implementation of new cataloging procedures, the retrospective conversion of existing separate records, and, if the catalog format is changed as well, the new display medium. Considering these components one by one, we can enumerate the elements of each and the costs they entail.

The Planning Process

The prime element of cost in the planning process is staff time. Involvement of higher paid administrative and middle-management level staff is essential to successful planning, and this is the most costly factor. On the other hand, the investment in careful planning can save much more money in poor implementation later on. If new staff appointments at higher levels are made to coordinate efforts, these salaries must also be added to the total of planning-hours-times-salary for all others. The planning process also involves money spent in preparing and disseminating information in the form of policy analyses, reports, surveys, budgets, personnel allocations, and so on. Eventually, the results will have to be translated into documentation outlining the final process to be implemented. Thus, the cost of designing, typing, and duplicating preliminary materials, and later, reporting the results of meetings and planning instruments for the next step in the process must be carefully assessed.

The fundamental costs of the planning process are:

- Staff hours spent in meetings, planning sessions, and workshops

- Staff hours spent writing and preparing planning documents

- Staff hours added (for new personnel)

- Supplies for preparing and disseminating planning documents and reports

Implementing New Procedures

The two main cost elements in the implementation process are staff training and the step-by-step evaluation that should accompany it. Each adjustment to procedures as originally conceived requires follow-up evaluation to insure the original goals and objectives are being served. Developing procedural manuals might be the responsibility of a catalog coordinator or a technical services department head. It takes time and experimentation to reorganize procedures and reduce them to a step-by-step manual that any staff member can understand and follow. Manuals also require staff time to type and duplicate. Their utility will probably be a function of their design, readability, and ease of use; therefore, attention must be paid to the physical format, appearance, and execution.

The training process, designed to acquaint all library personnel with the new catalog and cataloging process, may be well served by other materials in addition to the manuals. Some of these might be adapted for patron use, too. A single coordinator or technical services head might do most of the training, or it could be divided among several people. Time spent in training and being trained both have to be counted.

Reevaluation of new procedures as they are implemented is the final step. This is difficult to estimate because it is at least partly determined by the success of initial plans, their translation into step-by-step procedures, reduction to a manual of procedures, and training. Still another factor in the need for reevaluation is the flexibility of individual staff members to accept and establish new job responsibilities and tasks.

The implementation process thus requires assessing the following elements:

- Staff hours for training, including both trainers and trainees

- Staff hours for developing procedural manuals and other training documents

- Supplies for creating new procedural manuals and training documents

- Staff hours and materials for evaluating implementation of new procedures.

Retrospective Conversion

This component is a function of three factors: the level and quality of previous cataloging, the display medium of previous cataloging, and information sources available for new integrated cataloging. It is far less important what the display medium of the new catalog will be, and though the size of the collection will dictate the total cost of retrospective conversion, the per-record cost should not be affected significantly by it, unless it is done by a vendor, whose price is geared to the number of records. The age of the collections, the kinds of media represented, and previous access policies will affect the amount of work required to upgrade old cataloging to current standards.

If the library has a shelflist with sufficient information to identify each item, and a source for current cataloging information rich in older materials, then the amount of original cataloging involved in retrospective conversion may be small, and the entire project may be relatively inexpensive. If, on the other hand, no usable cataloging already exists for previous collections, or no cataloging source is available from which standardized data for these materials can be derived, then the other options for obtaining adequate cataloging are limited to original or commercially purchased cataloging. Naturally, original cataloging is expensive, and purchased cataloging may not be much less.

The importance of the medium of previous cataloging lies in its adaptability for continued use as well as ease of upgrading. If, for example, the previous cataloging is in machine-readable form, it would be easier to upgrade than if it were in a non-computer-based book or card format. It is more likely, however, that existing cataloging is in manual form, without computer assistance. Thus, the ability to use it depends on its quality. Brief listing, perhaps with author/title or short title only, an imprint statement, and an abbreviated physical description, may be difficult to identify uniquely if passed against a large database such as OCLC or NICEM, without the item in hand. This kind of situation requires original cataloging with items in hand rather than mere upgrading of old records. In some catalogs where the materials were stored on closed shelves and the catalog merely served to index subject matter and titles of a relatively small collection, there is very little value for upgrading in the entries.

The components of cost in retrospective conversion projects have been discussed at length elsewhere.[2] Costs can be divided into materials for which cataloging in current, standardized form is readily available and materials needing original cataloging. These two kinds of materials should be considered separately. For materials that require original cataloging, the same cost elements apply as for all other original work—time devoted to intellectual work by catalogers, time devoted to execution by support staff, supplies, and tools for cataloging. For those materials being upgraded, cost elements will depend on the kind of conversion method employed and the amount of work it entails. No standard set of cost elements applies to all methods or to all cataloging.

New Display Medium

If old separate nonprint catalogs are abandoned in favor of a single public catalog display, there may be a cost differential between the old and new display medium. If, for example, the old form was a card or book catalog and the new form is online, the per-entry cost could be significantly lower in the automated catalog. Once the cost of the hardware and implementation are absorbed, the cost of entering an individual bibliographic entry is minimal. There are no added filing costs for the computer-manipulated file as there would be for card files or added book pages (to say nothing of the expense of preparing new editions).

If the new format is cards rather than a manually-produced book catalog, some savings are still likely, particularly if the cards are not typed or printed in-house but are obtained from an outside source. Integrated book catalogs where previous separate, nonprint catalogs were in card form are likely to cost more to produce, even with computer assistance. If an online catalog is not an option, a COM catalog might be more cost effective.

It is also possible that a change in the form of both the separate nonprint catalog and the main public catalog is being planned in conjunction with the integration effort. Sometimes plans for making one improvement in access engenders others and simultaneous implementation, while not easy, enables a library to avoid undergoing several upheavals. The cost of the new catalog form is not attributable to the integration project, but to the desire to give better bibliographic service. Indeed, in many libraries, integration of print and nonprint cataloging is a result rather than the cause of plans to automate the catalog.

The most important investment is in the planning process. Sufficient funds for a thorough analysis of current and projected procedures, decisions on policy, training, implementation, and feedback from every level is essential. It is not enough for filers to be told they will have to interfile cards previously filed separately. If a change to an online catalog is implemented, filing may be eliminated completely. Without input into the planning process there may be no opportunity for free flowing communication between filers and administrators so the fears of the former and assurances of the latter can be exchanged. The alternative to communication is increased resentment and resistance. Expensive though it may be, broad-based participation in planning is the key to successful implementation.

Exercising the option of converting all old, separate, and possibly poor cataloging to currently acceptable standards is a different cost issue. An integrated catalog is most effective when it contains all holdings. Conversely, multiple files are, in themselves, a barrier to efficient access. The urgency of retrospective conversion is related to the use-potential of older holdings, i.e., if they are going to continue being used, they should be converted within some reasonable time frame. Unfortunately, costs of retrospective conversion are impossible to generalize, depending on the quality of old records and access to sources of standardized cataloging.

Implementation costs, including training staff, informing the public, and putting new procedures in place, are the remaining factors in the process of integrating the catalog. They involve development of support materials, training time, reorganizing the work flow and job responsibilities, and reallocating budgets which may have reflected the separate access systems. As new procedures are tried, a built-in test-and-evaluation process should accompany them to insure that they work as planned.

Naturally, if an online public catalog is planned to coincide with integration of bibliographic access for print and nonprint materials, it implies a significant commitment of funds to planning, decision-making, and implementing the new catalog system. The pattern of expenditure will follow, quite closely, that described in this chapter for integrating access, though it is complex and may require more far-reaching changes. The results of these efforts and expenditures should be increased service to patrons.

Notes

1. Calvin N. Mooers, "Mooers' Law or, Why Some Retrieval Systems Are Used and Others Are Not,"*American Documentarian*, 11 (July 1960, p. ii. For a more recent discussion of Mooers' theory plus more pertinent information, see also James R. Dwyer's "The Effect of Closed Catalogs on Public Access," *Library Resources & Technical Services*, 25 (April/June 1981), pp. 188-89. Though Rush's arguments support his position that non-*AACR2* catalogs be kept open and converted to *AACR2* standards in order to maintain the integrity of the public catalog, these arguments could apply equally well to other issues as well, both relating to the integrity of the public catalog as well as the more general question of how much effort will people expend in order to obtain information from any tool or tools.

2. Brett Butler et al., "The Conversion of Manual Catalogs to Collection Data Bases," *Library Technology Reports*, 14 (March/April 1978), pp. 109-206. Though dated, this is one of the best discussions.

Recommended Reading

Helpful guidelines for managing the change process are found in the following:

Butler, Brett, et al. "The Conversion of Manual Catalogs to Collection Data Bases." *Library Technology Reports*, 14 (March-April, 1978), pp. 109-206.

Carter, Ruth C., and Scott Bruntjen. *Data Conversion.* White Plains, N.Y.: Knowledge Industry Publications, 1983.

Corbin, John. *Developing Computer-Based Library Systems.* Phoenix: Oryx Press, 1981.

The Management Process: A Selection of Readings for Librarians. Chicago: American Library Association, 1983. See, especially, the sections on Control and Organizing.

Peters, Stephen H., and Douglas J. Butler. "A Cost Model for Retrospective Conversion Alternatives." *Library Resources & Technical Services*, 28 (April-June, 1984), pp. 149-62.

Library Trends, 21 (April 1973). "Systems Design and Analysis for Libraries," ed. F. Wilfrid Lancaster.

Chapter 9

Results of New Access Systems

W HAT benefits can we expect to reap from the effort of integrating bibliographic access? How will patrons be better served? Will the library function more effectively? More economically?

Let us look at these questions and consider their answers in view of the foregoing chapters. We have observed the many complex details necessary to alter existing procedures. Is it worth the effort? Do people really care? These questions also need to be answered, and to the satisfaction of library boards and directors who have to commit funds to planning and implementing the changes as well as to the public for whom all changes tend to be inconveniences, at least for the moment.

PATRON BENEFITS

An integrated access system, combining information about all of a library's holdings in one public catalog, enhances the catalog's ability to show what works are in the library as well as to collocate works of an author, editions of a work, and works on a topic. These two basic functions of the catalog can never be fulfilled by a single-medium catalog in a multimedia library.

Access to Multimedia Collections

It is highly unlikely that any library could return to the book-only orientation of yesteryear. The public is too accustomed to the presence of nonprint media in library collections to be satisfied with books alone. There are media items of importance in every academic and extra-curricular subject one can think of. In addition, many

243

storage and preservation problems are being addressed by converting print materials to nonprint formats.

For schools, the need to include nonprint materials in collections, and in the catalogs, seems clear. Public libraries, too, need to develop nonprint collections. Clearly, the issue is not whether or not nonprint items exist in library collections or even whether they are important to them. It is the elimination of the access barrier that separate catalogs have always posed for the library user who does not approach the collections with a particular nonprint item in mind. The traditional separation of print and nonprint shelving makes the catalog even more essential for locating nonprint items and, since that tradition is still strong, makes the omnimedia catalog beneficial to catalog users today. If librarians can justify providing patrons with bibliographic information to materials in other libraries which are not even owned by the home library, but can only be loaned to them, how can they justify *not* providing information for items actually owned and housed within their walls? Yet we appear to accept union lists of printed monographs and serials being made available to the public with greater urgency than integrating all of the library's files into one main public catalog.

Just as supermarkets capitalize on the idea of one-stop shopping, selling much more than the local grocery, so does the library offer a diversity of intellectual products. The integrated public catalog gives one-step access to them. In the supermarket, we expect to push our basket all over the store to obtain what we want, but in the library the catalog is supposed to give enough guidance to its users so that they do not have to make the rounds of every stack area.

Collocating Versions of a Work

Catalogs show the holdings of the library—all of them—when integrated. When nonprint catalogs are separate, they do not. This most basic and least complicated catalog function seems worth attaining because library patrons believe it to be true even when it is not. The opportunity to find a work in different physical forms (e.g., a Shakespearean play in printed form as a book, in aural form on a phonograph record, tape cassette or reel, in audiovisual form on a film or videotape or disk or a sound filmstrip) simply does not exist in a nonintegrated catalog. Someone seeking all the library's items by or about Shakespeare will not find them in an unintegrated catalog if any of them happens to be in nonprint form. The work—

that intellectual or artistic essence that does not have physical form itself—may well be identical in all forms, but they would not be represented together unless the catalog was integrated. When a librarian decides to purchase a phonograph record album of a complete version of Shakespeare's *Macbeth*, is the assumption made that it should be used by all patrons looking for a copy of that play, or only those patrons who want sound recordings and coincidentally are interested in *Macbeth*? The implication of excluding the sound recording of *Macbeth* from the public catalog is that it would not satisfy a person looking for this play because of its medium. In reality, many patrons would be eminently satisfied with the sound version, and some might actually prefer it to the print editions because they prefer listening, or want the opportunity to listen and read together to enhance their appreciation of a complex and beautiful work. Some people do not like paperback editions because they are hard to read. They might prefer the sound version, too. This first advantage of the integrated catalog to show all holdings of the institution is so obvious that it is difficult to understand why it seems to escape so many professionals.

The second advantage of integrating catalogs is equally obvious and fundamental: including entries for nonprint media items in the public catalog permits all editions of a work, all works of an author, and, to a lesser degree, all works on a subject to be collocated. Displaying holdings in this organizational structure—that is, collocating them by author, title, and subject—is supposed to enhance access for catalog users. Putting aside the question of whether the cost of doing this at all is justified or not, what reason would there be to claim the sound recording of *Macbeth* is not an edition or a version of the work? Suppose for a moment, that the *Macbeth* album is the only version of the work available for circulation during the week this play is studied in a literature course at a school, and it is not listed in the public catalog. Suppose it was only listed in the media center's separate catalog, in a separate department. How many students looking for *Macbeth* would be prevented from gaining access to the sound version because the public catalog did not collocate it with all other editions of the work? Probably quite a few. Does the lack of collocation with print editions create a barrier to access? I believe the answer to this question is yes. If we can accept the need to identify a work given several different titles, e.g., *Macbeth, The Tragedy of Macbeth, Shakespeare's Macbeth*, and *Laurence Olivier in J. Arthur Rank's Production of Shakespeare's Macbeth*, by a uniform title, we should be able to accept the same concept of a union of all physical manifestations of the work, too. If we think it is a barrier to access to scatter all of the possible titles of *Macbeth* in the various places in the alphabet they would fall, i.e., "T" for Tragedy, "S" for Shakespeare, "L" for Laurence, and "M" for Macbeth, how much more of a barrier is it to remove the nonprint version altogether and put it in a different location simply because it is not in the form of print-on-paper. The integrated catalog resolves the issue, collocating all editions or versions of a work and giving patrons the opportunity to select any that satisfy their needs.

Enhancing Use of Materials

A third and most important advantage to catalog integration is that increased access through the catalog usually means increased use of materials. Increasing circulation of the collections has multiple values to the institution. First, it usually means more people are satisfying their information needs. Second, it means that individual items are getting more use, presumably the reason they were purchased in the first place. Third, increased circulation can be used to demonstrate that the agency is more effective in serving the public. Circulation statistics and use patterns are, perhaps, the most frequently used method of allocating funds by parent institutions to libraries and by the libraries among branches, departments, subjects, or media. There are very few libraries that pay no attention to the use of materials when it comes time to make budget decisions, selection decisions, or evaluations of staff performance and future staffing needs. Greater use of nonprint materials would seem to indicate more attention to these kinds of library holdings as well as their contribution to increasing the overall visibility of the library itself. Paying more attention to nonprint and increasing allocations to media materials and personnel, however, do not always result from increased use, no matter how logical it may seem, because factors other than use often receive higher priority. It should certainly demand some response, however, consistent with similar actions in other areas, and this could not help but benefit library patrons. For that matter, if the result of increased access was decreased use, a valuable negative response could be made, in keeping with objectives of service more important than being "fair" to media collections.

A fourth advantage of integrated catalogs is bringing into the catalog material whose subject matter and content level relates to the print materials already represented there. Up to this point, we have been discussing collocating identical works in different media. Now, however, we look a step further, to works related by their content. When media materials are selected, what criteria and objectives govern their selection? Ideally, the same criteria and objectives that govern selection of books and printed periodicals and serials. It would seem to be productive, then, to include entries for books and media in a single catalog collocating materials on the same subject. Nonprint media can provide different approaches to a subject, supplementing printed materials, as well as simply duplicating or substituting for books. In medical education, for example, a videotape of a surgical procedure is not reproducible in print. In some areas of interest, the nonprint product is the more important material; in others, it is an adjunct to primary resources in print. Consider the importance of television materials in studying contemporary history; consider, too, the relationship of nonprint to print in the study of early history, say, of the seventeenth century. While nonprint artefacts will help provide some information, written and printed materials are probably more valuable evidence for researchers of that earlier period.

No one can rationalize the decision to maintain separate catalogs for media on the basis of content value. Integration clearly affords everyone the chance to select the most appropriate specific items that satisfy their particular needs. A library patron studying certain kinds of celestial phenomena might choose to look at charts of space, photographs of heavenly bodies, or other visual materials in addition to books and/or research reports on their subject. Similarly, an opera lover might select, in addition to a sound recording of a favorite opera, a book on opera production and costume design, a libretto, or a score to accompany it; or, perhaps, a biography of the composer, librettist, or both. Students of Shakespeare who want printed plays are also interested in visual material on Elizabethan stagecraft and costuming, as well as the ephemera associated with theatrical productions, such as posters, programs, drawings of stage sets, etc. The examples come from every subject area and include every kind of material.

MEDIA COLLECTIONS: TOGETHERNESS OR INDIVIDUALITY?

One of the problems often used to defeat proposals to integrate the catalog is the notion that a photograph, a chart, or a poster is not the equivalent of a book and therefore is not a suitable item for bibliographic description. The idea of cataloging each photograph or each disk in a collection or, for that matter, each floppy diskette in a series of microcomputer programs is somehow seen as inappropriate. There are two ways of looking at this kind of material to resolve the issue. The first is to treat the collection as a whole, in the same way that a group of books which together form a coherent whole such as an encyclopedia are treated as a unit. This would be appropriate in many cases because the individual items are part of a larger unit. Even the top tune collection, which changes its parts every week when the new ratings appear, can be viewed as a particular kind of serial collection, with periodic deletions as well as additions. The rules for bibliographic description make it possible to do this, but in applying them, it is important to keep in mind whether the patron who looks for the material will find what he or she seeks if it is treated as one unit. If not, the alternative is to enter each individual item as a bibliographic entity. This is also made possible by the cataloging rules.

The second alternative, entering the individual items in a collection as individual bibliographic entities, merely acknowledges that an intellectual, artistic, or informational unit may be small or large. Collections of small things like photographs, for instance, may be usable without cataloging them individually; but usually in such a case there is some attribute that links them together so they may be treated together. If not, and each one is discrete and different, no size prerequisite dictates they cannot be cataloged individually. If these materials are worth adding to the library's holdings, there should be adequate access to them.

The book as a unit of bibliographic description is only a matter of convenience. Some books are made up of groups of plays, stories, poems, songs, or similar, smaller units representing discrete individual works. Woe to the person who is not familiar with the reference tools used for accessing the individual works in such volumes, and who fails to enlist the help of a librarian in searching for one of the works. Few libraries provide, in the catalog, an entry for a play directing patrons to the various anthologies owned by the institution where it appears. Yet plays published separately do get separate entries in the catalog. To the patron looking for the play, it cannot make much sense. The cry of the catalog manager is usually that cataloging every song, poem, or photograph in a collection is a Herculean task, enormously time-consuming and extremely costly. This is definitely an important reason to consider individual full treatment carefully; but if not doing so effectively removes those works from library patrons' reach, can the task be avoided?

One of the most difficult achievements for a library catalog is consistency. Changes in cataloging rules, subject headings, and filing rules create problems of one kind, and the variant output of different catalogers create more. The whims of authors/creators and publishers/producers to vary spellings and name forms cause still more. All of these are hard for catalog users to comprehend and overcome. Librarians deal with these problems by adding cross-references, employing authority files to minimize inconsistencies in headings, and doing their best to help patrons cope. The definition of a bibliographic unit (BU), however, is poorly addressed and presents a large and sticky problem. How is it logical that a play published alone, paperbound, and quite small, may be considered a BU while the exact same work, bound with several others between covers, hardbound, in much larger form, is not? It is not the work itself, but the presentation that seems to count most in determining the BU. Sometimes, the anthology has a separate title entry for each story/play/song/poem it contains, but not always. This inconsistency must surely confound patrons, raising a formidable barrier to access. It does not prevent us from cataloging the anthology as a BU, sometimes with and sometimes without the analytics pointing to its individual works, but it ought to cause us a great deal of discomfort. Is consistency in any of these areas worth an investment in money, time and effort? In which area are the benefits greatest for information seekers? How far should the catalog go in imitating or duplicating the indexes and other bibliographic tools which, up to now, have provided the only keys that exist to individual works in anthologies and collections?

When patrons approach the catalog, they may assume they will find books (by their authors, titles, and subjects) or their equivalent, which may be films, visual or sound recordings, and so forth. They normally do not expect to find sections of these BUs, whether they are chapters, movements of symphonies, or scenes of plays. Treatment of anthologies in the catalog, however, varies widely depending on how many works are bound or recorded together, what the prevailing policies are in the individual library, the Library of Congress, and the bibliographic sources used by the library, as well as the economics of treatment, staff available for the job, and whether or not the cataloging department faces an enormous backlog or is up-to-date on most pending work. All of these factors can influence a decision to create additional access points for the works in anthologies or only an umbrella heading for all as a unit. Nor are these the only factors affecting such decisions. Sometimes the presence or absence of a collective title may affect bibliographic treatment; sometimes the subject area dictates a particular kind of treatment. There are probably other factors important in individual libraries or to individual librarians.

One of the arguments for cataloging only the overall unit is that the added work and resulting entries would be too costly and time-consuming to prepare and file. Another is that the size of the file would become unwieldy and difficult to search. These familiar points are raised with regard to integrating the catalog, with catalogers complaining that media are composed mainly of an-thology-style units, e.g., sound recordings with many short pieces on each side of a disk or tape. It may, indeed, happen with more frequency in nonprint than in print that a bibliographic unit is made up of works that could stand alone, though there are no scientific studies to prove it, but a number of book genres—poetry, plays, and short stories, for example—and virtually all printed serials are similar, yet they are not excluded from the catalog on those grounds. In most cases, though, they are treated as a unit, with little attention paid to the "works" they contain. Other tools have been employed to access the smaller works, or the more specific ideas and articles in books and journals, except when these were published in a stand-alone format, one play, one song, etc. We can continue to do this for the integrated catalog, too, following the same guidelines as for books of poems, etc., and deciding on an individual basis when to make exceptions. We can also reevaluate other options, asking ourselves whether it is possible and desirable to extend access beyond the bibliographic units we currently treat in library catalogs.

A case for limiting access to the book, film, or collection, i.e., of maps, photographs, songs, slides, or whatever, can easily be made if the physical limits of book or card catalogs are all we have to consider. It is easy to understand the expense of printing book catalogs with several times as many entries in them. It is equally clear that multiplying card files by two, three, or more would not only create expenses of preparation and filing, but physical problems of space as well as cost for the larger numbers of drawers, cabinets, and so on. Now, however, automation offers a new possibility, the ability to handle thousands of entries as quickly as hundreds and hundreds of thousands with equal ease, provided the system is large and powerful enough. If, in addition to integrating the catalog, it is also automated, other opportunities and capabilities move within reach. Catalogs cannot deal with the inconsistency of bibliographic units which may contain only one work or several. The BU varies in all media, but newer media, particularly those which hold a great deal of intellectual output in a very small space—microforms and videodisks are good examples—are the most problematic. Catalogs of the future will have to confront this problem. Increased use of media with high storage capacities will present more and more demands on catalogs to resolve the inconsistency of BUs. An automated catalog can control the larger numbers of entries which would result from establishing the work as the BU for all cataloging, as well as the added entries that would result from integrating media cataloging with books. But this is not the only benefit that would result from automating the integrated catalog. Let us look at how computerizing the data in the catalog can add to service patrons can receive.

BENEFITS OF AUTOMATION

One advantage of computerizing the bibliographic information that goes into a library catalog is the versatility with which it can be searched and retrieved. A second advantage is the computer's ability to handle a large number of entries in its files and indexes with accuracy and speed. Putting these two capabilities together, a computerized catalog can combine the kind of access afforded by traditional catalogs—author, title, and/or subject identification of physical embodiments of intellectual effort, i.e., books, films, recordings, etc.—and the kind of access afforded by indexes—author, title, and/or subject identification of works, parts of works, or even ideas contained within works, plus a range of approaches to them. Dates, publishers/producers, media, languages, or other bibliographic elements besides authors, titles, and subjects could be accessed. Summaries or abstracts could be searchable and might become commonplace for adult works as they are for children's materials and certain kinds of nonprint materials. The computerized file makes searching a rapidly executed, localized process, unlike manual searches which involve the scanning of many volumes of indexes, trips to the catalog for location information, trips to the shelves for the actual documents, and repetitions of this cycle for as many times as necessary to satisfy the objectives of the search. The manual search, in a large library with many floors of stacks, large card catalog, and departmentalized reference collection, could take hours, days, or weeks for a complex piece of work. Automating the process can mean considerable time savings.

More and Better Access

The depth of indexing done by reference tools designed to give maximum access to subject matter in periodicals, books, and other literature is costly to produce. It is unlikely that librarians in individual libraries would duplicate this work for their catalogs. What they could do, however, would be to index all the elements of a catalog entry designed to give access to portions of a BU, e.g., contents notes, summaries, and other informative notes. They could also transcribe all the authors in multi-authored works, chapter titles where such information enhanced access, and include all performers, producers, contributors, and individual titles to anthology-like items.

Machine capabilities require two new ways of looking at bibliographic entries. First, the elements may each be potential access points. *AACR2* acknowledged this possibility by removing choice of access points from its previous status in *AACR1* as the first step in establishing a bibliographic identity for a work and placing after the entire description is completed. The code does not suggest access points beyond the traditional main and added entries already common from earlier codes, but it is not hard to imagine broadening those concepts to include more elements to be "searchable," i.e., used as headings as well as all the authors and titles of a multiwork unit, or, all the authors of a single work when there are more than three. After all, these rules for choosing a "main" entry from two or more possibilities originated as devices to make catalogs and cataloging practicable and cost-effective functions; they did not relegate all second-named authors to oblivion out of the belief that they are less important than first-named authors. In a single entry catalog, only one of the two (or more) could occupy the main, i.e., only, filing point for an item. In fact, once multiple listings became common, they were accorded heading status, too, as "added" entries. All the computer enables us to do is to place all authors on the same footing. Depending on how a computer program is written for retrieving data, all names can go into one file, or authors can be indexed in a file separate from illustrators or editors. Corporate names may be in one file with personal names or in a separate file, again, depending on the instructions and organization of the system and its database.

Other elements not previously indexed in card or book catalogs could now be made searchable. Studies made of esoteric bibliographic elements catalog users would like to be able to search include language, date, medium, publisher, and more.[1]

AACR2 also provides for analytics—the identification, or analysis, of portions of a bibliographic unit which patrons wish to access independently of the whole unit.[2] Once again, traditional practice in most libraries rested on cost and other practical problems of doing analytics rather than a belief that they were undesirable or unworthy intellectually of being made. The computer furnishes a way of making access to these parts economically and practically feasible. Already, many manual indexes which gave patrons this kind of access are being automated to eliminate the high cost of manual preparation. Automating catalogs presents two possible methods for gaining access to analytics. One is by entering them as access points in the initial cataloging process. Another is by creating an interface between the automated catalog and automated indexes. Either way, patrons benefit by having access to the actual works in library collections, not merely to the physical packages in which they appear.

Searching in a computer database is very different from searching a card or book catalog in a number of ways. Patrons can benefit from the flexibility they provide not only in the number of searchable items, but also in the combinations of search terms, qualifications which can be introduced, e.g., only French-language versions of a work published in Canada, different ways of using partial information to find an entry, and free text searching in which any words can be searched alone or in phrases within an index. Addition of abstracts or, perhaps, inclusion of summaries for adult as well as children's works would provide more clues as to the nature and scope of the content of the works.

Saving Time and Effort

The computer does not require patrons to move from place to place while conducting a search. A large card catalog can stretch for a block or more, and divided catalogs, where subjects are in their own file, can add to the distance patrons have to go to move back and forth through the alphabet. If status information is attached to the catalog records, trips to the shelves may also be avoided. All of the distance traveled represents time—the time it takes to find what one is looking for, first in the catalog and then on the shelves. Needless to say, for staff users, time is the library's money; but for other users, it is their own time and money saved. The ideal time-saver would be to provide catalog information to homes, offices, or schools where people have the equipment to receive it. Eventually, such an information network for materials held in the library may emerge, though direct access to the full text of many documents may enable information seekers to skip over use of the library catalog altogether. A scenario can easily be imagined in which libraries keep the full text of some materials in machine-readable form for those people who want access to them directly and others only in their original forms with bibliographic citations online. Even in the more immediately foreseeable future, however, the fact that a catalog user can sit in a comfortable place with a terminal and be given enough information to prevent fruitless trips to various other places—the shelves, other catalogs, indexes, the circulation desk, etc.—is benefit enough for most people.

The interface with other library systems, acquisitions' order files, in-process files, and circulation files, for example, gives the catalog an entirely new dimension. This enhancement is a valuable addition to the more limited information in a traditional catalog. Many institutions include temporary slips in their catalogs for items in the process of being cataloged; some also use temporary slips for materials on order which have not yet arrived, but not as many. Still fewer include holdings information, i.e., the number of copies available in the system; and no library with a traditional catalog can give status information on the availability for loan of each copy of each title in the collection.

Most people, though not all, are interested in obtaining one or more documents as a result of their use of the catalog. Up to this time, they would not expect this tool to tell them more than if the title is a part of the collection and, of course, the bibliographic description, location, and a very general idea of the subject content. When a title does not appear in the catalog, one can assume it is not part of the collection, but at least two other files, the order file and shelflist or in-process file, have to be consulted before determining whether it was ordered or received but not yet processed. Furthermore, if the title does appear in the catalog but is not on the shelf, circulation and/or shelflist files must be consulted. The best that can be managed in some libraries is an educated guess, though others have recall systems that enable them to do better. Usually, patrons are told to leave their names and addresses so they can be contacted when the item is returned, since even libraries with recall systems cannot be certain if or when the materials will be brought back. The idea of having order, in-process, catalog, and circulation information in a single tool seems an impossible dream. The fact is, however, that the impossible dream can now be realized either by means of separate but interconnected computer systems for the three technical service functions or through the use of a single integrated computer system for all three functions. The value to patrons and staff should be significant. And now, the person who wants an item that is out in circulation might be able to initiate the recall and/or hold on the item without the assistance of a staff member and without the need to fill out forms.

Linking With Other Systems

Beyond the expansion of the catalog into a more versatile tool containing full information about works from their entry into the system as orders, through each use after they are received, to their final de-accession, lies the possibility of adding information from sources outside the library—union catalogs, bibliographies and indexes, etc., to the store of in-house information. The capacity for interfacing different computer systems with one another already exists, but each connection presents a series of problems to be solved and complex instructions to be created before the connection can be made. There are "black boxes" that allow an OCLC or WLN entry to be automatically entered into a different circulation or acquisition system, but there is no universal black box that can work for all kinds of systems. Each library must begin with what it has and what it can plan to add to its existing equipment. In the case of commercially owned or controlled systems, individual libraries have no means of getting the information they need to create an interface, but it may prove advantageous to those who have the information, i.e., the vendors, to do so. No one knows what path future research into the subject of computer-to-computer links may take, but expert Frederick Kilgour[3] believes it will not be a quick or easy one. Still, enough progress has been made already to point to achievement of some success, though not with every system and every desirable link. A good deal of time has already been invested in creating a link between the bibliographic utilities.[4]

Filling Different Needs

Several times, the differing needs of catalog users has been mentioned and the computerized catalog's flexibility in filling them should be pointed out. Many catalog users are looking for location information so they can borrow an item, or at least use it in the library if it cannot be borrowed. Others, particularly staff members using the entries, need a detailed series of bibliographic elements to satisfy them. Card and book catalogs present the same entry to everyone who uses them. The full-entry unit card goes back to the early years of this century when the Library of Congress began to sell packs of unit cards to the library community. Departures from unit card entries are usually those in which only the main entry has full information while all subject and added entries contain an abbreviated version. In a sense, the person using the catalog can select the full or partial entry format by deciding whether to look under the main entry or an added or subject entry, but in actuality, this is not what happens. It is more likely that the search is conducted under the only information known to the person, rather than a deliberate selection from among alternative headings. The computer system can be designed to furnish the level of information needed by the patron regardless of the heading used to access the entry. The choice of information level, from minimal (only the call number, author and title) to a full MARC record with enhancements, could be made by the searcher as part of the search process. It would also enable only the desired data to be printed, either on the terminal display or a hard-copy printer. In either case, it takes more time for full entries to print than abbreviated versions, so printing more than necessary defeats the purpose of using computers to save time. On the other hand, full entries may be needed for all sorts of reasons and the abbreviated entry formats of some existing nonstandard systems simply would not suffice. Thus, if a choice must be made, it would be short-sighted to opt for brief entries only in an online catalog.

LEARNING TO USE ONLINE CATALOGS

To be effective, searching on a computerized catalog needs to be simple and easy to do in addition to being flexible, rapid, and giving access to more information than traditional catalogs. The term usually applied to computer systems that are simple and easy to operate is "user-friendly." Unfortunately, very few of the computer systems for bibliographic data are sufficiently user-friendly for people to use them without training. This is true of the three major reference databases, DIALOG, ORBIT, and BRS, and it is also true of the bibliographic utilities, OCLC, RLIN, WLN, and UTLAS. It is mostly true for turnkey systems, too, but vendors of turnkey systems and software system packages are rapidly changing the image of their systems as they progress toward the development of integrated multipurpose systems. One extremely important component of an integrated and/or multipurpose computer system is a public access catalog.

The catalog, actually a product of technical services activity as well as a bibliographic service to the public, is a key link between technical, behind-the-scenes services, and public services. It has often been a source of conflict and irritation between them as well as between librarians on the one hand and the public on the other. Many librarians believe that the catalog is not meant for the lay public, but only for professionals to use in helping them; that it is too complex and arcane to be well-understood and effectively used by most nonlibrarians. The first opportunity to teach the use of the catalog usually falls to children's librarians, who assume one or two demonstrations of how to use the catalog will keep most children out of their hair for all but their most difficult problems. The second opportunity is frequently part of collegiate orientation week. If they do not go to college, there may never be a second opportunity, though some junior and senior high schools also offer library instruction. Even if a relatively thorough job is done of teaching a young person the rules of a particular catalog, they are likely to change over time, so "refresher courses" are needed to keep patrons abreast of catalog code revision, new filing rules, subject heading revisions, and local departures from all of these. If patrons use several libraries in the course of their educational and recreational pursuits, each one is likely to have its own combination of headings and structural arrangements to be learned.

In addition to the general lack of comprehensive programs of bibliographic instruction in all libraries, patrons have problems with the controlled vocabularies used to provide subject access. Aside from the difficult issues of headings that are sexist or offensive to minorities, some of the language is outdated and changes are made very slowly, there is no consistency in the use of natural language or inverted order for headings, new words are added very slowly, and few catalogs contain the access points of only one set of descriptive and subject heading codes, but are amalgams of several introduced over all the years of the life of a catalog. Recataloging is expensive, and so is authority work. These are often the most expendable components of organizational services when something has to go.

A third impediment to patron success with the catalog is their lack of familiarity with the form of authors' names used for headings, which used to be the fullest form under the first *Anglo-American Cataloguing Rules* and is now the one by which they are best known. Although that simple change seems eminently practical, it results in fragmenting the works of authors who write under several names and will not help the patron whose reference is under a form not used at all. Other difficulties occur when names are misspelled, remembered incorrectly, or are only partially known. Partial or incorrect information for titles is a frequent cause of failure, too.

Thus, librarians have some good reasons for asserting that library catalogs are not really meant for the public. Following their logic, a case could be made for ignoring user-friendliness, since it is an extremely costly programming problem, and professionals have learned to deal with the user-unfriendly systems we already have. But does this benefit patrons? Perhaps it will not matter to the hardcore nonusers of the catalog, or those who are accustomed to demanding that searching be done for them. Most people, however, make an attempt to find what they want in the catalog even though studies show that they don't persist very long in the effort. Assuming for a moment that these are in the majority, it is clear that there is much to be gained from making the catalog more intelligible to nonlibrarians, and incorporating strategies for enhancing the possibility of success.

User-Friendliness

Two kinds of user-friendliness need to be considered, then: (1) The intellectual content of the catalog in terms of its headings and organizational structure; and (2) the operation of the computer system in which the catalog resides. Obviously, the choice and form of headings are determined by rules outside the scope of the individual library. But they can be mitigated to some degree by the ability of the computer to accept partial data, or to provide a larger number of cross-references than a manual catalog could, as well as its ability to furnish more accessible elements, delimiters, and combinations of access points. No one argues the greater versatility of computerized catalogs over card and book forms.

The operation of the computer system is another issue, involving more or less knowledge on the part of the operator according to the kind of programming designed for it. User-friendliness cannot be obtained without a prior investment of time and effort in development of solutions to the many problems underlying easy and simple access. These problems include the following:

- Self-contained tutorials

- "Forgiving" entry modes

- Online assistance

- Browsing functions

- Different search modes for beginners and more sophisticated searchers

- Use of lay language

Let us consider the implications of each problem on this list, which is by no means exhaustive.

Self-contained Tutorials

A computer system with self-contained tutorials should not require additional offline training to operate. When a searcher approaches the system, an intelligible message—intelligible to the lay person, that is, not a jargon-filled message decodable only by a computer expert—should lead the person either to a simple online lesson on how to use the system or additional messages that "walk" them through their search. There are two general approaches for accessing information from a computer, the menu approach and the command approach. In the menu approach, a list of all the available alternatives is presented to the searcher and the desired option must be selected. The option may be numbered or letter-coded, or the whole word or phrase might have to be entered to make a selection. In some systems, a separate key must be pressed after the option has been identified and entered, and in others, only the correct option identifier needs to be typed in or touched. Additional keys to be pressed add to the complexity of operation and should be programmed out if possible. In the command mode, the searcher has to enter proper command words to execute the search. Sometimes commands are in English-language words or their abbreviations and sometimes commands are coded, e.g., the command which selects the desired index of OCLC to be searched is embedded in the format of the search key used. Though the menu approach sounds simplest, there are advantages to the command mode, too, one of which is the avoidance of a large number of steps that may have to be executed to get to the desired information. Ideally, both approaches should be available so patrons can use whichever one they prefer, or some combination of both should be used to enable the advantages of each to be realized.

At the 1983 Annual Conference of the Association of American Library Schools (now the Association of Library and Information Science Education), Michael Gorman described a microcomputer black box which translated searchers' natural language inquiries into the codes and search keys required for searching the OCLC and Library Control Systems in place at the University of Illinois. The microcomputer system was designed initially by a humanities professor who wanted to short-cut the encoding process through which a person mentally transforms a citation into a series of computer-acceptable search keys. This type of interface may solve problems for existing systems whose programming is too costly to change into "friendlier" operation for the public. But it would be less complicated to develop new systems with friendlier operational modes as integral parts of their design.

In concluding his paper, Gorman pointed out a basic philosophic choice between designing online catalogs which require patron instruction to use—he called it the "bibliographic instruction approach"—or simplifying catalog systems to the point where no instruction is required. Librarians in this country have traditions of providing instruction in the use of the catalog that could easily be put forth to rationalize ignoring user-friendliness in favor of a more arcane and less intelligible system than the card catalog. Continuing to adhere to the bibliographic instruction approach, however, implies a disregard for the lay public that librarians have sometimes been accused of having to an unfortunate degree. There is more than enough need for librarians to interpret for patrons the intellectual potential of the catalog as a tool beyond the obvious finding-list feature to keep professionals endlessly busy without adding complications to its simple use for known-item lookups.

"Forgiving" Entry Modes

One of the greatest problems with operating computer systems is the necessity to type in absolutely accurate, error-free data in exactly the right order, including every required punctuation mark, space, and entry key. A "forgiving" system would supply forgotten code characters or correct spacing so the information would not have to be re-entered from the beginning. Beyond this, common typographical errors could be overlooked, such as mistaken upper or lower case letters, missing initials, misspellings, and omission or substitution of insignificant words in a title, e.g., *Incidents of History* in place of *Incidents in History.* People who make more than one or two typographical errors could be presented with a soothing message to encourage them to relax and take their time in entering essential data accurately. The forgiving system keeps this essential data down to a minimum, particularly the system-related punctuation and spacing which doesn't make much sense to the lay public anyway.

Online Assistance
Most people resent having to admit to a librarian that they cannot work a machine others are using with ease. It is frustrating to do your best to be precise and accurate and receive a response that either doesn't make sense or only tells you that you are wrong— which you already know. The way the computer handles errors is both a delicate issue in public relations and a complex programming problem to produce adequate assistance for inexperienced or careless users. Error messages should identify, however briefly, either what was done wrong or what should be done to correct it, or possibly both. If entry codes were missing or incorrect, an error message should specify the error and ask for re-entry. If the user entered too many characters, or a space where one didn't belong, this should be apparent from the error message they receive. Every error message and every decision point should be accompanied by an option to get help by typing "help" or touching an appropriate key. Help should automatically be given to someone who repeats the same error several times, similar to the OCLC response to incorrect entry of its log-on conventions that tells the operator to "please see your representative if you are having trouble logging on." A catalog user might be asked to see a librarian without disturbing the screen, or a printer might be activated to record the sequence on the screen, for the patron to show to a catalog staff member. In this way, the user's error is documented for correction. The way that online assistance is provided, i.e., through error messages that inform users how to proceed, through a general help message available at all times to review any or all of the internally programmed instructions for users, or through a set of specific help messages designed to review specific procedures, is a determinant of its friendliness to users. All three kinds of help can be used to serve different purposes. All should be worded in simple, but not simplistic, language and should

assume the user wants to correct the error. The inscrutability of a machine must be overcome by attending to the problems of including the best online instruction and corrections that can be devised.

Browsing Functions

When we are not sure of the information we bring to a manual catalog, we can leaf through it in hopes that we will find the desired entry by chance or by coming close enough to find it in a search of that general area. Computers may enable us to do this type of searching, too, in one of two ways. First, partial information can be entered, called "truncation" or "masked searching," in which all the entries satisfying the words or characters entered are produced in answer to the query. Usually, many more entries will satisfy a partial request, e.g., if the subject is "banking," but the user cannot remember whether it was *banking, banks* or *banks and banking,* one could enter *bank-* and retrieve, in addition to these, *bankers, bankrupt/bankruptcies, bank tellers,* etc. The larger the file, the more unwanted entries would be retrieved along with the one sought, but with time and patience, each entry could be scanned until the one sought was found. Another method is to scan the indexes, moving forward or backward from any selected spot, until the desired one appears. This can be as time-consuming a process online as it would be in a manual file, but sometimes it is the only way to locate the desired material. People need to be able to browse, to jog the memory or make up for incomplete or inaccurate information in the catalog, and an online catalog should be designed to allow it.

Different Search Modes for Beginners and Advanced Searchers

User-friendliness may be acceptable for someone's first try at using an online catalog, but it could quickly become tedious as a searcher gains facility with the computer system. There should be alternative methods of searching for experienced users either to speed up the search process or to allow them to make more complex inquiries. One way to do this would be to allow patrons to select the kind of access that suits their level of expertise, e.g., a system that might allow either a direct command mode or a menu mode in which each decision point is presented in turn and prompts tell users what to do next. Another way to accomplish the same thing is to make intermediate steps dispensable for those with knowledge of the system. Abbreviation of commands or search keys help to speed up the process for knowledgeable users, keeping required keystroking to a minimum. One of the problems with the keyboard-less CLSI touch-sensitive terminals is that you cannot simply key in (or use a scanner to read in machine-readable information) a desired name or title in order to retrieve known items from the file, but have to go through several steps to zero in on the item within its file narrowing the search as you proceed. A combination of touch-sensitive and keyboard CRTs offers both kinds of searching. Addition of a scanning device also enables bar-coded or optical character recognition (OCR) labels to be automatically read into the system, bypassing both keystroking or touching the CRT screen to get a response. The type of searching done should be related to the user's knowledge and ability to manipulate the computer system in various ways.

Use of Lay Language

The last element in user friendliness is the ability to seek responses by using ordinary English words instead of a restrictive vocabulary full of arcane computer jargon. Prompts should be couched in understandable terms, e.g., "name and address code" rather than APATID, used in the CLSI system to identify a name-address search key for patrons, and entry of a person's name and/or address should be permissible in addition to the search key made up of several letters from each. Someone who uses the system as a catalog should be able to "ask a question" as well as "enter an inquiry." Error messages should be worded clearly, politely, and in lay language. Commands might be programmed to accept "author" or "name" interchangeably. It should be enough that patrons can identify a name without having to distinguish between personal and corporate entities. Authority files online are useful, but all possible forms of a name or subject heading should be usable, not only the authorized form. When an unauthorized form is entered, the computer system should produce the same response that the authorized form would have elicited with an announcement to the user of the correct, authorized heading. The user should not have to reenter the request using the authorized form, as they do, in effect, in a manual catalog. In other words, the authority file should be invisible to users, except to inform them that there is an authorized form and what it is for future reference. If they forget the correct form on the next occasion, they will still get a response, with the information about the correct form, once again.

These kinds of operating characteristics are not easy to design, but if they are not part of the online catalog then the burden of accommodation is shifted to the catalog user. The reason online catalogs are being implemented is partly to give better service to all catalog users. Staff or professional users of the catalog can be trained to use unfriendly catalogs and can act as intermediaries for the lay public. However, this negates the value of the change to on-line systems for the majority of the public, who have been told since childhood, "Go look in the catalog!" and it does not take into account and capitalize on the interactive nature of computer systems which users need to direct for their own benefit.

CONCLUSIONS

This chapter examines a number of questions about integrated access: Will patrons be better served? Will the library staff and their operations function more smoothly? More effectively? More economically? The first question may be answered yes, for several reasons.

Serving Patrons More Effectively

The twin purposes of the catalog, to be the patron's finding tool and to bring together works related by author, title, or subject, are better fulfilled by an integrated catalog. The word "works" does not imply only books, though many library catalogs seem to interpret it as if it did. So long as libraries collect materials in all media, the catalog should offer access on an omnimedia basis without imposing arbitrary limits on the public's bibliographic access.

Integrated catalogs are also likely to lead to greater use of materials in the library's nonprint collections with a corresponding increase in satisfaction of informational or recreational needs. This increase in the use of materials is a clear indication of more effective public service. Should the result of catalog integration be decreased use of the materials, one would certainly question the value of the materials and elicit a corresponding negative response. Bringing information about nonprint materials into a closer relationship with entries for print items containing similar content or with related identity adds to the research value of the catalog. Materials are not missed, and the combination of various kinds of materials may be essential to particular kinds of inquiry.

Finally, an argument used to keep nonprint catalogs separated from (main) print catalogs has been the large number of individual items that would need to be included, e.g., the individual photographs, maps, or sheets of music. This argument fails to recognize the same situation occurring with books and serials, and the general lack of consistency in treating the "work" as the fundamental bibliographic unit, rather than the packages in which it appears. The lack of consistency in defining a bibliographic unit creates problems for catalog users regardless of the medium involved. Integrating the catalog may well motivate librarians to reassess the definition of bibliographic units to try to achieve greater consistency.

Automating the integrated catalog adds more to its potential for service by adding to the number of search options and access points. The computer's ability to hold and manipulate large numbers of entries quickly and economically enables it to treat all entries for all holdings and even to deal with the still larger number of entries resulting from using works as bibliographic units in all formats. This would bring a consistent treatment of works to the catalog it has never enjoyed until now, even when only books were entered into it.

The space-saving benefits of online catalogs are twofold. For the library, it frees the area taken up by large card or book catalogs. The patron is able to access all the information in the catalog from a single terminal. If the catalog contains on-order, in-process, and circulation data, this can save fruitless searches in the stacks for materials that are not there. Terminals can be located anywhere a power supply is available and the right equipment can be assembled, including public buildings, dormitories, departmental offices, classrooms, offices, and private homes.

In addition to the inclusion of data other than purely local bibliographic and location information in an online catalog, local data can be enriched with similar information about holdings in other libraries, encouraging and facilitating resource-sharing and other cooperative uses of the information. Although some people criticize this aspect of online catalogs, since the material from other libraries is not immediately available and obtaining it creates more work for the local agency, it affords users of smaller collections or those with materials less relevant to their needs another means to satisfy their information requirements without the effort of traveling elsewhere or the cost of obtaining catalogs and indexes of other collections.

The greater the number of access points and searching options available, the more flexible people's searches can be, and the more individually tailored to their specific intellectual or physical needs. Integrating nonprint materials into the files is an important component in the process of customizing service to the public, furnishing primary or complementary resources for many subject disciplines, and materials relating to available print resources. Automating the integrated catalog makes this already valuable tool much easier to manipulate in complex ways and extends its effectiveness along the lines already described. However, it brings to the fore another issue—the complexity of the new catalog system and operation of the equipment in which it is housed. It should not be beyond the capability of ordinary people to use and the ease with which they can operate it unaided is its measure of user-friendliness. User-friendliness is a function of the programming of the system. If the instructions that tell the computer system how to operate are written to give assistance in the form of prompts and tutorials, accept less than perfect information from the user, and offer help throughout the process of searching, then the need for a specially trained professional intermediary should be minimized, though some people will always prefer mediated searches.

The new online integrated catalog will reflect more holdings, giving patrons more choices; have more access points, giving them more flexibility; and offer a wide variety of options to satisfy their needs. The catalog should achieve greater consistency in identifying works as the bibliographic unit to which it gives access. All of these qualities, plus the greater speed with which the entries can be accessed, benefit the people who use catalogs, whether for personal research or recreation or staff operations.

The second question, whether library procedures and staff operations will be benefited, too, can also be answered positively, since staff searchers have most of the same needs that patrons do. User-friendliness may be the only dispensible feature of online integrated catalogs as far as staff use is concerned, and for new staff, tutorials and prompts online may be equally valuable, perularly if this system can be bypassed by a more sophisticated user. For staff users and the productivity of their search time, the fact that online integrated catalogs can contain all holdings and collocate works, not merely their physical packages, is one advantage. The speed and flexibility of searching in online catalogs with full holdings is another. Perhaps even more significant are the possible interfaces with other internal and external bibliographic systems, connecting the catalog with acquisition and circulation files and/or online indexes. Easy access to these systems should increase the effectiveness of searching as well as insure good coordination among internal operations. Analysis of internal operations should be facilitated by interfacing systems, with the result that bottlenecks can be identified and problems resolved.

The question about whether integrated and automated catalogs are economical is more difficult to answer. In the short run, the cost of integrating and automating the catalog cannot be absorbed quickly enough to show any savings. In fact, they are likely to cost a great deal, especially the automation project. The economic advantages are only realized over a longer period, and part of their benefit lies in the greater amount of service that can be rendered by the same, or even a smaller, staff. Other savings may be made in the simple integration process, without automation, particularly if standardizing the cataloging enables it to be done more efficiently, or if it can be done via an OCLC terminal or other cooperative or central service, which tends to lower the cost per unit cataloged.

It is hard to put a dollar value on the additional services rendered by an integrated manual catalog, but the number of requests it can fill should be higher, and the cost of maintaining it may well be lower, since only one set of rules applies and one session of interfiling needs to be done rather than two, three, or more. Although some people believe that it takes measurably longer to file entries in a larger file (and this may be true for files beyond a certain size), in experience as a card filer, I found that it took less time to interfile a number of cards into one file than to interfile half of them in one file system and half of them into another. The cost of revising the cards would also be lower, again, since one session using one set of rules would be done for all materials. The question of economics depends on the size of operations, since efficiency of scale is a relative thing, realizable only up to a point, after which increases in volume result in a decrease in efficiency.

The Need to Care

The last questions, is it worth the effort? and do people really care? have to be answered yes. Predictions of the demise of libraries as we know them are largely attributed to the ability of other information providers to give "better" service to the public. While technology plays a major role in new methods for furnishing information services, it is rather the differences in attitude toward service and the client that separates traditional library agencies from the innovative information providers. Two critical manifestations of traditional library attitudes are the unwillingness to market one's services overtly and the extremely slow development of new services and products. Private sector promoters try to anticipate the wants of their market and then advertise, reaching out to the largest possible number of consumers. Both kinds of activities have been deemed beneath the high intellectual plane of library professionals. Also, libraries are mostly bureaucratic organizations where change is resisted, often quite successfully, and the weight of tradition is a palpable impediment to it. This is true or has been true, I believe, in all types of library organizations save, perhaps, corporate libraries. Thus, the notion that technology should be employed to facilitate the development of new products and services and also, perhaps, to reach out to more clients to consume those goods and services is a more or less uncommon one. There have always been librarians who recognized the value of anticipating client needs, even as far back as Cutter, who recommended using up-to-date, commonly used terms for subject headings so that the client's vocabulary would be reproduced in the catalog, making it easier for it to be searched. Others of equal eminence have reminded us of the client's needs in every area of service throughout the years, and yet we never seem to have acquired a clear focus of effort in this direction or spent very much time and money planning to amaze clients with sparkling new ways to cater to their needs. Even now, there is doubt about the appropriateness of home delivery of biblio-graphic services via computers and/or cable television, just as there is about the value of video and film and rock music and computer games as library materials. But we should have no doubts as pro-fessionals that it is indeed worth the effort to develop new systems to serve the public more effectively and more completely, in more ways with more products and in fancier packages than previously done.

Media management must become central to the library's manage-ment concerns, so that it serves the same objectives in the most ef-fective ways that can be devised. Separate media catalogs and separate acquisitions, circulation, and public service policies and processes can never produce the same results, overall, as coordina-ted activities under a unified management system. Crucial to the success of such a coordinated operational structure is a unified catalog in which medium is not an arbitrary barrier to access. As the automation of catalogs is contemplated, unification of separate catalogs is more critical, since one of the byproducts (or perhaps one of the main products) of such systems is management information. This information can and will be used as the basis for decisions of many kinds, undoubtedly including fund allocations and collection evaluations. Indeed, the automated catalog has the potential to be a management tool. An integrated catalog permits collections to be viewed as a whole rather than as a series of disparate parts and may well bring to the attention of managers some surprising revelations about the function and use of their media materials.

Reports from an automated, integrated catalog are enriched with the information about those sections of the holdings that not only complement and augment the books in the collections, but also offer unique ideas, information, or aesthetic experiences, and which should relate to the whole collection the library is aiming to develop. Left to their own devices, media managers are free to go their own way, and the media collection becomes an end in itself, with no real relationship with the print materials. The more fragmented media collections are—since we could easily dream up a series of separate film collections, music collections containing scores and musical recordings, slide collections, filmstrip collections, poster collections, computer software collections, etc.—the less likely they are to serve the same goals.

No sensible collection manager allows individual departments to dictate their own rules, objectives, methods of operation, and services; yet, that is exactly what happens with media departments that are separated from the rest of the institution's processes. That is exactly what happens with managers who say "collections" when they mean "books" and assume that media are not important or have little to offer the library user except as special materials with limited uses. Evaluating media collections can and should be done on the basis of the same criteria as book collections, with similar results. If only the book entries are automated, or if the book and media entries are not compatible with one another, then how can such unified evaluations be made easily and without a great deal more effort and money? Integrating the catalog should produce much more than better access to media materials. It should also produce, in the long run, a more coherent and coordinated overall collection, capable of serving the public more effectively.

Media point the way to the twenty-first century. They give us the means to store millions of pages on a few small disks, to watch history unfolding all over the world and beyond, to communicate instantaneously with millions of people. The library can harness the power of media to serve the public in new and different ways with new and different products, but retain and improve those services and products in which print materials are the fundamental information medium, too. Print and nonprint are not separate and mutually exclusive resources in the world at large, nor should they be in our libraries. Integrating them into unified bibliographic systems helps to establish a new and more ambitious program of library and information services with which to meet the future.

NOTES

1. Though many studies have been made, a brief and easily understood discussion is contained in Josefa B. Abrera's "Bibliographic Structure Possibility Set: A Quantitative Approach for Identifying Users' Bibliographic Information Needs," *Library Resources & Technical Services*, 26 (January/March 1982), pp. 21-36.

2. *Anglo-American Cataloguing Rules*, 2nd ed. (Chicago: ALA, 1978), Chapter 13, pp. 270-73.

3. Frederick G. Kilgour, "Public Policy and National and International Networks," *Information Technology & Libraries*, 2 (September 1983), pp. 239-45.

4. Literature on the subject goes back a number of years. See, for example, Henriette D. Avram's "Toward a Nationwide Library Network," *Journal of Library Automation*, 11 (December 1978), pp. 285-98. A more recent examination of part of the linking effort may be found in Wayne E. Davison's "The WLN/RLG/LC Linked Systems Project," *Information Technology & Libraries*, 2 (March 1983), pp. 34-46.

Appendixes

Highlights of Professional Media Activities, 1940-1965

1941 – 1943	Carnegie Corporation funds ALA Film Forum Project.
1946	LC produces first *Copyright Film Catalog*.
1947	Fitchburg, Massachusetts, Public Library is first to circulate films.
1947 – 1951	Carnegie Corporation funds ALA Film Office.
1948	Catalog of commercial sound recordings, *Phonolog*, begins publication.
1948 – 1949	First two educational film circuits established with Carnegie funds in Ohio and Missouri.
1949	*Schwann Record and Tape Guide* begins publication.
1949	LC/ALA's cataloging rules include music and maps, noting that "Rules are still lacking for the cataloging of . . . sound recordings, motion pictures, manuscripts, prints and photographs, and books for the blind." (*Rules for Descriptive Cataloging in the Library of Congress*, vi.)
1949	ALA publishes Margaret I. Rufsvold's *Audio-Visual School Library Service: A Handbook for Librarians*.
1951 – 1953	LC begins printing and distributing catalog cards for films and filmstrips; it also publishes preliminary editions of its rules for cataloging films and sound recordings.

1955	ALA publishes *Films for Public Libraries.*
1956	ALA's *Standards for Public Libraries* contains provisions for collections and services based on non-print materials.
1958	ALA and MLA jointly produce cataloging rules for sound recordings.
1959	LC publishes cataloging rules for graphics.
1962	ALA publishes *Films for Libraries.*
1963	LC establishes separate Recorded Sound Section within its Music Division.
1963	ALA publishes Mary D. Pearson's *Recordings in the Public Library,* a manual of practice.
1964	ALA's Library Administration Division includes a panel on audio equipment in the second annual Library Equipment Institute.
1965	Congress passes the Elementary and Secondary Education Act (ESEA) providing funding for library media acquisitions.

Multimedia Cataloging Codes

1967   *Anglo-American Cataloging Rules,* sponsored by the American Library Association, the Library of Congress, the (British) Library Association, and the Canadian Library Association.

1968   *Standards for Cataloging, Coding and Scheduling Educational Media,* sponsored by the Department of Audio-Visual Instruction of the National Education Association.

1971   *Standards for Cataloging Nonprint Materials,* second edition of the above, sponsored by the Association for Educational Communications and Technology, successor to DAVI/NEA.

1972   *Standards for Cataloging Nonprint Materials,* third edition, sponsored by AECT.

1973   *Nonbook Materials: The Organization of Integrated Collections,* sponsored by the Candian Library Association.

1973   *Non-book Material Cataloguing Rules,* sponsored by the (British) Library Association and National Council for Educational Technolgy, and called the LANCET rules.

1975   Revision of Chapter 12 of *AACR1,* sponsored by the Library of Congress and the American Library Association.

1976   *Standards for Cataloging Nonprint Materials,* fourth edition, sponsored by AECT.

1976   Revision of Chapter 14 of *AACR1,* sponsored by the

Library of Congress and the American Library Association.

1978   *AACR,* second edition, sponsored by the American Library Association, the British Library, the Canadian Committee on Cataloguing, the (British) Library Association, and the Library of Congress.

1979   *Nonbook Materials,* second edition, sponsored by the Canadian Library Association.

Survey Questionnaire

This survey is designed to determine public librarians' attitudes towards bibliographic access to nonprint materials and current practice in their libraries, issues of importance in the library profession. Your participation through completion of this questionnaire is essential to an accurate assessment of these attitudes and practices.

No answer will be used to identify you personally or the institution with which you are affiliated. All replies will be analyzed anonymously.

Each reply is coded for the geographical region from which it comes and the size of population served, in order to validate applicability of the conclusions of the study to all kinds of public libraries in the United States.

The questionnaire has four parts. Please respond to every question in each part by writing the number of the response which most closely reflects your situation or attitude.

There are no "right" or "wrong" answers. Please respond as frankly and thoughtfully as you can.

PART 1: OCCUPATIONAL SITUATION

1. How many years have you been a professional librarian? (That is, since receiving your professional degree or, if you do not have a library degree, since starting your first professional level job)

1. Less than 1 year
2. 1 to 3 years
3. 4 to 6 years
4. 7 to 9 years
5. 10 years or more

2. How long have you held a professional post working with nonprint materials?

1. Less than 1 year
2. 1 to 3 years
3. 4 to 6 years
4. 7 to 9 years
5. 10 years or more

3. Does your job involve cataloging

1. Print and nonprint materials
2. Only printed materials
3. Only nonprint materials
4. No cataloging

4. Does your job involve

1. Using print and nonprint materials with the public
2. Using only nonprint materials with the public
3. Using only printed materials with the public
4. No direct interaction with the public

5. *Has your professional training included*

1. Formal or informal courses, institutes or workshops in media librarianship
2. Some courses, institutes or workshops and some on-the-job training with media
3. Only on-the-job training with media

PART 2: BIBLIOGRAPHIC ACCESS PROVIDED

6. *Is cataloging for nonprint materials available to patrons in your library?*

1. Yes
2. No (If not, skip to Question 44.)
3. Other (specify) _____

7. *Does your library have a written cataloging policy?*

1. For all its materials
2. No written policy
3. Other (specify) _____

8. *Are bibliographic records for all materials filed in one public catalog?*

1. Yes
2. No
3. Other (specify) _____

9. *If bibliographic records for all materials are NOT filed together, are separate catalogs or lists for nonprint materials available to the public?*

1. Yes
2. No
3. Other (specify) _____

10. *If separate catalogs for nonprint materials are available to the public,* are they located in the same place as the public catalog?

1. Yes
2. No
3. Other (specify) _____

11. *In what format is the public catalog?*

1. Book catalog
2. Card catalog
3. COM catalog
4. Other (specify) _____

12. *If nonprint bibliographic records are available in separate catalogs, in what format are they?*

1. Book catalog
2. Card catalog
3. COM catalog
4. Other (specify) _____

13. *If your library has separate catalogs for nonprint materials, how many are there?*

1. One for all nonprint media
2. One for each different medium
3. More than one, but not as many as one for each medium

14. *Are most printed materials cataloged in-house?*

1. Yes
2. No
3. Other (specify) _____

15. *Are most nonprint materials catalogued in-house?*

1. Yes
2. No
3. Other (specify) _____

16. *Does your library use OCLC, RLIN, WLN or any other bibliographic database for cataloging?*

1. Yes
2. No

17. If a bibliographic database is used in your library, is it used for cataloging
  1. All library materials
  2. Only printed materials
  3. Only nonprint materials
  4. Other (specify) ─────────

18. If most printed materials are NOT cataloged in-house, how is it done?
  1. Central service
  2. Commercial processing service
  3. Other (specify) ─────────

19. If most nonprint materials are NOT cataloged in-house, how is it done?
  1. Central service
  2. Commercial processing service
  3. Other (specify) ─────────

20. What rules are followed for original cataloging of print materials?
  1. *AACR1,* including revised chapter 6
  2. *AACR2*
  3. Other rules or modifications of the above (specify) ─────────

21. What rules are followed for original cataloging of nonprint materials?
  1. *AACR1,* including revised Chapters 12 and 14
  2. *AACR2*
  3. Other rules or modifications of the above (specify) ─────────

22. If your library is not already implementing AACR2 *for printed materials, are plans being made to do so in the near future?*
  1. Yes
  2. No

23. If your library is not already implementing AACR2 *for nonprint materials, are plans being made to do so in the near future?*
  1. Yes
  2. No

24. To implement AACR2, *will your library*
  1. Close the old catalog and maintain two catalogs
  2. Upgrade all old entries
  3. Interfile old and new entries and link them with references
  4. Other (specify) ─────────

25. Does your library share its materials with any other library, library system or network?
  1. Yes, all materials
  2. Yes, some materials (specify)
  ─────────
  3. No

26. Catalog entries for printed materials contain the following bibliographic elements if applicable:
  1. Title proper, parallel titles and other title information
  2. Title proper and sometimes additional title information
  3. Title proper only

27. Catalog entries for nonprint materials contain the following bibliographic elements if applicable:
  1. Title proper, parallel titles and other title information
  2. Title proper and sometimes additional title information
  3. Title proper only

28. General Material Designations prescribed on Page 20 of AACR2 *are used in the catalog entries*

1. For all materials cataloged
2. Only for nonprint materials
3. Never used for any materials
4. Sometimes used for some items (specify) _____

29. Statement(s) of responsibility are used in catalog entries if applicable

1. For all materials cataloged
2. Only for printed materials
3. Only for nonprint materials
4. Sometimes used for some items (specify) _____

30. Edition statement(s) are used in catalog entries if applicable

1. For all materials cataloged
2. Only for printed materials
3. Only for nonprint materials
4. Sometimes used for some items (specify) _____

31. Physical description statements are used in catalog entries

1. For all materials cataloged
2. Only for printed materials
3. Only for nonprint materials
4. Sometimes used for some items (specify) _____

32. Series information appears in catalog entries if applicable

1. For all materials cataloged
2. Only for printed materials
3. Only for nonprint materials
4. Sometimes used for some items (specify) _____

33. Complete notes including information on contents, summary, audience level, related works, etc., are usually present in catalog entries

1. For all materials cataloged
2. Only for printed materials
3. Only for nonprint materials
4. Sometimes used for some items (specify) _____

34. Standard numbers (ISBN, LC, etc.) and similar identifiers are usually present in catalog entries

1. For all materials cataloged
2. Only for printed materials
3. Only for nonprint materials
4. Sometimes used for some items (specify) _____

35. Alternate elements relating only to particular nonprint formats, such as director, date of first release or airing, performers, matrix numbers, etc., are used in catalog entries if applicable

1. Always, if known
2. Sometimes
3. Never

36. Main and added entries are made

1. In the same way for all materials being cataloged
2. Differently for different kinds of materials (specify)_____
_____

37. If cataloging is done outside the library, do you add more headings to those on the prepared entries?

1. Yes
2. No
3. Other (specify) _____

38. What subject heading list is used for printed materials?

1. Sears List of Subject Headings
2. Library of Congress Subject Headings
3. Other subject heading lists or locally developed subject headings (specify) _____
_____

39. Is the same subject heading list used for nonprint materials?

1. Yes
2. No
3. Other (specify) _____
_____

40. What classification system is used to arrange printed materials in your library?

1. Dewey Decimal Classification
2. Library of Congress Classification
3. Other (specify) _____

_____

41. Is the same classification used to arrange nonprint materials?

1. Yes
2. No
3. Other (specify) _____

42. If a different arrangement is used for nonprint materials, please describe it briefly:

_____

_____

43. Are your nonprint materials on

1. Open stacks
2. Closed stacks
3. Other (specify) _____

_____

PART 3: ATTITUDE SURVEY

The following statements are designed to elicit your views of bibliographic access and nonprint materials. Please enter the number of the response that most closely reflects your level of agreement or disagreement with each statement according to the scale listed below:

1. STRONGLY AGREE
2. AGREE
3. NO OPINION
4. DISAGREE
5. STRONGLY DISAGREE

44. I want to see entries for everything in the library in one catalog.

45. Each information medium should have its own catalog.

46. AACR2 is an improvement over previous cataloging codes.

47. It is difficult to apply AACR2 to nonprint materials.

48. When seeking information, public library users prefer using printed materials to nonprint forms.

49. Sometimes the best information is not in a book, but in a film or a recording or other nonprint item.

50. Nonprint materials are used primarily for recreation.

51. The subject headings used for printed materials are inappropriate for nonprint materials.

52. The classification used for printed materials is inappropriate for nonprint materials.

53. Nonprint materials cost too much for the library to afford.

54. Public libraries should spend more of their budget on nonprint materials.

55. Public libraries should spend more of their budget on the equipment needed to use nonprint materials in-house.

56. Public library users like using nonprint materials when they have equipment available.

Please indicate your preference of the pairs of alternatives that follow, by writing the number of your response in the box provided.

57. In order to serve the public better the library should

1. Put all catalog records into one public catalog
2. Maintain separate catalogs for each informational medium

58. In order to serve the public better the library should

1. Use AACR2 for all cataloging
2. Tailor cataloging rules to local use

59. In order to serve the public better the library should

1. Expend more resources to improve the cataloging of printed materials

2. Expend more resources to improve the cataloging of nonprint materials.

60. If cost and space were no barrier, the public would be best served if

1. Nonprint materials were intershelved with books and reading areas were also equipped with nonprint hardware.

2. Nonprint materials were not intershelved with books and reading areas were not equipped for viewing and/or listening, but separate areas for housing and using nonprint materials were provided.

61. The public is best served if the library

1. Keeps its nonprint materials on closed shelves and provides more staff to help users obtain desired items.

2. Keeps its nonprint materials on open stacks and provides more

frequent replacements for damaged or stolen items.

PART 4: PERSONAL PROFILE

62. Age:

1. Under 25
2. 25 to 30
3. 31 to 40
4. 41 to 45
5. Over 45

63. Sex:

1. Female
2. Male

64. What is your highest level of educational achievement?

1. Less than a bachelor's degree
2. Bachelor's degree
3. Master's degree
4. More than a master's degree

Thank you for completing this questionnaire. Your participation in the study is greatly appreciated.

Sheila S. Intner
Investigator

List of Acronyms

AACR	*Anglo-American Cataloging Rules* (usually used to refer to the first edition, published in 1967)
AACR1	Specifically, the first edition of *Anglo-American Cataloging Rules*
AACR2	Specifically, the second edition of *Anglo-American Cataloguing Rules,* published in 1978
AECT	Association for Educational Communications and Technology
ALA	American Library Association
ANSI	American National Standards Institute
AV	Audiovisual
BALLOTS	Bibliographic Automation of Large Library Operations using a Time-Sharing System
BRS	Bibliographic Retrieval Service
BU	Bibliographic Unit
CC:DA	Committee on Cataloging: Description and Access
CCS:	Cataloging and Classification Section (of RTSD)
CIS	Congressional Information Service
CLA	Canadian Library Association
CLSI	CL Systems, Inc., previously Computer Library Systems, Inc.
COM	Computer-output microform
CRT	Cathode-ray tube
CTI	Computer Translations, Inc.
CUFC	Consortium of University Film Association
EFLA	Educational Film Library Association
ERIC	Educational Resources Information Center
FLIC	Film Library Information Council
GMD	General material designation
IFLA	International Federation of Library Associations and Organizations

ILL	Interlibrary loan
ILLINET	Illinois Information Network
ISBD	International Standard Bibliographic Description
ISBD (CM)	International Standard Bibliographic Description (Cartographic Materials)
ISBD (NBM)	International Standard Bibliographic Description (Non-Book Materials)
ISBD (PM)	International Standard Bibliographic Description (Printed Music)
ISBN	International Standard Book Number
ISSN	International Standard Serial Number
JSCAACR	Joint Steering Committee for the revision of the *Anglo-American Cataloguing Rules.*
LA/NCET	Library Association and National Committee for Educational Technology
LC	Library of Congress
LCSH	Library of Congress Subject Headings
LITA	Library and Information Technology Association (of ALA)
LP	Long playing
LSCA	Library Services and Construction Act
MARBI	Committee on Representation in Machine-Readable Form of Bibliographic Information
MARC	Machine-readable cataloging
MLA	Music Library Association
MOUG	Music OCLC Users Group
NCLIS	National Commission on Libraries and Information Science
NICEM	National Information Center for Educational Media
NTIS	National Technical Information Service
NYSCAT	New York State Catalog (for film and video)
OCLC	Online Computer Library Center
OLAC	On-Line Audiovisual Catalogers
OPAC	Online Public Access Catalog
PAC	Public Access Catalog—also called OPAC
PAIS	Public Affairs Information Service
RASD	Reference and Adult Services Division (of ALA)
RLIN	Research Libraries Information Network
RTSD	Resources and Technical Services Division (of ALA)
RTSD/AV	Audiovisual Committee of RTSD

SDC	Systems Development Corporation
SDI	Selective dissemination of information
SOLINET	Southeastern Library Network
TESLA	Technical Standards for Library Automation Committee, a committee of the (ALA) Library & Information Technology Association
UBC	Universal Bibliographic Control
UTLAS	University of Toronto Libraries Automated System
WLN	Washington Library Network

Glossary of Terms

Access point A heading filed in the catalog such as a name, title, subject, or other element.

Accession number An identifying number assigned to materials according to their order of acquisition.

Added entry Access points derived from the bibliographic identification of a work in addition to its primary access point.

Alphanumeric Letters of the alphabet or numerals.

AMIGOS Regional bibliographic network located in the southwestern United States.

Analytics Bibliographic description and access for parts of works, e.g., a song on a record album.

Archive tape The record, produced on magnetic tape, of a library's cataloging activities online with a bibliographic utility; also called archival tape or archival magnetic tape.

Audiovisual materials/media Physical forms of library materials in which intellectual or artistic content is presented in aural, visual or both aural and visual form.

Authority control Maintenance of only approved forms of headings in a catalog.

Authority file; authority work A file containing records of headings used in library catalogs, which may be names, subjects, or other access points, as well as cross-references; the work involved in creating the entries in authority files.

Automated bibliographic system A computer-based and -manipulated system of bibliographic information.

Backup; backup system A system or set of procedures used during downtime; also, a second database or multiple copies created to insure against loss of data in the event of a failure.

Bar-code Machine-readable labels with unique identifiers used to identify materials for a computer system.

Baud rate Speed at which information is transmitted.

Bibliographic access   The availability of information about library materials; may also be called mediagraphic access to emphasize its applicability to more than just books.

Bibliographic control   Accumulation and organization of information about library materials, especially books.

Bibliographic description   The identification of a work as a physical and intellectual entity.

Bibliographic utility   An organization that generates bibliographic data and disseminates it to participants by means of a computer network.

Boolean operators   The terms AND, OR, NOT, which, when added to multiple searching terms, define a particular search pattern, e.g., public AND libraries. Boolean searching refers to the use of these terms in searching a database or catalog.

Brief listing   A shortened form of entry, including fewer elements than required by *AACR.*

Call number   A shelf location device consisting of the classification number plus other locational marks, e.g., author numbers, dates, collection symbols, etc.

Cartographics   Materials related to geography, e.g., maps.

Cathode-ray tube (CRT)   A kind of computer terminal with a visual display similar to a television screen.

Central processing unit (CPU)   The part of a computer system in which the actual computing is done.

Circulation control   A system for monitoring borrowing of library materials, usually applied to computerized systems.

Classifed catalog   A library catalog in which entries are arranged according to their content or subject matter.

Closed shelves   Stack areas in which the public are not permitted.

CODEN   A unique six-character name for a serial title.

Codes of communication   Media used to convey information.

Color coding   Identification of materials by the assignment of colors to the various categories.

COM catalog   A catalog in micrographic format produced by a computerized system.

COMPENDEX   A database containing bibliographic information for engineering materials.

Configuration   The arrangement and connections of hardware and software in a computer system or network.

Connect time   The length of time the user is connected to an on-line database, recorded automatically by the computer.

Control number   A unique identifier assigned to an entry.

Controlled environment   A physical space in which such things as temperature, humidity, and light are maintained within limited ranges and air pollutants are filtered out.

Controlled vocabulary   Headings in which a prescribed form of subject words and names must be used.

Corporate body/name   An entity/name of an entity used to identify people acting together as a group; not the same as the legal definition of a corporation.

Crash   Failure of a computer system.

Customized cataloging   Cataloging adapted or modified to fit the specific needs of an individual library.

Cutter; Cuttering   An identifying symbol derived from alphanumeric tables originated by Charles A. Cutter; the assignment of such a symbol.

Database   A collection of information in machine-readable form organized according to a systematic structure.

Database management system   Software designed to enable people to enter, organize, and manipulate data in a computer database.

Deacquisition   Removal of materials from a library's database.

Descriptor   A word defining the subject matter of a work.

Dial access; dial-up access   Access to a computer system at remote sites by means of telephone lines.

DIALOG   A computerized reference system containing many databases in various areas, i.e., subjects, disciplines, or industries. Originally part of the Lockheed Corporation.

Dictionary catalog   A catalog in which all entries are arranged in alphabetical order in a single file.

Direct access   Terminal with uninterrupted connections to the computing unit, as opposed to dial access. Also called hard-wired.

Discography   List of titles of sound recordings on disks.

Disk   A storage medium for sound, video, or computer data.

Disk drives   The machinery into which disks, diskettes, or disk packs are put when they are being used by the computer; also called "drives."

Disk packs   Computer data storage medium consisting of several disks mounted together in a single unit.

Diskettes   Microcomputer data storage medium consisting of single disks, smaller than those used in larger computers.

Distributed processing   A computer network system in which some of the computing work is done by each participant.

Divided catalog A library catalog consisting of more than one alphabetic file.

Document delivery Services for getting library materials into the hands of clients, e.g., circulation, interloan, SDI.

Documentation Material accompanying computer software explaining its structure and/or use.

Down; downtime Not operating; time when a computer is not operating.

Dummy A false item substituted on the shelf for the real material, containing its call number and information about its actual location.

Dump (verb or noun) Automatic entry of data from one automated system to another.

Electronic mail Online communication system for individuals to send messages to one another.

Electronic media Materials dependent on electronic communications and playback systems for transmission and use.

Field In a computer entry, a portion of a record devoted to a specific kind of information, e.g., a title field contains the title of a work.

Fixed field A part of a computer record with a predetermined number and order of characters in it.

Floppy; floppy disk A flexible disk used with microcomputers to store programs and data.

Free-text searching In an online search, the ability to access any word or phrase in a record, not only the headings.

Graphics Any of a large number of visual materials, including pictures, photographs, posters, cards, charts, filmstrips, etc., covered in *AACR2*, Chapter 8.

Hard copy Computer output printed on paper, rather than in electronic form.

Hard data In research, the basic measurements on which statistical analysis and interpretation are based.

Hard disk A rigid disk used for data storage with microcomputers.

Hardware Computer equipment or machinery; also used generally to denote any kind of equipment or machinery.

Hard-wired Terminal which has a direct and uninterrupted linkage or wire to the computing unit.

Head In a disk drive, the device that "reads," "writes," or erases data from the disk.

Head crash Failure occurring in the reading and writing process by a head, often affecting the data stored there.

Hit   An entry in a database satisfying the characteristics of a search key.

Host; host system   A central computing and data storage facility to which access is provided by means of terminals located outside the facility.

Imprint   Part of a bibliographic entry giving the place of publication, name of publisher/producer, and date published.

INFORM   A database containing bibliographic information for business management literature.

Input (noun or verb)   Data entered into a computer; the act of entering it.

Integrated access   Bibliographic access which includes information for materials in all physical media.

Integrated catalog   A catalog in which entries for materials in all physical forms are interfiled.

Integrated system of technical services   A computer system for performing the functions of acquiring, cataloging, and circulating library materials.

Interactive   A system in which a dialog is possible between computer and user.

Interface   A point of connection between people and machines or between different machines.

Interlibrary loan   A circulation transaction in which one library lends its materials to another library's patrons, abbreviated ILL. Also called interloan.

Interloan   Interlibrary loan.

Intershelve   Place together on library shelves.

Key-title   A coded version of a serial title standing for one particular serial, even if others exist with the same title.

Keystroke   The typing of a character on a typewriter or typewriter-like keyboard.

Keyword   An entry consisting of a significant word in an element of a record.

LANCET rules   The British cataloging code for nonprint media published in 1973.

Lightpen   A device for scanning bar-code labels; an input/output device.

Local notes   Notes relating to a particular item in hand.

Machine-readable   Material in a form in which it can be read by a computer.

Machine-readable data file   Computer software

Macrocomputer   A mainframe computer.

Main entry   The primary access point derived from the bibliographic identification of a work.

Mainframe   One of the largest computers in terms of its data storage and computing power.

Main memory   The amount of space for holding data in the CPU itself, without the additional secondary storage units such as disks.

Manual   Without computers; refers to data entry, cataloging, or other processes.

MARC format   A structure for encoding bibliographic information for entry into computer systems.

Materials booking system   A computerized system for making advance reservations for materials that are lent for limited time in rotation, often done for films.

Media   Formats of library materials, not usually intended to include books; may also be called audiovisual media, nonbook media, or nonprint media.

Media librarianship   The part of the profession of librarianship focused on the development and use of nonprint media materials.

Mediagraphic control   Accumulation and organization of information relating to nonprint materials.

Mediagraphy   Listing of nonprint materials.

Memory   In a computer, amount of data that can be stored.

Microcomputer   The smallest type of computer with limited power and storage space.

Microcomputer software   Instructions for microcomputers.

Minicomputer   A computer in the mid-size range, larger than a microcomputer but smaller than a mainframe or macrocomputer.

Modem   Shortened version of MOdulator-DEModulator, a device that translates a computer signal into a telephone signal and back again.

Monomedia   Devoted to titles in only one physical format.

Multimedia   Including more than one physical format.

Natural language   The use of ordinary words in the order they occur as search elements in a database or catalog, as opposed to the use of subject headings or descriptors.

Network; networking   A group of libraries sharing a computer-based bibliographic database system for various cooperative purposes; the act or process of doing so.

Nonbook materials/media   Physical forms of library materials other than books; usually intended to be exclusive of other printed materials such as periodicals, pamphlets, and printed sheets as well.

Nonprint materials/media Physical forms of library materials other than print; used in this book interchangeably with audiovisual or nonbook materials and usually including printed maps and music.

Offline catalog A catalog prepared with the services of a computer system, but displayed in a form that does not require a computer to access; e.g., a computer-output-microform or computer-produced card catalog.

Omnimedia catalog A catalog containing entries for materials in all physical media; multimedia catalog; integrated catalog.

Online catalog A computer-based library catalog maintained in realtime, interactive systems; also called online public access catalog (OPAC).

ORBIT A computerized reference system containing databases in various areas, i.e., subjects, disciplines, or industries, part of the Systems Development Corporation.

Original cataloging Cataloging in which the data are taken directly from the item being cataloged.

Output Information produced by a computer, as opposed to input.

Participatory management Incorporation of nonmanagerial staff members in management processes.

Phonolog A loose-leaf, permuted index for sound recordings on disks with entries for song titles, album titles, and performers.

Physical access The ability to go into an area and/or take materials from the shelves; the ability to actually have items in one's possession.

Postings The number of entries satisfying a search request.

Processor Central processing unit.

Program Instructions to a computer system enabling it to perform various desired operations; also called software.

Program language One of several systems for writing instructions for computer operations; sometimes shortened to just "language."

Public catalog The main catalog(s) provided for use by a library's clients.

Realia Real objects, e.g., stones, skeletons, etc.

Realtime Rapid data processing enabling responses to guide a user or control a process.

Resource-sharing A program whereby a library shares its materials with other libraries.

Retrospective cataloging The cataloging of materials already in a library's collections; also called retrospective conversion.

Response time   The length of time elapsing between a user's request and the computer's response.

Retrospective conversion   The alteration of bibliographic data for materials already in a library's collections, usually used to describe its change to machine-readable form, but also applied to other departures from pre-existing forms.

Search key   A structure for coding data for a search in a computerized database.

Search statement   The data entered when searching for an entry in a computer database.

Selective dissemination of information (SDI)   A document delivery service in which the library sends users information about new materials in selected subjected areas.

Shelflist   A listing, arranged by call number, of the materials in a library collection.

Software   Computer programs, i.e., instructions and/or data enabling the computer to perform various desired operations.

Subfield   Part of a field, e.g., in a title field, the portion devoted to title proper.

Subject access   Availability of information relating to the subject content of library materials.

Subject cataloging   The assignment of subject headings to materials.

Subject heading; subject heading list   An access point identifying the subject matter of a work; a list of acceptable terms to be used in identifying the subject matter of materials.

Subsystem   Part of computer system's range of activities devoted to a particular function or functions.

Surrogate   A substitute for the physical work, in a library catalog, a record containing a description of the physical and intellectual/artistic content of a title.

Terminal   A device used for communicating with a computer.

Thesaurus   A list of subject terms usually confined to a single discipline or subject area.

Truncation   The use of partial information to search in an online system.

Turnkey system   A computer system package containing hardware, software, and varying levels of training, implementation, and maintenance support, which presumably could be purchased, installed, and used by merely "turning a key" to start the computer.

Tutorial; online tutorial   An instructional module designed to teach the use of the computer system; such an instructional module, available in the computer system itself.

Uncontrolled vocabulary Headings in which no prescribed form is used, but any subject words or forms of names are used.

Union catalog; union list A catalog combining records of more than one library collection.

Unique identifier A number, word, or alphanumeric entity bearing a one-to-one relationship with an entry in a database, e.g., an accession number, control number, or key-title.

Universal Bibliographic Control A system of accumulation, organization, and dissemination of bibliographic data, on a global basis, under the aegis of IFLA.

Up; uptime Operating; time when a computer is operating.

User Usually applied to persons who use a computer system, but also to those who use any library service.

User group An organization made up of representatives of libraries using a particular computer system.

Variable field A part of a computer record in which the number and kind of characters entered may vary.

Vendor Usually used to refer to someone who sells equipment or materials, especially computer systems, to libraries.

Vertical file The library's collection of pamphlets, etc., kept in filing cabinets, usually arranged by broad subject areas.

Video display terminal A computer terminal with a visual display; a cathode-ray tube terminal.

Video software Videorecordings designed to be played back on appropriate equipment; not to be confused with computer software.

Subject Index

216422